THE BOOKS OF

GEORGE JEAN NATHAN

ഔ ഔ

In Collaboration with H. L. Mencken

≋(THE ENTERTAINMENT OF A NATION)≋

GEORGE JEAN NATHAN

THE

Entertainment

OF A NATION

OR

Three-Sheets in the Wind

NEW YORK   *Alfred A. Knopf*   1942

Manufactured in the United States of America
Published simultaneously in Canada by The Ryerson Press

FIRST EDITION

CONTENTS

CONTENTS

{(THE ENTERTAINMENT OF A NATION)}

The Status of the Male Playwrights

S. N. Behrman's ability as a writer of the higher comedy is duly recognized; he is the best we have in the nation, as he has already sufficiently attested. But his last produced effort, *The Talley Method,* hardly increases his laurels. It has its virtues. It again indicates its author's gift for character delineation, his command of the language, his cultivation, his superior approach to the dramatic theatre, and his contempt for any kind of cheapness. But it also again indicates his more recent arbitrary determination to sacrifice the artist to the appellant, his conviction that a well-wrought comedy is in itself not enough and that it must in one way or another provide a commentary on and criticism of the immediate faults of the world, and his substitution of personal resentment, albeit here and there artfully concealed, for suave implication and suggestion. And it further indicates, strangely enough for Behrman, an occasional tendency toward "literary" writing.

The leading figures in the play are an eminent surgeon and the poetically minded woman he would make his second wife. The not unfamiliar conflict is accordingly one between hard pragmatism and compassionate idealism.

Contributing factors are the surgeon's son and daughter whose attitudes toward life their father cannot comprehend and a Central European refugee whom intolerance and lack of sympathy drive to suicide and who thus brings the play's thesis into focus. So far, perhaps so good. But in his passion to have his play Say Something at all costs, Behrman periodically argues it out of natural flow and makes it just a little disconcerting. The net impression is of a Stokowski glancing over his shoulder every now and then to make certain that Dorothy Thompson is still in her seat.

Behrman continues to do himself and his dramatic art an injustice in thus following the principle of his associates in the Playwrights' Company that plays must inevitably deal with the indignations of the moment or flounder. With his colleagues the Messrs. Sherwood, Anderson and Rice let him not fail to reflect that *The Blue Danube* will probably prosper much longer than the *Horst Wessel* song, that long after people have stopped reading Eddie Bernays' *Speak Up For Democracy* they will doubtless still be reading *David Copperfield*, and that maybe even *Twelfth Night* will be interesting people some little time after they have completely forgotten *American Landscape, Journey To Jerusalem* and *There Shall Be No Night*.

I lead off with these observations on Behrman because he provides me with the theme of this introductory chapter, to wit, the unhappy circumstance that, with not more than one or possibly two exceptions, our leading more serious American male playwrights not only suggest not the faintest sign of growth but, more, definite symptoms of deterioration. O'Neill, of course, is in a class by himself. His work shows a steady inner progress and a greatly increased depth. This, as will again be amply proved when his monumental cycle of nine plays known generally as *A*

Tale Of Possessors Self-Dispossessed is produced, is in a measure due to his high artist's contempt for problems of the immediate moment and his sole concern with humanity in time unending. And long before the cycle will be ready for production, it will be attested to with an almost equal force in two plays he has completed apart from the cycle: *The Iceman Cometh* and *Long Day's Journey Into Night.* The only other exception is, perhaps, Robert Sherwood. Sherwood, even though he has mounted guns on the ivory tower and seems for the time being to be set upon dropping propaganda leaflets on his audiences in lieu of drama, appears nonetheless to offer intimations, however periodically dim and confused, of some future quality.

Apart from this duo, however, the graph is in a descending, or at best a static, line. Take, for example, Elmer Rice. If we overlook the agreeable little comedy, *The Left Bank,* produced in 1931, his work in the main shows a progressive decline since *Street Scene,* his best play, done two years earlier. His latest exhibit, *Flight To The West,* is typical of the bacillus which since then has often infected him, as it has others, and which has increasingly invalidated him as a dramatist of critical esteem. That bacillus is the one I have already alluded to: the preoccupation with the headlines of the moment and the consequent conversion of drama into mere editorial comment. As in the instance of a number of his fellows, Mr. Rice has accordingly become largely a compère of current indignations, a three-dollar writer of 10-20-30 melodrama who has substituted Nazis and Fascists for the old peanut-gallery villains and Yankee Doodle and the Jews for heroic Jack Desmond and the Orphans of the Storm. Thus, *Flight To The West,* like certain of his plays preceding it, presents itself as little more than *PM* journalism on glossy paper.

Save for a moment or two when he whips out the old pistol, this *Flight To The West* is basically the melodrama of our boyhood merchanted in terms of oral instead of physical conflict. Laid in a transatlantic clipper flying from Lisbon to New York and carrying a cargo of assorted Americans, Nazis, refugees, Jews and Gentiles, its three acts resolve themselves, except for the aforenoted momentary flash of the revolver, into an editorial debate on the political and racial points of view of the various passengers, with the Jews—as is usual in contemporary melodrama of the polemic species and as has been signified—in the role of Little Nell.

Although Mr. Rice's sincerity is unquestioned and although he succeeds in evoking a share of the audience reaction automatically resident in his materials, his play remains mostly a succession of literal quotations of his assembled company of topical stock characters. The impression I could not get out of my head while looking at it was of some such old popular naval melodrama as *The Ensign* with its conflict between British and American seamen alternately converted into one between Nazis and Americans, Fascists and anti-Fascists, and Aryans and non-Aryans. The writing only increased this impression. Where in *The Ensign* the American seaman was hissingly insulted by the British seaman and yelled back, "Maybe we Americans ain't got no manners, but we can fight like hell!", in *Flight To The West* when the American airship officer is hissingly insulted by the Nazi official with, "You Yankees, some day we will teach you!", he simply indicates an improvement in American manners by saying nothing in reply, contemptuously. And so on. Further, the devices wherewith Mr. Rice seeks to give melodramatic suspense to his extended discussions are the all too recognizable ones. One character thus permits a look of trepidation to cross her features and apprehensively remarks, "I feel something is going to happen." Another observes ominously, "I don't know, but I am sure I've seen that man somewhere before." And a third, who evidently saw George Arliss in *Disraeli* and liked the curtain line to one of its acts, puts on a puzzled look when in a quandary and says, "I've got to do *something!*" and in reply to "But what?" returns, "I—don't—know."

Mr. Rice more and more seems to become a mere dramatist of popular hot collars. And popular hot collars are the province much less of the artist than of the commercial melodramatist. He sells back to his audiences the prejudices they already have when they enter his theatre. The worthy dramatist makes his sale, rather, after they have been sitting skeptically in the house for some time.

Maxwell Anderson, a considerably superior writer who has also been bitten by the bug, is essentially a dramatic artist but one whose stubborn conviction that he must arbitrarily, whatever the occasion, express himself in mayonnaise verse has given many of his later plays the appearance of suffering badly from the gout. Abjuring simple and relevant expression, his work has progressively taken on a swollen quality that, while it may not be the result of deliberate pretentiousness, nevertheless has often induced that feeling. Since *Winterset*, his best play—if we forget the Stallings collaboration, *What Price Glory?*—his stage syntheses of analogical sermonizing and choir singing have become less and less effective, and when for the nonce he has partly abandoned them in favor of prose adventures like *The Star-Wagon* and *Candle In The Wind* what has emerged has been either sheer box-office whiffle or patently requisitioned compromise.

It is not unfair to several of these playwrights, I think, to observe that, while they have progressed far beyond utilizing the old theatrical hokum implicit in Mother, the Baby, and perhaps to some extent even the Flag, they still freely surrender themselves to the newer hokum implicit in Lincoln, Democracy and Racial Persecution, to say nothing, for extra measure, in that obliquely resident in Hitler, Stalin, Franco, Laval and Lindbergh.

The majority of my colleagues, I find, entertain a critical point of view opposite to mine and argue that dramatic journalism of the species mentioned is not only desirable in this period of world crisis but even superior to a more aloof aesthetic. That it may be publicly desirable, I shall not argue the one way or the other, but that has nothing to do with the appraisal of drama as a fine art. For fine drama is timeless and merely journalistic drama, however good and however interesting, as evanescent as news itself. This disguised journalistic drama that so many of the critics raptly endorse can enjoy no more lasting life than the Living Newspaper drama of the late Federal Theatre Project. The Living Newspaper drama said its effective say and then properly passed into limbo, like yesterday's newspaper itself. Today's headlines are ever tomorrow's few sticks on an inside page.

The decline of George Kelly, the static position of Paul Green, the retrogression of Marc Connelly, the status quo of Sidney Kingsley, the declension of Clifford Odets, the bust-up of John Howard Lawson and Robert Ardrey, the enervation of Irwin Shaw and so on all further concern the immediate historian of our theatre. And out of that concern two things become signally apparent: first, that more and more the artistic vitality of that theatre must seemingly depend upon the new and independent writing blood that may come into it, and second, that only our deliberately lighter and gayer playwrights indicate the development that their more solemn brothers fail to suggest.

✿

We have, to reiterate, had enough now of Lincolns used to remind us analogically of the tragedy of subjugating and enslaving a race, of Connecticut real-estaters employed to hint at the possibility of the invasion of the Fascist idea, of Finland held up as an admonitory mirror to our American way of life, of Spanish war deserters meeting up with Hitlerian counterparts in the Florida keys and roused to a realization of danger to home and mankind, of even comedies like Behrman's *No Time For Comedy* elaborately self-doubtful of their own validity in the present time of world stress and of musical shows that identify the racketeering politics of Peter Stuyvesant's New Amsterdam with those of the New York of today. To say nothing of Christ sacrificed to make a Roman holiday by way of intimating the eventual triumph of presently oppressed and persecuted Jewry.

This returns us to Maxwell Anderson who is responsible for the Christ play in question, *Journey To Jerusalem.*

For all those qualities which his sympathetic critics have long freely allowed to him—sincerity, dignity, lofty aim, etc.—it becomes increasingly and disturbingly apparent that this Mr. Anderson as playwright remains largely a small boy strutting about in an adult's frock coat and that, whatever the noble thoughts that agitate him and the noble acts that inspire him, he is unable to make them in written performance seem other than whimsically juvenile. It would, as I have noted, be unfair to say that he is always pretentious; he is not. But the unhappy fact, as also noted, is that he frequently gives off that impression. It also would be unfair to say that he is most often merely rhetorical when he would be poetically eloquent. He sometimes is not. But here again even when he is eloquent his eloquence has in it something of the infelicitous effect of a woman's purple dress in the strong, hot sunlight or of a too heavy perfume in the morning. He suggests, in short, a very expensive enameled egg-beater functioning brilliantly over a large soufflé bowl that contains only half the white of one egg, a dribble of milk, and no butter, flour, or sugar.

In *Journey To Jerusalem,* treating of Jesus' pilgrimage at the age of twelve to the annual Passover feast and His borning consciousness of His future tragic mission on earth, along with the parallel with the plight of modern Jewry noted, Anderson brings even further deficiencies to his already deficient craft. He merely states his play, failing save in one brief instance—the meeting of the young Jesus with the bandit Ishmael—even faintly to dramatize it. Except for that one moment there is not a single dramatic situation, nor a flicker of suspensive action. In the way of poetic imagery, the playwright is further guilty of some of the worst clichés sounded in the theatre since Virgil Geddes last embarrassed the rafters of the Provincetown playhouse in Macdougal street, and in his excursions into philosophical meditation the situation may most politely be expressed by allowing that he is not materially profounder or much more pregnantly original than Channing Pollock, author of that great art-work, *The Fool.* It is not fifteen minutes after his play begins that the effect is not progressively and dismayingly like that induced by Walter Hampden's annual Players' Club one-hour-and-a-half oral treatise on Edwin Booth, with the name of the Saviour substituted for the actor's. It is, in short, simply reverent ham.

In a program foreword to the play, Mr. Anderson discoursed learnedly on the languages spoken at the time along the eastern coast of the Mediterranean. "Greek," he explained, "was still the language of diplomacy and culture; Latin was the speech of the Roman soldiers, tax-gatherers and officials who governed the region for the Caesars; Hebrew was spoken among the priests of the temple at Jerusalem and taught in the religious schools of the Jews; but Aramaic was the common speech, known to all and heard at every market place and street corner. Aramaic was the speech of Jesus Himself, and when he stood as a child in the Sanhedrin and conversed with the judges, his native dialect and Galilean accent may easily have caused some smiling among the learned men."

Aside from the fact, such things being as they are in the theatre, that the role of Jesus was played by a young actor hitherto active in the gangster play *Dead End* and on commercial radio programs whose speech which caused some smiling among the learned men was considerably less Aramaic with a Galilean accent than Broadway with a Vyvyan Donner microphone accent—aside from this fact there was the same old general refractory trouble when any playwright seeks to suggest in English and for use by English-speaking actors a variety of alien tongues. The result, in this specific case, was that the Roman soldiers, tax-gatherers and officials who were supposed to be speaking Latin sounded as if they were translations of Sallustius Crispus by Westbrook Pegler and that the priests who were supposed to be talking in Hebrew seemed to be carrying on their colloquies in something that sounded suspiciously like Zoë Akins dialogue recited by the Harvard Dramatic Club. As for the Aramaic, it ran the actor gamut all the way from Jerome Weidman to Aimée McPherson and from Arthur Kober to Archibald MacLeish.

I hope that one of these days playwrights will in this direction at last see the error and futility of their ways. I always on such occasions think back to the manner in which Ludwig Lewisohn once tried to indicate the nature of the Silesian dialect in his translations of certain of Hauptmann's plays and upset the equilibrium of our tympani with such exotic delicatessen as "the vicious critters"; "nothing is his'n"; "you know, y'understan', we get a powerful lot o' tramps here right along"; "the impident hussy"; "don' knows I c'n blame you"; "crooked beast!"; "sich a critter"; "beast of a scythe!"; "out with the brazen hussy!"; "she just gits kinder rough now an' then"; and—as God is our judge— "we don't have to be thinkin' and thinkin' before we spends a penny, no, nor before we spends a pound neither."

There's *echt* Silesian for you, Gerhart!

Both this *Return To Jerusalem* and his directly antecedent *Key Largo*, of which more presently, have made us again speculate if their author has not been very greatly and carelessly overestimated. I do not mean in the last few years alone, for since *The Star-Wagon* and *Knickerbocker Holiday* there has been manifest a considerable headscratching and backsliding. I mean in the years before, when the critics (myself in part on at least one occasion among them) went to town for him with what seems to have been a questionable rapture. That his *Winterset* had some definite merits and that his *High Tor* was a fairish effort in the way of legendary drama we may freely admit. But that even the former was quite all we thought we saw in it, I wonder. Not only, as must at length be clear to a blind man or even to certain of the critics, is Mr. Anderson's position obviously not in the very remotest degree to be compared with

O'Neill's, but it is, I believe, further acutely debatable in comparison with that of other playwrights in our theatre. Surely Behrman is critically the finer artist; surely Sherwood is a more adroit hand at thematic hypnosis; surely young Saroyan has an immeasurably greater imagination; surely Anderson's old collaborator, Stallings, had immensely more dramatic drive and force; surely Lillian Hellman has a final deeper grasp on character; surely the novice John Steinbeck in his sole play has evoked a much more profound commiseration and pity; and I, for one, am not entirely certain that Paul Green and Robert Turney haven't something in the way of honest poetic expression that Anderson most generally lacks.

Key Largo, to revert to that example of the Anderson craft, represents, it seems to me, all that is best and worst in its author. And through it we perceive the reasons for the amused skepticism regarding the man and his plays long expressed, to the quondam irritation of his local advocates, by visiting English critics. In those days we local critics were given to such a determination to boost the American theatre, which was coming along pretty nicely at that, that I fear we sometimes started cheering before the football was even out of the locker room.

This *Key Largo* indicates the same high purpose and intention which its author's name generally guarantees and which in the past have often induced his critics to praise him for what he has tried to do rather than for what he has actually done. As in the past, too, it indicates a dramatic ambition not matched by the talent behind it and which consequently fails to reach the meridian to which it aspires. Two things, it seems, are instrumental in causing Mr. Anderson to stumble. One is his conviction that he is a sizable philosopher when he is rather simply and usually a naive expounder of the oldest and most worn stencils of the defeatist doctrine. The second is his already noted frequent passionate adherence to the free verse form, often not only questionable in its relevance and appropriateness, but sometimes internally dubious.

As for the first, we find sufficiently fecund illustrations in this play. I quote several essences:

1. "No way squares with the rules . . . you're thinking of the old rules . . . Men don't live by faith or honor or justice . . . that's revoked . . . they live as they can, as the animals they are."

2. "Our cause is lost . . . maybe because there isn't any God."

3. "They say there's just one test for whether a man's a fool—it's how long he lives and how well."

4. "The soul—or psyche—has the same composition as eggs and butter."

5. "If it's like all the other faiths I've ever known . . . it's nothing. A pocket of air under the vest."

6. "The sky's quite empty . . . the scientists have been over it with a fine-tooth comb and a telescope and the verdict is, No God, nothing there."

7. "There's no faith sure if you test it often enough . . . no love of woman or love of man that won't dry up in the end."

8. "The mind has but one purpose, to defend the body and ward off death."

9. "And Christ hangs dead on the cross, as all men die, and Lenin legislates a fake paradise, and the girl holds out her arms and she's made of sawdust, and there's sawdust in your mouth!"

10. "Then why would one live—woman or man or beast? To eat and sleep and breed."

11. "Where this voyage started we don't know, nor where it will end, nor whether it has a meaning, nor whether there is good or evil, whether man has a destiny or happened here by chemical accident," etc.

(Footnote: Mr. Anderson's defeatist mouthpiece makes a sudden Pollyanna about-face at eleven o'clock, but that has no bearing upon the critical point.)

As for the second, we may question the integrity of blank verse which, as in this *Key Largo*, incorporates into brusque colloquialism like "sons of bastards," "eat dirt and be damned," "we'd better hump it," "some sob story," "the hell with it," "hell, we're not here for fun," "I got it," "nutmeg alma maters," "you God damn fools," "Jeez, this bird's an amateur," "hand over fist," "belly-button," "comfort stations," "that's my meat," "God damn service," "this thing was on my chest," "barge in," "how's tricks, pardner?", "oh, boy!", "hot damn," "disappearing like a bad smell," "look, bo" and "cause a stink"—we may, as I say, question the integrity of blank verse which interlards such lingo with words and phrases like these: "expiation," "the least approximation," "idiot ideologies," "I had some reluctance about deciding," "without warrant, without reason, incessantly," "allergic," "faces draining white under the moon," "dead white light from the dead moon," "cleansing the earth," "a demon that lives in my soul," "the earth's shell," "a parting curse," "beyond all begging," "interminable branching highways," "shriven," "over-simplified," "ophidian," "satrap," "casuistic brain," "envisioned," "magnanimity," "under the rose," "limitless tensions of the sky," "rope of sines and cosines," "Wells' Martian polyp," and "unathletic periphery."

And, please, let us not hear the argument that if Shakespeare could do it why can't Maxwell Anderson.

These, I appreciate, are hard and disobliging words to write of a dramatist whose resolve is as brave as Anderson's, but more and more he reminds me of a charming, if social-pushing, host who invites one to dinner, ushers one in to a table beautifully and promisingly set, and then —after some palate-whetting hors d'oeuvres—seeks to make one oblivious of the absence of any further food with a lot of fancy conversation. It would take genius to write the plays Mr. Anderson essays to write, and all he brings to them is a little talent.

Frequently, when it comes to dramatic art as represented by Mr. Anderson and merely box-office art as represented by such playwrights as the Messrs. Kaufman and Hart, give me the latter. This is not affected lowbrowism calculated to endear myself to the proletariat. I leave such amiable chicane to Billy Phelps, Gilbert Seldes and other such critical contact-men. I mean it quite as I do when I say that I'll take Jerome Kern's *Music In The Air* in stead of Verdi's *Simon Boccanegra,* de Caillavet's and de Flers' *The King* in place of Congreve's *The Old Bachelor,* to say nothing of Behrman's *The Second Man* over both, and the dancing of Renée De Marco above that of three-fourths of the women in the Ballet Russe.

There is often a lot of nonsense in critics' talk of the difference between a writer with high aim and one with a lesser one. The best anti-aircraft gun in the world, even if embossed with gold and embellished with the pictures of the Twelve Apostles and an aquamarine carved in the pattern of Buddha's navel, isn't worth a hoot unless it has the necessary ammunition. To praise a playwright, irrespective of his competence to do anything about it, simply because his aim is a lofty one is as ridiculous as it would be to praise me, for example, for a desire to be a Beaumarchais when the best I can do—as has been amply and disenchantingly proved—is to be merely a Nathan. There is no question that Anderson's aim is immensely higher than Kaufman's and Hart's, but there is also no question that most of the time it remains all aim and little else.

The Kaufman-Hart witticos evidently have no aim higher than to amuse us with cleverly imagined comedies and in the process to make some money out of us. O.K. They often do amuse us; they amuse us in an intelligent manner; and if they did not make some money out of us for doing so we would be pretty ungrateful. What is more, in their own chosen line they show a craftsmanship and talent superior to that shown by Anderson in his. So why criticism should still go in for the notion that good comedy is fundamentally never so important as poor drama, if only the latter concern itself with some august theme and express itself in the verse form, I am afraid I would not know. Nor would I know why so many otherwise judicious folk continue to believe that there is somehow something just a little cheap about laughter. The idea that loud laughter is the mark of a moron and that any playwright who can make the kind of critic who believes it weep is not only something of a dramatic genius but miraculously purges that critic into a creature of profound tragic heart and mind evades my metaphysic. Mark Twain, to be childishly banal about things, didn't aim nearly so high as his contemporary, Mrs. Humphry Ward; worse, he was a comedian; yet which is to be picked for win, place and show?

However, nevertheless, Deus misereatur, Ilias malorum, il rit bien qui rit le dernier, and dammit, the latest collaboration of our exaggeratedly anointed twain isn't at all what it should be. Called *George Washington Slept Here*, it has some funny stuff in it and it again provides some evi dence of the Kaufman-Hart skill, but on the whole it isn't anywhere up to its authors' previous peak. It is moderately good but it isn't good enough, either for them or for critical us. This is particularly true of its comic invention. The best the authors can do about their couple who with patriotic pride buy an old house in the Pennsylvania countryside in which Washington is reported to have slept is suddenly to floor them with the news that it wasn't Washington but Benedict Arnold. This is serviceable enough for a momentary laugh, but the boys surely could have done better. Just by way of a little impudent constructive criticism, wouldn't it have been more fruitfully amusing to have the couple learn to their and the community's moral consternation that it was George who slept there all right but that someone else slept there with him, and that that someone —as would be amply justified by the copious personal and historical record—was a lady of color?

As for Sidney Kingsley, his last disclosure up to the time of writing, *The World We Make*, derived from the popular Millen Brand novel, *The Outward Room*, is simply another stencil in the lengthy catalogue of the drama of regeneration. That drama is divided into two classes: physical regeneration and spiritual regeneration. In the first, we have a cripple who hasn't been able to rumba for years or an invalid apparently suffering from everything from myxomyoma to galloping smallpox finding a sudden and complete bodily regeneration induced by Faith, the triumph of the aforesaid therapeutic Faith being theatrically indicated just previous to the character's corporeal metamorphosis by a gradual sunrise effect, a shaft of calcium white projected sharply downward from the sky-cloth, the sound of church bells in the valley below, or the shadow of a cross on the backdrop. In the second, we have someone, frequently either a minister of the Lord whose doubts have caused him to abandon the cloth or a harlot sunk to the lowest depths of iniquity, or both, finding an equally sudden and equally complete mental and spiritual regeneration through Love, the eventual triumph of the aforesaid therapeutic Love being in turn indicated by the redeemed one's fixed, transfigured stare at the peanut gallery, his or her demise with a countenance illuminated by an unwonted blissful and beatific smile, or the regenerated twain's hand-in-hand egress into a Roman lion pit, far-flung mosque, or off-stage daisy field.

There is also a third class. This is made up of exhibits combining the first two classes. In this third and somewhat hybrid class we find both the physical and the moral, mental and spiritual regeneration facilely accomplished by a visit in the bucolic regions with artless, simple and lovable country-jakes (vide *Turn To The Right, The Fortune Hunter*, et al) or by a mere climb to the top of a mountain and a deep breath of God's clean air (vide *The Great Divide*, et al).

Mr. Kingsley's exhibit at least enjoys the novelty of falling into all three classes at once. His heroine is in need of physical, mental and spiritual regeneration all rolled into one, that regeneration she ultimately finds in Faith, Love and a visit with artless, simple and lovable folk all rolled into one, and the triumph is theatrically and duly registered by the rapt gaze at the balcony, the countenance (though here still undemised) illuminated by the unwonted blissful smile, an imminent hand-in-hand egress into the new world, and, by implication, all the rest excepting maybe only the shadow of the cross and the Cheyne-Stokes breathing on the mountain top.

Conspicuous in the daily prints in the earlier years of the present century were the advertisements of one Munyon, by title Dr. and by economic profession the dispenser of a patent medicine guaranteed to cure most of the ills of humanity. Invariably accompanying the advertisements was a cut of the eminent gent himself, magnificently aflow with mustachios, overpoweringly imposing in frock coat, and with forefinger raised solemnly to the heavens. The caption read: "There Is Hope!"

Robert Ardrey, of whom much was originally expected, has turned out to be an offspring of the eminent doctor, his pocket bulging with a like nostrum. His most recent panacea bears the label *Thunder Rock* and takes the form of introducing into the fancy of a cynic, retired symbolically to a lighthouse, various ghosts of the American past and through them inducing in him, despairful of the future of mankind, a profound conviction that all is not lost and that Munyon and his finger were right. The spooks, it appears, theoretically so valorous in his imagination, were cowards in their mundane incarnations, which revelation causes our hero peremptorily to pack up his kit, abandon his ivory tower and go forth into the world, presumably to consolidate the infinite glory of the future by getting Asiatic cholera in Chungking while writing a book arguing that the Japs are scalawags.

Not only, unfortunately for the puissance of his optimistic evangel, does Dr. Ardrey's writing suggest a Simon and Schuster book advertisement but his dramatic invention intimates that he must be an omnivorous reader of the plots of plays compiled over the decades by Mr. Burns

Mantle. His device of ghostly characters colliding with the protagonist's imagination harks back at least a quarter of a century to Thaddeus Rittner's *The Man In The Prompter's Box* and encounters on the way a quorum of dramatists ranging from Pirandello and *Six Characters In Search Of An Author* to Benjamin Kaye and *On Stage*. His protagonist, in turn, utilizes the reflective memory shenanigan of John Balderston's *Berkeley Square*, as his ghosts utilize the comportment of Elmer Rice's in *American Landscape*. And for good measure he includes the prognostication hocus-pocus out of several of the Priestley opera. All of which might not much matter if he visited a fresh and vital mind upon the materials, but the mind he visits may best be indicated by his ponderously lofty pronouncements that if Darwin had not contributed the theory of evolution to science someone else would have, that if Lincoln had not freed the slaves someone else would have, and, by implication, that nothing so effectively clears the head for lucid philosophical introspection as a skinful of powerful schnapps.

To continue with the younger men, Irwin Shaw's latest reviewed work, *Retreat To Pleasure*, again discloses the talented short story writer as a deficient playwright. The tale of three men in pursuit of a girl, it resolves itself into the kind of play Saroyan might write if he were foolishly to write the kind of plays certain of his critics demand. That is to say, plays slightly better ordered and definitely more plotty than those he presently confects and, in addition, plays that contain what the aforesaid certain critics contemplate as intellectual content.

This intellectual content, in Shaw's case, consists largely in utilizing as parsley for his supposedly meaty reflections the names of writers like Gibbon, Cabell and Hemingway and, further, in investing his mouthpiece character with

philosophies compounded of a diluted mixture of Karl
Marx, Elbert Hubbard and Richard Halliburton. And his
emotional content, in turn, consists for the major part in
such stereotyped and familiar scenes as, for example, the
one in which a man and woman who have loved and
separated sentimentally recount to each other tender episodes out of the past: the little house by the sea with the
sound of the waves penetrating into their room, the picnic
lunch, the delight in listening jointly to Mozart, the ride
on top of a Fifth Avenue bus, etc. Two or three episodes
in the play are original and have some merit, but for the
rest all we get is a short story composer's attempt to develop a single note into a fugue.

Lynn Riggs has now got the play about incest out of
his system—something many of the younger playwrights
have to do sooner or later—and he is accordingly left free
tranquilly to pursue the rest of his life's work. What is even
more good for him, he has now also and simultaneously
purged himself of the play about the grimly evil female
who wrecks the lives of all those with whom she comes into
contact. The physic was called *The Cream In The Well*;
it was smeared with traces of an improperly assimilated
acquaintance with Ibsen, Strindberg, O'Neill and Lillian
Hellman, to say nothing of a thoroughly assimilated acquaintance with Virgil Geddes and other such later Provincetown Playhouse tragedians; and it was bad, very bad.

This Riggs is usually no slouch when it comes to playwriting, as his *Green Grow The Lilacs* and *Russet Mantle*,
despite what they may have left to be desired, have proved.
But in this, his latest exhibit, he not only got in over his
head but made so many peculiar loud noises trying to get
out that his erstwhile critical sympathizers could only stand
embarrassedly on the beach and insouciantly scratch their

noses. Essaying to adapt to his tragedy the Strindberg technique of intensification, Riggs, as others before him, managed to achieve only exaggeration, which is a quite different matter. Unable to hit off the technique in character, except superficially, he slipped into the error of applying it merely to external action. The result, as is always the result, was something that gave off the occasional aspect of travesty. His characters made all the suitable Strindberg faces but their accompanying actions were little more than a high-school rewrite of inferior Ibsen and worse Wedekind.

As for Clifford Odets, he continues grievously to disconcert those critics who early in his career hailed him as a new great genius in American playwriting. Each successive play of his not only adds to their wounds but finds them growing more and more dizzy trying to invent explanations and apologies. Not all of them, to be sure, for there are one or two who, heads buried in the critical sand, are apparently determined to save their faces by insisting that they weren't wrong about him and who will probably go on endorsing him as a gift from heaven even if he writes plays that they would hammer the life out of if written by anyone else.

Night Music, one of their genius' latest works, the story of still yet another boy and girl from the outlands who meet in New York and desperately try to make a place for themselves against the customary stage odds, follows the conventional basic pattern of plays of a kidney and is not only the poorest play its author has concocted but one beside which even Elmer Rice's *Two On An Island* and Arthur Wilmurt's *Young Couple Wanted*, recent essentially similar plays, take on unexpected comparative values. Here and there Odets reveals faint glints of his older aptitude for quick character delineation, of his feel for dramatic effect, and of his ironic humor—how often in the case of his later plays have we written those same words, to say nothing of those now to come—but by and large his exhibit goes critically to pieces on the rocks of juvenile sociological dialectics, benzedrine-fed drama, and aimless volubility.

Some critics have praised Odets for turning in this play from his accustomed pessimistic and cynical attitude to a warm optimism. That optimism, however, amounts merely to superficial and bogus theatricality, due either to careless or deliberately hokum thinking. I give you an example:

His play ends with the boy and girl, both destitute and out on a perilous limb, harking to the look-upward philosophy of a friendly old member of the metropolitan police force, proclaiming their resolve to conquer the future, and gaily going off, arm in arm, toward what we are invited to imagine are fame and riches. Inasmuch as the girl and boy are completely down and out financially, as both have just lost their jobs, as we have been shown throughout the evening that neither has any particular talent for anything, as the boy is a mere windbag without an ounce of hard sense in his head and the girl a softy, and as, finally, their adviser, cicerone and future helper is plainly stated to have slaved patiently and dumbly in the police department for thirty-five long years without getting anywhere—inasmuch as we have been previously and emphatically impressed by the author with all this, it is pretty hard to wonder if Odets' optimism regarding their future and the future of all boys and girls like them doesn't stem less from a clear and honest appraisal of their estate than from a hopeful recollection of the box-office happy-ending drama of an American theatre long since critically gone to the ashcan.

And as for *Clash By Night*, revealed most recently, it offers nothing to alter one's opinion of its author's current standing.

We come, in conclusion, to certain necessary qualifications in the case of our endorsed Mr. Sherwood.

If the Federal Theatre Project gave us what with considerable exactness was called the Living Newspaper, Sherwood is giving us what with at least a measure of exactness may be called the Living Editorial. Neither, however, is in form the least like the other and both differ further and widely in the fact that, whereas the former was contrived with plan and deliberation, the latter is the hapless consequence of dramaturgical insufficiency. For though it is plain in *There Shall Be No Night*—as in some of his antecedent *Abe Lincoln In Illinois*—that Mr. Sherwood's intent assuredly was drama rather than editorialization, the result is insubordinately and very considerably more the second than the first.

It thus follows that while the exhibit as editorial is satisfactorily eloquent it leaves something to be desired as drama. When Mr. Sherwood is lecturing on the insanity of man in terms of war, when he is pleading for God and rationality in the face of barbarism, when he is denouncing the evils of Moscow and Berlin with invaded Finland as a background, when he points with hope to the salvation of mankind in phrases from the Book of Revelation—when he is about such business he is, while rather platitudinous and not overly profound, sufficient unto the mob demands of the occasion. But when he is about the somewhat more important and more relevant business of jelling it all into drama, he is less auspicious.

So far as drama goes, Mr. Sherwood communicates whatever of it may be implicit in his editorialism mainly by means of such Sardouish subterfuges as the radio, letters, and reports from the outside brought in by suddenly introduced and partly extraneous characters. And when periodically he realizes the necessity for some straightforward dramatic diversion from his editorializing he falls back upon such makeshift and outworn devices as the man who, with an ache in his heart, forces a quarrel with a woman he loves so she may leave him and be spared future pain, as the young girl desperate when she finds herself with child, and as the playing upon a piano to relieve a scene of emotional tension.

Despite these obvious critical deficiencies, any such exhibit as *There Shall Be No Night* naturally gets the facile audience response that nearly always results from a dramatization, however faulty, of any topical subject about which the audience feels particularly indignant. Al Woods, on an infinitely lower level, capitalized pretty handsomely on that sort of thing many years ago when he rushed upon the stage overnight dramatizations of sensational news events, often of a criminal nature, about which the public felt hot under the collar. On the higher level aforesaid, Mr. Sherwood in *Abe Lincoln In Illinois* capitalized the current threat to democracy, as he in this instance capitalized the hatred of Hitler and Stalin and the sympathy for the ravished little neutral countries.

I am not, let me say, by any means here climbing on an ivory pedestal and alleging that I am an elegant fellow fastidiously remote from any slightest similar reaction to such things. Far from it. But for good or ill I happen at the same time to be a hired dramatic diagnostician and as such it is my duty to announce that it remains the bald fact in these malefic matters, rather than Mr. Sherwood's stage contribution to them, that induces my reaction. In much the same way, while I, like almost everyone else, react powerfully against such things as dictatorships, racial persecutions and poor little girls cruelly driven out of house into snowstorms, in my professional capacity I still nevertheless scratch my ear in some critical doubt over *A Passenger To Bali*, *Waltz In Goose-Step* and *Way Down East*.

In sum and by way of general commentary on critic and criticized.

The room was beautiful. The orchestra was softly playing a Strauss waltz. The girls in their flowered late summer dresses looked lovely. The champagne was excellent. I went over and sat with Dorothy Thompson. "What," she instantly and peremptorily demanded of me, "is your opinion of Molotov, Voroshilov, Kalinin, Malenkov and Timoshenko?" "I read Sean O'Casey's new play, *Purple Dust*, this afternoon," I said. "It is rich in poetic imagination."

She looked at me over her champagne glass with profound disgust. "What is a mere play, even one by O'Casey, in times like these!" she exclaimed.

"But," scared half to death, I allowed, "it happens that my job is dramatic criticism, and the play interests me."

"A critic!" she scoffed, as the waiter refilled her glass. "There is no place today for a mere kibitzer in life."

Politely, nay with ineffable chivalry, refraining from observing that the only perceptible difference between us was that Dorothy was a critic-kibitzer in the field of war and politics whereas I was one in the field of the theatre and drama, I bowed elegantly at the middle, kissed her on each cheek, for I have long entertained a personal regard for her, and departed in the direction of the bar. There, after a brief colloquy with the bartender on the respective merits of Joe Di Maggio and Alphonse Daudet, the latter a great favorite of my bartending friend, I stood and meditated.

Why, I wondered, in a world grown cruel and ugly and

so famished for even a little glimpse of the old peace and
fineness and beauty, why this paradoxical sudden wide dis-
taste and even contempt for the artist and for those who
would defend and champion him? Why, I pondered—and
my bartending friend sympathetically pondered with me
—this belief that there is no place in the world today for
men and women who steadfastly hold themselves professionally, if mayhap not personally, aloof from the current
confusion and who steadfastly hope and try to keep alive
the inspiriting old artistic traditions? And just how, my
friend and I further ruminated, is the contemptuous attitude of the Dorothy Thompsons toward the artist essentially different from Hitler's?

The fact, nevertheless, remains the fact. There is little
general patience these days with any novelist, essayist, poet
or playwright who does not allow his work in one way or
another to reflect his concern with what is immediately
going on around him. And as we unfortunately have few
spirits independent enough to resist the market clamor,
the result is often something pretty painful. A dubious
journalism has usurped the chair of Melpomene; Thalia
wears a V sweater; Calliope grows to look more and more
like Winston Churchill; Euterpe sings *The Last Time I Saw
Paris*; Terpsichore runs a Bundles For Britain ball; Erato
chalks derisory limericks about Hitler on the lavatory wall;
Clio gives public readings of the Gettysburg Address; and
Polymnia patriotically hisses Wagner.

No one, surely, wants to see Nazism beaten and liberty
and democracy preserved more than I do, and no one is
more willing and fully eager to do his small share toward
that happy end, but I'll be good and bedamned if I can
see how it is going to be done, or even helped to be done, by
the simple process of converting the fine arts into New York

Post editorials. The Dorothy Thompsons and their boy-friends may write their heads off and yet they can no more bring down a single Messerschmitt with their propaganda screeches than they can bring up the estate of the drama with their propaganda plays like *Another Sun*.

It is, as I write, still too early in the theatrical season of 1941-42 to tell just how far the stage will again go in for plastering the ivory tower with indoctrinatory three-sheets. But unless all signs fail the analogy, parallel and straight-out propaganda playwrights will once more be with us in sufficient numbers and, as heretofore, will for the most part make us overpoweringly homesick for the days when the drama was still an art and not a rally. When I say us, I of course speak within narrow limits, for all too evidently there remains a great audience to be capitalized on with dramatic repetitions of the afternoon's newspaper editorials, hams made up to look like Jefferson and Lincoln, old-fashioned Germans heroically going back home to kidnap Hitler, pianists in the little invaded nations drowning out the Stukas with brave renditions of Sibelius, cloak and suiters identified spiritually with Jesus Christ, Free French-men beholding again the angel of Mons in the bottoms of their wine glasses, and illiterate cockneys suddenly brought to a realization of the grave danger to the civiliza-tion of Shakespeare, Milton and Warwick Deeping, shoul-dering a 22-calibre pistol, and gallantly going forth to beat off the full force of Goering's Luftwaffe and save the Empire.

Since themes matter little and treatment matters much, all this might conceivably be acceptable even to such fowl as strangely persist in esteeming *Romeo and Juliet* above *Flight To The West* or even *Shenandoah* and *The Girl I Left Behind Me* if only the playwrights who are busying themselves with the themes were sufficiently gifted dramatic artists. But the most of them are very far from that, and the consequence has been and threatens to continue to be a succession of defense campaigns, spiritualist cabinet materializations of Tom Paine, testimonials to the valor of our English and Chinese brothers, and hot-foots to Adolf artlessly masquerading as reputable drama, and fooling nobody but the actors and maybe a million or so other people.

This, obviously, as intimated, is of course solely the point of view of a professional critic of the drama, but how any professional critic of the drama can possibly entertain any other point of view and still hold his job with his head up is rather hard to make out. Yet the fact remains that there are plenty such, and that their heads still peculiarly brush the ceiling. For it is their stout conviction, regularly expressed, that if drama does not center itself upon the events of its immediate time it is not worth its salt and should be relegated to the library, where, presumably, it may languish forgotten along with all the great classic and modern literature there that similarly did not center itself upon the events of its immediate day.

This journalistic critical attitude, already spread through the nation like hot-dog stands and doing an equally rush business, is the most discouraging and malignant thing that our young dramatic artistic aspiration has to face. I know at least a half dozen young fellows of considerable talent who have come to me lately, in their eyes the look of little dogs lost and bewildered in a traffic jam, and who have speculated if there was any use in trying to write the plays closest to the hearts of their imaginations with contemporary criticism waiting around the corner with a blackjack.

The records of more modern dramatic history suggest

that good propaganda plays—and there have been good
ones—have for the larger share been written not during
the fact but considerably after it. Meditation and reflection
have thus distilled what was mere stark propaganda into
the tincture of philosophical dramatic literature. Heat
makes reporters; calm makes poets.

The usurpation by most of our leading playwrights,
duly encouraged by the majority of our critics, of the profession of newspaper editorial writers, cable editors and
Mecca Temple Ciceros seriously threatens that advance of
the American drama which began so auspiciously twenty
years ago and which, until lately, promised to grow apace.
Only O'Neill stands stubbornly, courageously and brilliantly apart from the salesmen of popular indignations and
therapeutic cure-alls, remains resolutely in his ivory tower,
and to the ultimate greater credit of the native drama looks
amusedly down at the swarm of neo-Aristotelian ants scur-
rying aimlessly among the day's newspaper files, frantically looking up the definition of analogue in the dictionary,
and voraciously nibbling large chunks out of *Mein Kampf,
Blood, Sweat and Tears* and the hundred and one *I Saw
France Falls*. And only O'Neill does that drama a disservice
by failing to give to it, in its hour of greatest aesthetic need,
those fine, aloof plays which he has completed in the unholy
dramatic din about him and which yet thoughtlessly he
insists upon keeping from the stage.

As for the rest, contemplate the picture. Sherwood, as
has been pointed out, uses Lincoln as his stooge to sell us
Democracy, and invaded Finland to sell us Preparedness.
Anderson looks up and discovers the meaning of analogue
and uses Christ to sell us the error of racial persecution and
oppression, and further drafts France to sell us a psychic
lesson. Hellman wins the critics' prize for merchanting the

need for some neo-Schurz to return to Germany and take
a pot-shot at Hitler. Rice charters a transatlantic clipper
and sells us tolerance of Zion and hatred of the Nazis in
terms of a set of stock-company angels at stage right and
a set of stock-company devils at stage left. Behrman also
looks up and finds the meaning of analogue and auctions
us antagonism to the totalitarian doctrine in terms of a
heartless surgeon. And he also sells us the philosophy that
this is No Time For Comedy by forgetting for the moment
that he is a dramatic artist, turning special pleader, and
writing a very poor comedy. Kingsley sells us the Constitu-
tion through an actor listed in the program as Thomas
Jefferson. And Odets peddles us again one of his sociological panaceas boiled from herbs grown on the old *New
Masses* lot.

Look further at some of the others. Barry vends the pre-
ciousness of American freedom through a parable in which
a red-headed young actress called Liberty Jones is chased
around the stage by ferocious characters representing
Nazism, Fascism and Communism. Irwin Shaw hawks an
allegory in which oppressed Jewry is shown to triumph over
persecution, typified by a Brooklyn gangster, by luring the
scoundrel to Sheepshead Bay and with sudden bravado
hitting him over the head with a lead-filled blutwurst.
Robert Ardrey sells us the idea that we shouldn't rely on the
traditions of the past, shouldn't lull ourselves into a false
security and should bestir ourselves to fight for world order
by exhibiting to us four or five actors designated as ghosts
of the intrepid yesterday and then having them comport
themselves like so many Joe Webers being poked in the eye
by Lew Fields. John Howard Lawson retails the glory of
the Communist ideal in terms of the old foreclosure of the
mortgage and the cruel eviction of the poor hero with his

wife and little child. Robert Turney hopes to recreate in us the Spirit of '76 through enough waving of the flag to give even George M. Cohan goose-pimples. Ben Hecht sells us the determination to battle the forces of Fascism by presenting to us a bravo who finally rouses himself from lethargy and goes forth against the enemy armed with a mandolin.

Continue. Ellis St. Joseph joins the Newcastle Coke and Coal Importing Co. by exposing Hitler in the person of a spurious clergyman who persuades the crew of a ship symbolizing Old Point Comfort, Va., or something of the sort, to mutiny. Burnet Hershey proffers us the hypocrisy of the Nazi Aryan doctrine by bestowing upon us a high-class Nazi whose mother's maiden name is discovered, to his glowering abashment, to have been von Levy. Even the customary humorists, the Messrs. Kaufman and Hart, seek to sell us patriotism with a tear-brewery in which an old German-American even more excessively amorous of the United States than Nathan Hale or Walter Winchell is beaten up by a gang of Fifth Columnists. And girls like Ayn Rand, Clare Boothe and Dorothy Thompson help sail the coal schooners to Newcastle with the aid of windy plays demonstrating, respectively, the virtues of the pure Russians, the despicability of Nazi consuls, and the pitiable plight of refugees from the dictator nations, including, presumably, such starving and pathetic creatures as Baron Rothschild, the Countess Szechenyi and Pola Negri.

And they say *Saroyan* is crazy.

II

The Status of the Female Playwrights

Her last play, *Watch On The Rhine,* proves two things. It proves again that Lillian Hellman is the best of our American women playwrights and it proves that even the best of our women playwrights falls considerably short of the mark of our best masculine. This statement will of course cull a smile from the girls at large, since they will attribute it, as is the custom of the dears, to the male's besetting theory of the general superiority of his sex and to his arbitrary collateral condescension. But though the beauties may be fully correct in some other directions, I am afraid that in this particular one they are wrong. For the facts pretty substantially demonstrate the probity of the obnoxious impeachment.

Why it should be that women, when it comes to the confection of drama, are most often inferior to their boy-friends—or at least to their boy-friends in the same play-writing categories—I do not know and, what is more, shall accordingly not, as is frequently the critical custom, develop into a scholarly treatise implying that I do. But, as we all too well recognize, they are, and the best I can manage under the circumstances is to venture a few guesses, possibly wrong.

My first guess—and even the pre-eminent Miss Lillian seems to give it some support—is that a woman dramatist seldom succeeds in mastering an economy of the emotions. Give her an emotion, whether tragic or comic, and she will stretch it not only to its extreme limit, but beyond. It is for this reason, I believe, that the drama of most female playwrights, Miss Lillian among them, often resolves itself willy-nilly into melodrama, and that the comedy of others often edges up closely to farce. I appreciate that there are exceptional cases, but as a general rule I think that the criticism holds.

This generic feminine inability or perhaps disinclination to hold the emotions within bounds has been responsible in Miss Hellman's case for the unwitting excess of melodrama in *The Children's Hour, The Little Foxes,* and this *Watch On The Rhine.* I say unwitting because I doubt if the author herself would recognize it for melodrama and admit that it is melodrama. She would in all likelihood take to injured task any critic who so dubbed it and would argue that even if it be melodrama it is definitely appropriate and relevant. There is the feminine blind-spot. For while it may be appropriate and relevant in the lesser dramaturgy it is more than suspect in the higher drama that is its author's aim. Its theatrical value may be unquestioned, but its critical dramatic value allows for many interrogation marks.

And do not in this connection try to confound me by bringing up the names of such dramatists of the past as Strindberg. The difference there is that the over-intensification and elaboration of emotion to the point of melodrama was the result and direct purpose of a deliberate dramaturgical technique. The difference here is that it is unintentional, or at least unavoidable by nature.

My second guess is that it is apparently very difficult

for a woman playwright to see her leading characters with a complete objectivity. Why this should be, I also do not know, since certainly women novelists often seem able to negotiate the business. But the record shows that in the instance of our women dramatists the opposite is the rule. A Clare Boothe may be carelessly praised for achieving such objectivity in a play like *The Women,* but shrewder criticism has little trouble in distinguishing between scrupulous objectivity and indiscriminately presenting a lot of female characters as simon-pure bitches. A bucket of black paint may be amusing if splashed all over the stage, but it hardly constitutes sound appraisal of character and amounts in sum merely to a melodramatically inversed sentimentality.

I may be mistaken, but I can at the moment recall no play pretending to quality written by an American woman in the last dozen years whose central characters have not at one point or another suffered critically from the personal sympathy or personal dislike of their author. In howsoever small a way they intermittently become not their authentic selves and betray their creator's personal prejudices. Nor does it matter whether they are male or female.

My third and associated guess is that it appears to be almost impossible for a serious American woman playwright to handle a theme save she be positively committed that one side of it is absolutely right and the other side absolutely wrong. There can be no middle ground, no flicker of doubt, no dispute of reason or justice. Black must be black, white must be white. And however artfully she may try to conceal her arbitrariness her womanish prejudice remains transparent. That is the way of the ingrained melodramatic emotion. If there is a woman hereabout who has dramatized or could conceivably dramatize some such theme as, say, that of *Strife* as Galsworthy dramatized it,

I invite her to supper tonight and, after the sixth bottle of champagne, offer to propose matrimony on the spot. (No sarcastic letters, girls, please.)

But enough of guesses and to a general survey.

Returning to Miss Hellman, I hope that my animadversions may not be thought too severe. For, as I have said, she is in this estimation not only far to the forefront of her local playwriting sex but very considerably in the van of a sufficient number of the lesser uglier gender. If she has the dramatic faults inherent in her gender, she also has virtues in advance of those of members of her gender and profession. She has a mentality superior to the majority; she has an incorruptible honesty and honor; and she knows how to write. These qualities along with the dubious ones are again made evident in this *Watch On The Rhine*. The tendency to extend a tensional scene considerably beyond its effective limits, sometimes found in her plays, is again painfully in evidence. It is, in fact, in such evidence that the last half of her third act, given over to the sad farewells of her protagonist, induces the impression that the curtain got badly stuck at 10:40 and that the actors are sparring for time until it is fixed and may be lowered. Here Miss Hellman piles on the blues in a succession voluptuously suggestive of a juke box into which someone has put ten dollars in nickels. The lugubrious goodbyes of her hero, visited seriatim upon his old mother-in-law, his brother-in-law, his wife, his three children and others, take on a perverse resemblance to the old Weber and Fields Music Hall act with the dialogue: "I am going away from here" —"What, you are going away from here?"—"Yes, I am going away from here"—extended to some fifty times its old length.

Miss Hellman's induction to her play about an anti-Fascist who returns to his native Germany to further the underground movement against Hitler, with death a certainty, is similarly unduly prolonged, dispersed and dilatory. She indulges in so much preparation that when her drama eventually gets going it has to meet and triumph over her audience's tedium and restlessness. But when that drama does get under way the author's gifts come plainly and forcibly into view. Her dialogue flashes; her characters, hitherto more actors than human beings, take on sharp life; her action achieves beat and vitality.

Of our other presently active women playwrights, Rose Franken seems to me, albeit on a less important plane, the possessor of one of the likeliest talents. Like the others, she is given to some of the deficiencies that have been mentioned, but she indicates an appraisal of character that has rather less compromise in it than most of her sisters', and a resistance to the exaggeration which gives birth to melodrama measurably greater, and a gift for making the apparently casual internally dramatic that is quite unusual.

The general modern tendency to evaluate drama in proportion to the size of its theme rather than in proportion to the merit with which a theme, big or little, has been treated is responsible for some freakish critical performances. It is thus that a play like Miss Franken's *Claudia*, which is in the main well wrought, is arbitrarily derogated in favor of a play less well wrought but whose theme bulks larger in immediate journalistic importance. It is by this standard that Miss Franken's play about a young girl's difficult adaptation to the marriage state is, however ably it be done, automatically considered a less worthy achievement than an inferior play which concerns itself with some such subject as the racial problem, the struggle between capital and labor, or the threat of Communism in Scappoose, Oregon. It is thus that a poor play like Mr. Rice's *Flight*

To The West or an even poorer one like Mr. Lawson's *Marching Song* is stubbornly esteemed, at least in their secret hearts, by many drama critics above some such very much better play as this *Claudia*, or some such other as, say, Saroyan's *My Heart's In The Highlands* and *Love's Old Sweet Song* or Osborn's *Morning's At Seven*. That some of the world's finest plays have had themes relatively insignificant in comparison with some of the world's worst plays is a philosophy seemingly lost upon the doctrine of present-day critical appraisal.

Susan Glaspell, who for some years was looked to as a figure of potential importance among our female playwrights, never realized herself, doubtless for the reason that the drama seemed always to be an alien field to her, and she awkward and uncomfortable in it. Her plays remained less plays than plans for plays. The direct articulation essential to drama was absent. She has not been heard of for some time and accordingly does not fall into any critical operation upon the current working girls.

Rachel Crothers, a prosperous box-office artisan, began her career years ago with serious intention and seemed for a while destined to amount to something. But it was not long before the great god Success found her bowing and scraping before its altar, with the result that there came from her a succession of plays painstakingly calculated to make money and let serious quality go hang. She is a shrewd woman at her job, but no play she has contrived since her early days has been other than trivial and occasionally amiable pastime. To a somewhat lesser degree than her sisters is she violently prejudiced either for or against her leading characters and she is, further, sometimes a likelier hand in the matter of keeping her comedy within rational bounds. But one may readily allow her comedies to criticize themselves simply by placing them in critical juxtaposition to those of, say, a male writer like Vincent Lawrence. The bold perception of human beings that Lawrence indicates becomes in Miss Crothers mere box-office appeasement.

Lula Vollmer, save for a disastrous reappearance several years ago with *The Hill Between,* has been in retirement. She started out with some promise as a writer of folk drama, but the bacteria of melodrama and emotional prodigality soon infected her as they have many of her playwriting sex and her plays became less and less valid. As for Sophie Treadwell, the bacteria were in evidence from the very beginning. In *Machinal,* one of the most negligently over-estimated plays in the modern American theatrical record, they expanded themselves like circus balloons and presently burst all over the stage. It may be that in her newest play, *Hope For A Harvest,* which has not yet been shown at the time of writing, things will be different, but the statistics up to the moment prove her to be just one of the girls.

Zoë Akins, when it comes to emotional economy, takes on the aspect of a 2 a.m. barroom choir in the throes of *Sweet Adeline.* And when it comes to prejudicedly falling in love with her leading characters her passion has hardly been exceeded since the days of Charlotte Chisholm Cushing. Even when she leaves off independent enterprise and goes in for the adaptation of foreign plays she apparently can not entirely resist squirting in the cologne and molasses in extra doses. The majority of her exhibits, accordingly, are essentially little more than Milne with a champagne jag and with half a dozen orchids supplanting the forget-me-nots in their lapels. *A Texas Nightingale,* a thoroughly intelligent comedy, is one of the few exceptions.

We come to the leading collaborators: Edna Ferber (with George S. Kaufman), Dorothy Heyward (with her husband, Du Bose), and Bella Spewack (with her husband, Samuel). And here we get into some difficulty, since there is no immediate personal way of knowing the exact nature and measure of the ladies' contributions to the team-work. So let us proceed as best we can.

First, Miss Ferber. Her two sole solo plays, *Our Mrs. McChesney* and *The Eldest*, amounted to nothing. It was only when she took on Mr. Kaufman as a helper, in the cases of *Minick*, *The Royal Family*, *Dinner At Eight* and *Stage Door*, that she managed to get anywhere—and of these plays only *The Royal Family* achieved any critical quality.

Secondly, Mrs. Heyward. Before marriage she wrote a number of plays, the only one to be produced being *Nancy Ann*, which had no merit. Following this independent production, she collaborated with Dorothy De Jagers on something called *Cinderelative*, which was rubbish. Then came the association with Du Bose Heyward and things began to look up. *Porgy* and *Mamba's Daughters*, both dramatizations of novels by husband Du Bose, gained favor, and Dorothy could go around with her head up.

Thirdly, Mrs. Spewack. I have no record of any play or plays written by the lady on her own. Her collaborations with her husband, antecedent to the highly amusing farce, *Boy Meets Girl*, were these: *The Solitaire Man*, *Poppa*, *The War Song*, *Clear All Wires* and *Spring Song*. All were inferior stuff, with only *Clear All Wires* showing the faintest glimmer of value and with *Spring Song* so overemotionalized that the tears of the actors cascaded over the footlights and nigh drowned the audience. Following *Boy Meets Girl* came *Miss Swann Expects*, a complete dud.

There is the girls' record. I leave the jury to its meditations, misgivings, and wonder.

III

And in this Tent, William Saroyan

Is Saroyan crazy? That is the question which for some time now has been occupying the nation. There are two opinions. The advocates of one maintain that Saroyan undoubtedly is. The advocates of the other indignantly deny any such thing and maintain that he is only half-crazy. Both argue their convictions with what they believe to be equally convincing proofs. And, illogical as it may seem, both present much the same evidence.

Exhibit A is their Specimen's unremitting proclamation, usually accompanied by a loud pounding on the table and a kiss handsomely bestowed upon the nearest waiter, that he is a genius. Even some of the critics who admire his writings enormously assert that this is an unmistakable sign of the fellow's insanity. No man who is really a genius, they say, goes around telling people he is. It's not polite.

Exhibit B is their Specimen's oft printed remark that the main difference between himself and Shakespeare is that Shakespeare wasn't an Armenian. Bernard Shaw years ago said that the main difference between himself and Shakespeare was that he knew how to write much better plays than Shakespeare. And, argue the alienists, everybody knows that Shaw is crazy.

Exhibit C is their Specimen's various published statements of his Credo. "The American theatre has been waiting for me, me Saroyan; no one else in it knows how to write plays. I am happy and proud to come to its rescue." . . . "I have just gotten up and have had no coffee. So I want to explain everything in six or seven words. The world is *the* theatre. The other theatre—the one which charges admission—is *not* the world. Therefore, the theatre does not exist. Only the world exists. Therefore, there is no point in going to the theatre. There is no art in the world, therefore; or in the theatre; or in people; or in nature." . . . "I learned by the end of seven days that to enter a saloon and belong you had to be completely aloof. I got the idea from alley cats, whom I had watched carefully."

Further items under Exhibit C: "By the time I was nine and in the third grade I was well along in the art of satire, parody, subtle contempt for ignorance and pomposity, and kindly recognition of virtue and charm.". . . "I read *Lady Windemere's* (sic) *Fan* when I was fourteen and the same day wrote a very good play in imitation of that worldly and brilliant style.". . . "What I mean is, it's a cinch *something* is delighted by the delightful, saddened by the sad, and so on.". . . "I have especially liked the *bad* bad play, the unmitigated lousy play, with superbly lousy characters. I have liked this kind of play more than the finest fine play." . . . "To hell with the gag, What is truth? Everybody knows what it is.". . . "How to make a movie for $300? Frankly, I don't think it can be done."

Still further items under Exhibit C: "Mr. Medford became my movie agent before I had a chance to drop my hat and asked me if I had a story on the new type of locomotives and Pullman cars the Union Pacific was introducing. It so happened that I had just such a story. It was a love story.". . . "Light a match and you see beauty so amazing it is almost unbelievable, and you know there is nothing like it even in art any more: in music sometimes there used to be, but no more. Now we have jit, which is O.K., but strictly a gadget, too.". . . "The kicking and turning of Follies girls should by now be in decline as *the* American rhythm, the tempo and calculation of American life. It's all right, but it doesn't get anywhere.". . . "The writing of plays is an art. Eating a herring is, too. Let's not be dull about anything. Everything can and should be an art."

Exhibit D is their Specimen's complete disregard for plot in the plays he writes. Take *The Time Of Your Life*, for example. It may be a fine play, they say, but it has no plot. Why? Take *My Heart's In The Highlands*, for another example. It may be a beautiful play, they say, but where's the plot, the meaning? Take *Love's Old Sweet Song*. Take *The Beautiful People*. Same thing!

Exhibit E is their Specimen's assertion that it takes him only a few days to write a play. And as for a musical show, why, he wrote all the sketches for a projected Minelli one in an afternoon. And as for the ballet—there is nothing he will not tackle—well, he wrote *The Great American Goof* in exactly thirty-three minutes, including the time he lit half a dozen cigarettes, ate two frankfurters, and read the sports pages in the *World-Telegram*.

Exhibit F is their Specimen's program note to the afore-mentioned ballet: "The dancers in a ballet ought not to be mistaken for people . . . Even so, in writing this ballet, I was not able to forget that the living inhabit the world. This happened no doubt because I don't know the first thing about ballet . . . As I see it, the living probably deserve nothing better than they get, although this irritates me personally. It irritates me because nobody other than myself seems to understand that the world is not real. That in reality there is no such thing. What I myself do is ignore the world, keeping a clear eye on it all the time, of course. In everything I have ever written, from psalm to saga, I have mentioned the world only because it gets in my way. What I say is, What world? What this ballet says is that you need six or seven thousand years to get this place out of the idiot nightmare it's in now. By the way, for all we know, there may be a place in which it will be possible for the living really to live, instead of having all this Shakespearean fun they're having all the time. In addition to this balletplay, I have written another. It is called *The Poetic Situation In America Since Alexandre Dumas*. It may or may not be accompanied by music and choreography some day. Even so, it is something that can be read for itself. I plan to continue writing for this form. As *I* write it, it is a new American form."

So much for the evidence provided by those who think that Saroyan is crazy and by those more charitable and humanitarian persons who think he is only half-crazy. Now for those of somewhat broader vision who think he is only one-third crazy.

Those who give him two-thirds of the benefit of the doubt offer in his defense the following evidence:

EXHIBIT A: If Saroyan frequently publishes philosophies that give pause to the judicious and hint that he is a bit bughouse, consider these fulminations from other loons:

1. "Not to go to the theatre is like making one's toilet without a mirror." Schopenhauer is the particular hazelnut responsible for that one.

2. "If a second- or third-rate play is performed by second- or third-rate actors, no one can wonder if it is utterly ineffective." Goethe is the papiya who pulled that hot one.

3. "The word tragedy is derived from the Greek word which means goat and the Greek word which means song. Tragedy is then, as it were, a goatish song—that is, foul like a goat." That one is the cerebration of the screwball Dante.

4. "The reason is perspicuous why no French plays, when translated, have succeeded or ever can succeed on the English stage." The sage in the straitjacket who negotiated that one is Dryden.

5. "Good music is a remedy against tediousness." And that one is the profound, original and novel philosophy of the loco Napoleon Bonaparte.

EXHIBIT B: If Saroyan is entirely crazy, so, admittedly, was Strindberg, yet Strindberg is regarded as the greatest dramatist of his day. If Saroyan writes plotless and meaningless plays so at times did Strindberg, and the critics have long esteemed them as classics. Perhaps, therefore, observing the plotty and meaningful plays so many presumably sane, if stupid, writers are producing and further observing the plays regularly denounced by the critics, Saroyan isn't so crazy after all and is sagaciously and deliberately strindberging himself and writing the kind of plays the scholars and critics in secret honesty admire.

EXHIBIT C: The breakneck speed at which Saroyan boastingly writes his plays, etc. Lope de Vega and Goldoni among others—and they weren't especially hypped—often beat him at it.

EXHIBIT D: Is the personal proclamation that one is a genius always and inevitably proof that one is not only

crazy but a negligible writer? If so, Shaw is not only crazy
but a negligible writer. And what of Nietzsche? And of
Swift? And of Jean-Jacques Rousseau? Of course, there are
always Ezra Pound and Maxwell Bodenheim, but we'll skip
them.

EXHIBIT E: If Saroyan's program notes on his ballet, because of his bumptiously confessed ignorance of the ballet,
sound foolish, consider these in the same program by Alexandre Benois, who was responsible for the world-famous
Diaghileff *Les Sylphides*: "High noiseless flights, full of
tender, slightly devitalized grace, give a definite impression,
and this in spite of the lack of any story, of a strange, phan-
tasmal romance, a hopeless infatuation of disembodied
beings, who know neither fiery embraces nor sweet kisses,
and for whom all that is bacchic or passionate has been re-
placed by a sad tenderness, by the merest fluttering suspicion of physical contact."

Is that so very much clearer than loony Saroyan's, "The
world which everyone other than myself seems to have
identified and accepted as the world is in reality a figment
in a nightmare of an idiot. No one could possibly create
anything more surrealistic and unbelievable than the world
which everyone believes is real and is trying very hard to
inhabit. The story of my ballet is on this theme. The figure
of the attractive but unkind woman is not a symbol of
beautiful women in the world. What she really is is the
bright potential in all things which in the world is never
visible to men. She takes on the architecture of the beautiful female body in the ballet because that is the easiest
way out, and no harm to anybody. And because if there is
to be a misunderstanding, it isn't likely to be the worst in
the world, inasmuch as, for those who choose, she *could*
be simply a magnificent wench who cannot be taken by

rape, acrobatics, or gentle words."

So much, in turn, for the testimony introduced by those who believe that Saroyan is still a few steps this side of the asylum. And now, again in turn, for those who do not consider him at all cracked, among whom I number myself, which probably proves that I, too, am cracked.

Let us admit right off that Saroyan is peculiar. So am I, very. So, for that matter, in all probability, are you. If perchance you are not, you are just another human nonentity and may as well go on being an insurance salesman, bookkeeper or society portrait painter for the rest of your life. Saroyan's peculiarity in insisting that he is a genius, for example, is peculiar only in that he does his insisting publicly. Most of the rest of us writers do it in private. We tell ourselves we are geniuses, and he tells us he is. That is the only difference. Well, is he, though, a genius? No. But he has a fine and original talent and it is only natural, relative youth that he is, that he should grandly mistake it for genius. When I was very young—around ten, I think—and wrote a kid school piece that was posted by my teacher on the school bulletin board as a commendable instance of belles lettres, I was sure that I was a genius and lorded it about for a whole week. Even my parents were rather persuaded that I was on the way to becoming a second Walter Pater, which numerical status convinced me they weren't so very perceptive and still had a great deal to learn about the relative eminence of literary masterpieces. If Saroyan thinks he is a genius, let him think it. He will either get over it in time or prove to us that he is right. Meanwhile, such a belief in himself is a good thing; it will drive him into a higher resolve.

Saroyan's complete freedom from the customary inhibitions surrounding the punctilio are further mistaken for a loose screw, especially by those given to a strict adherence to the accepted social procedures. If, for example, a critic denounces one of his plays, he will not only write a voluminous letter to the critic pointing out the excellent, aye, the really remarkable, qualities in it that the critic overlooked but will insist that the fellow view the play again in his company in order that he, Saroyan, may explain to the fog-head what the latter could not discern for himself. I can't see any particular harm in this, save that it is a waste of precious time on Saroyan's part, inasmuch as if the critic does not recognize a good play when he sees one he is a dolt not worth bothering with and if, on the other hand, he recognizes a bad play for the bad play it is, he is not going to bother with Saroyan anyway.

Saroyan's gasconade in print may not be in the best of tact and taste, but tact and taste have nothing to do with mens sana. J. B. Priestley is often just as boastful and tactless and tasteless as Saroyan and, while he is nowhere the latter's equal as a playwright, he is certainly otherwise very far from identity with the Cuculus canorus. If Saroyan's manifestos are at times silly, which they are, they reflect not upon his sanity but solely upon his momentary intelligence and lack of experience. Yet even at his silliest I doubt if Saroyan has been any sillier than such nationally accepted philosophers as Dale Carnegie or such internationally accepted ones as Frank Buchman. The trouble with Saroyan is simply that when he expresses a thought, whether intelligent or unintelligent, he is firmly convinced that he is the first man to be on deck with it, like a youngster who with his first girl discovers the only true meaning of love. No harm in that either. We have all gone through that phase and we all, with increased wisdom and experience, grow out of it. Well, maybe not quite all. I can name at least two gross of writers of maturer years who still believe that their platitudes are new tablets from Jehovah.

If Saroyan, it is argued, were completely balanced he would write plays that could more readily be understood. Dismissing the excessive and unnecessary point that bean-brains are still trying to understand certain of the plays of Ibsen, Pirandello and other such crackpots, it remains that Saroyan's produced plays to date are so easy and simple of comprehension that they are veritable A B C. Their very absence of so-called plot only makes them easier of that comprehension. Plot is sometimes confounding rather than clarifying, as witness such recent instances as Elmer Rice's *American Landscape*, Dostoievski's *The Possessed*, Lonsdale's *Foreigners*, Harold Igo's *Steel*, Paul Vincent Carroll's *Kindred*, Gustav Eckstein's *Christmas Eve*, and Syd Porcelain's memorable barbouillage, *Alternate Current*. Plays like *My Heart's In The Highlands*, *The Time Of Your Life* and *The Beautiful People* are purely dramatizations of emotion, and as such are essentially much more readily assimilated than emotion dramatized in terms of thought—or, more usually, what passes for thought. Relevantly, they are drama in terms of human music and music doesn't have to be understood to be felt and appreciated, save by pundits, senescent critics, and intellectual posturers.

But even to the determined ratiocinator it must occur that Saroyan's plays, superficially aberrant though they are, present less difficulty to intelligent understanding than any number of presumably more clearly defined plays. Surely in none of Saroyan's plays—and that includes *Love's Old Sweet Song*, which incidentally has all the plot the dullest dope may cry for—surely in none of his plays is there any such thematic muddledness and obscurity as is to be found in Maxwell Anderson's *Key Largo*, with its meditative, war-tortured, cosmically agitated and cowardly protagonist finding hearty resolution in the challenge of a petty Coney Island roulette-wheel faker transplanted to a Florida tourist dump. Or in the aforementioned exhibit by Elmer Rice wherein the ghost of Moll Flanders, of all people, comes to Connecticut and persuades an American not to sell a plot of ground to the Nazis. Or, to shorten what might be a long catalogue, in some such play as Carroll's aforementioned *Kindred*, which contends that the world should be run by artists and then offers as its representative of these heavenly creative spirits and potential world managers a cadging violinist who plays nothing but jalopyan tunes on his fiddle, who sponges on decent tradesfolk, and who is the epitome of bounderism in every respect.

Saroyan is regarded as shatterpated because he has gone in for writing a ballet without knowing anything about ballet. Well, he went in for writing a play without knowing anything about playwriting and in *My Heart's In The High-lands* wrote the best play of its year. His ballet, true enough, is pretty dreadful; it is, despite his conviction that it is tasty stuff, nothing but an old hokum modernized morality play, the kind that Henry W. Savage and Morris Gest used to sicken the critics with, with Doubt relabeled American Goof, Temptation called The Bright Potential, Ignorance dubbed Old Man In Prison, and Tradition relabeled The Dummy. Having the dancers speak a few words now and again may be a novelty—Saroyan proudly announces that it is a "new form"—but, while it may be a novelty and a new form in the sense that serving flat beer in a cupped phonograph record is a novelty in the case of the beer and a new form in the case of the phonograph record, it is at once gratuitous, irrelevant and impracticable. A ballet should no more be spoken than a play should be danced. The mood established by choreography is dissipated by speech. In addition, as the presentation of this talk-ballet fully demonstrates, it is as quixotic to expect ballet dancers to be proficient in the reading of dramatic lines as it would be to expect Lunt and Fontanne satisfactorily to comport themselves in Mordkin's *Voices Of Spring* or, for that matter, in even Cole Porter's *Begin The Beguine*.

It isn't that Saroyan wrote a ballet that counts against him. It is merely that he wrote a bad one. But so also for that matter did the great Marius Petipa, the founder of the Russian ballet; he composed not one bad one, but at least thirty-five out of a total of sixty.

And so we give over the great Saroyan case to the jury. But before the jury leaves the room to retire to its five minutes of reflection and six hours of portentous time-killing pinochle at the expense of the tax-payers, I wish to say a few words on all four sides of the question.

On behalf of those who think the defendant is crazy, I wish to quote, with the defendant's suspiciously ready and even eager full permission, a program note to another play he has written and which still awaits production. The title of the play is *Sweeney In The Trees* and here is the note: "This is a play, a dream, a song, a poem, a travesty, a fable, a symphony, a parable, a comedy, a tragedy, a farce, a vaudeville, a song and dance, a statement on money, a report on life, an essay on art and religion, a theatrical entertainment, a circus, anything you like, or whatever you please." Yes, sir, that's the note! What is more, on behalf of these same persons who think the defendant is crazy,

I wish further to quote, similarly with the defendant's suspiciously ready and even eager full permission, a program note to yet still another play he has since written and which also awaits production. The title of the play is *Jim Dandy* and here is the note: "This play is for babies, the enwombed and the long since unenwombed, the now full-sensed and perishing who constitute the present immortality of living things. It contains no characters, no imitations of people, and no plot . . ." Yes, sir, that's the note! Furthermore, the scene is described as "A portion of what we choose to call the fiction room of the Public Library in San Francisco but is actually no such thing." (Further still, the play suddenly concludes in nubibus with the line, "The writer got bored, so the play ends.") Yes, sir, that's the general idea!

On behalf of those who think the defendant is only half-crazy, I wish to point out that that happens to be exactly what the first play really is and what the second honestly at least partly is.

On behalf of those who think the defendant is only one-third touched, I wish to hint that there is some very good stuff in both plays.

And on behalf of those who think he isn't crazy at all, I wish to say that if he only will work on the scripts a little longer and with more patience and will give them just a little more organization and direction, he will have produced two other highly imaginative and deserving contributions to the American drama, and two which will doubtless make the fish who now consider him crazy believe that he is crazier than ever.

In conclusion, a few words on behalf of myself. In this William Saroyan, crazy or not crazy, the national theatre,

I believe, has discovered its most genuinely gifted new writer. His plays singly and in combination have disclosed and further argue a talent which, as yet undisciplined, vainglorious, cockeyed and pigheaded, is nevertheless the liveliest and most bouncing that has come the way of the local stage in some equinoxes. In that talent, which still resembles a fountain contending against a strong headwind and helplessly splashing itself all over the place, we engage a whimsical imagination, a lenitive sentiment, a fertile humor and a human wonder and ache uncommon to our drama and which in sum make his plays, whatever their occasional critical subordinacies, such welcome additions to the file of American playwriting.

He is a peculiar mixture, this young Saroyan, one of the most peculiar it has been my adventure to experience among writers for the lighted platform. Although as unabashedly sentimental at heart as the inside of an old-fashioned lace valentine, he has the dramatic gift of making his emotional syrups not only palatable to the most realistically minded auditor but immensely moving. Although his dramaturgy is sometimes as sketchy as a child's drawing of Santa Claus or a moo-moo, he not only gets the effect more usually contrived by the more precise artisan but here and there achieves it with a doubled power. And although he seems superficially to sustain his characters, orchid-like, on the thinnest of thin air, they come to us at the end rounded, whole, and completely intelligible. He writes much too hurriedly and impatiently, a symptom of his brash overconfidence. And his plays, accordingly, are not fully what care and meditation might make them. But I, for one, would rather have them in all their relative crudity than any ten dozen others sedulously polished, like old pairs of cheap shoes, into a surface acceptability.

IV

Exit Sophistication

The difficulty about writing of theatrical trends is that often no sooner have you firmly proved this or that than the theatre the very next day embarrasses you by proving in turn that you have talked through your hat. Time and again we critical Nostradami have conclusively predicted that realistic dirt was done for, whereupon a *Tobacco Road* has popped up the following week and impudently started on a run of more than seven years; that the old so-called well-made play was out, whereupon a *The Little Foxes* has promptly sneaked in and become a roaring success; that the grown-up American public would no longer accept the kind of English plays that London audiences were wild about, whereupon a *The Corn Is Green* has presently made us look pretty foolish; and so on, disgustingly. Nevertheless, being a fiend for punishment, I shall take another chance and remark that, unless all signs fail again, it looks as if what goes theatrically by the name of sophistication is now as dead as yesterday's newspaper or tomorrow's *PM*.

By sophistication I mean, if any explanation is necessary, the superficial attitude which makes a philosophical virtue of boredom and a critical vice of interest, which

accepts with a languid resignation what is normally regarded with enthusiasm, and which views with worldly
disdain the affectionate beliefs and little incidents of the
common run of mankind. It takes various concrete forms.
In the plays of the Noel Coward English school, for example, it has been a consequence of mental and emotional
taxation without sexual representation and has summed up
as a café society version of the drama of Wilde and Pinero,
liberally interspersed with superior catalogues of the more
recherché champagnes, motor cars, yachts, spas, duchesses,
and diseases. The tone has been that of an infinitely weary
young man giving his bride the hot-foot on their wedding
night and then sitting down to the boudoir baby-blue piano
and playing Tschaikowski so loudly that the poor girl can't
get to sleep until dawn. And all to a counterpoint of whiskey
and soda sallies which have issued a fastidious horselaugh
to orthodox courtship, marriage and sexual relations, along
with whimsical sideswipes at the Ritz, the Carlton, the
George V and the Riviera, the whole inspirited by a miscel-
laneous employment of the word bitch.

In the American manifestation, sophistication or what
passes for it has occupied itself chiefly in converting ordinarily quiet and reputable Long Island into a development
populated entirely by the Everleigh sisters, Polly Adler, the
Haig and Haig distillery and the Ted Peckham Escort Service. The moment one has observed from the program that a
play is laid on Long Island, one has come to know pretty
definitely that Mrs. X will be up to no good with young Y,
a polo player, that Mr. X will be up to no good with Z, who
is either the Mrs. in the house across the way or a dancer in
a night-club, that everybody will get drunk by ten-fifteen,
and that, save for a denunciation of the whole gang at ten-
twenty sharp by some young revolutionary who believes in

Communism, Socialism, Semitism or Pure Love, the general conversation will from first to last be confined to saying yes to whatever people habitually say no and no to whatever they conventionally say yes.

More recently, Connecticut and Westchester have occasionally been substituted for Long Island, but the evenings have remained largely the same. The clothes the women wear will not be so expensive as those worn by the girls in the Long Island plays, the men will frequently show up in velvet smoking jackets instead of evening dress, and the young polo player will be an aviator or maybe only a writer or painter, but for the rest it will be the old familiar sex reconnaissance, the old familiar sousing, the old familiar young daughter of the household who either clocklike defends her mother's dereliction in terms of her father's dereliction or rushes tearfully out of the house to spend the night with her school chum, and in conclusion, the old familiar wisecracks about cuckoos mistaking themselves for roosters and dead ducks posturing as rabbits, periodically interrupted by the routine debonair allusions to one character or another as a dog of the female species or the son of one.

Sophistication in the instance of the musical shows has usually centered itself industriously upon the lyrics. In the English importations these long concerned themselves chiefly with impertinences on presentations at Court, the sex life of various fashionable hussies at Biarritz and Cannes, the peregrinations of the Duke of Manchester, the luncheon habitués at Claridge's, and the European social activities of Mrs. Laura Corrigan, of Columbus, Ohio. In the American exhibits of Cole Porter and such of his followers as E. Y. Harburg—even, indeed, oddly enough in the periodic case of Lorenz Hart—the lyrics have invited us to wink knowingly over the intimate mention of the names of well-known social personages and other figures in the upper metropolitan life. In place of the onetime June, moon and spoon we have accordingly been put on confidential terms with Mrs. Astor, Mrs. Vanderbilt, Elsa Maxwell and Lady Mendl; in place of the former love, dove and stars above we have had Walter Winchell, Lucius Beebe and Cholly Knickerbocker; and for the quondam hearts apart and shade of the sheltering palm we have been vouchsafed Daisy Fellowes, Barbara Hutton, Peggy Joyce, Mabel Boll, Brenda Frazier, Herbert Swope, Jock Whitney, Serge Obolensky, Tommy Hitchcock, Doris Duke, the Grand Duchess Marie, William Rhinelander Stewart and almost everybody else who can get a table in the front section of the Colony restaurant or enter the Stork Club without a visa.

This species of sophistication is a tony paraphrase of the old Lew Dockstader protocol, and is calculated with much the same purpose in end, which is to say, to instil in the audience, nine-tenths of whom live in Brooklyn, the Bronx and West 110th Street, the implication that they are the very part and parcel of the high life of the town and are to be accepted and treated as persons fully privy to all its esoteric goings on. In Lew's case—Lew's idea of society being anybody who wore a necktie—the names were those of a town's more eminent cops, bartenders and aldermen. But Lew's plebeian audiences for some time were just as tickled by his wily intimation that they were on buddy terms with them as have been the later audiences in the instance of the somewhat more soigné confidences.

The Continental sophisticated school, represented by such playwrights as Molnár, Guitry, et al., permitted their dichotomous ennui an expansive occupation with sex. In their exhibits it has been not the stork that brings babies so to speak, but the wolf. However and nevertheless, being *very* sophisticated, their wolf, for all his lupine machinations, has been indicated to have a liberal streak of the bird in him. This was known as the charming and delicate Continental approach. Thus, a lady had an affair with a man less with the man himself than with her romantic idea of him. Thus, especially with the French school, contraband physical love was for years generally less the result of passion than of a droll epigrammatic bout, accompanied by the necessary amount of Pol Roger, in a cabinet particulier, of the mere mention of Deauville, or of a husband who wore whiskers and was a member of the Chamber of Deputies, which held night sessions.

This Continental sophistication long resolved itself into four more or less specific catalogues. In the first, a philandering husband was duly put in his place by a wife who herself took a fling, or at least insinuated that she had taken one. In the second, a lover and his mistress differed amiably over her interest in a young man and wound up with her going off with the latter and with the lover complacently making a rendezvous over the telephone with either a former flame or the midinette who delivered milady's hat in Act 1. In the third, two married couples discovered an interest in each other's wives and husbands and, after two hours of amorous hide-and-seek and after the men had elaborately lied to each other over numerous cognacs and the women had equally elaborately lied to each other and to the men that they were really in love with, respectively, Raoul and Etienne, two young art students who up to then had not figured in the conversation, the couples again went whimsically on their old way. That is, save for a last moment hint that the afore-noted Raoul and Etienne, or their equivalents, might very possibly soon be waiting around the corner. In the fourth catalogue, a man and woman met at a bal masque, in an opera box, or something of the sort, fell under each other's spell, made an assignation, and thereafter returned to their own firesides with such a transcendent luminosity in their eyes and with such a sudden accretion of charm that their wife and husband hardly knew them.

That all this quote sophistication unquote has now pretty well had its day is suggested by, among other things, a line that Molnár himself has incorporated into his last play. When his wife in the second act begins to speak much the same kind of pseudo-cynical stuff that Molnár got away with for years, his husband is made to return with considerable impatience, "For Heaven's sake, no more of that sophisticated talk; I'm sick of it!" In point of fact, Molnár indicates his belief that sophistication is theatrically done for by turning turtle so completely that you can barely recognize the once sardonic old fellow. His play is so sentimentally soft and sticky that it wouldn't surprise us if he changed his name, now that he is in refugee exile here, to Milnar.

If the curtain is not yet wholly down on sophistication, it surely is descending rapidly. The road to the storehouse is paved with epigrams on love and marriage. The door of the storehouse has the latch out for sex with its toenails painted red and a perfumed cigarette dangling superciliously from its lips. The storehouse dray horses relish as tasty oats songs about Dwight Fiske, Dorothy Parker and Tommy Manville. And the late Mr. Cain rolls over in his grave whenever he hears again from a stage so much as a faint mention, even nostalgically, of St. Moritz, the Berkeley, Bea, Gertie, El Morocco, the international set, Schiaparelli, the Duke of Windsor, Hispano-Suiza, Cartier's, Antibes, Juan-les-Pins, chemin de fer, sidecars, stingers, baccarat, Como, Monte

Carlo, Elizabeth Arden, 21, Mrs. Otis, Theodore, pâté de fois gras, the Queen's milliner, Mouton Rothschild '98, Capri, Cairo, Aiken, Southampton, Palm Beach, or even Fanny Ward.

V

Enter Sentiment

Sentiment, the last remaining despairful refuge of the cynic in the modern world, has again after years of intellectual ostracism come into its theatrical own. The *again* might perhaps better be left out of the sentence, for the new dramatic sentiment is of a different kidney from that which once drove the judicious to the antidotal bottle. The old mush has been drained of its surplusage of the milk of human kindness and what once made even audiences of an intelligence quotient of more than one-half of one percent gag has been converted into acceptable and palatable provender.

The disrepute into which sentiment fell was due, first, to many of the plays and novels which merchanted it and, secundus, to the school of critics whose operations in and directly before the 1920's embarrassed it out of countenance. The aforesaid plays and novels, written not only by hacks but here and there by literati of some moderate standing, so often and greatly confused sentiment with sheer goo that one didn't know whether to read it or use it as a massage cream. The plays in particular, frequently dramatized from the novels, were so doubly cute that it was almost impossible for the actors to stop sucking their thumbs long enough to speak their lines, which were in turn so oversweet that the actors got such bellyaches their understudies had to be rushed in to finish the evening. As for the aforementioned disquieted school of critics, it not without some warrant, considering the engulfing flood of pap, offered as its remedial ideal a United States populated chiefly by Dreisers, preferably unshaven and without collars, and with their progeny of Hemingways beating up the Harold Bell Wrights and Robert W. Chamberses in every corner saloon, Farrells swimming nude in the nation-wide gutters, and Faulkners maneuvering esoteric corncobs in every countryside backyard.

The plays and novels on the one hand and the critics on the other combined gradually to disgust the more literate public with the prevailing literary and dramatic cockyleeky, and it wasn't long before the merest mention of a poor little orphan in a play or the merest allusion to a starlit pool in a novel was sufficient to induce a nauseous taste of sodium amidotriazin-sulphonate. That the critics exaggerated things somewhat may have been true and that the public's disrelish was also exaggerated may have been similarly true, but nonetheless there was ample justification. For matters had come to the pass where honest sentiment had been so effeminized that it became not only unmanly but emotionally downright indecent to allow it more than a half-inch of critical ground.

The sentiment that the drama by and large now goes in for is far removed from the tearjuice of yesterday. In it there is a truer comprehension of humanity, a mentality more shining, an emotional keyboard of white along with the black keys, and a new prophylaxis of humor. A critic can now look it straight in the eye and not tell it to go to hell. And that is one more mark of the advance of our American drama. When and if some of the old malt is offered, it quickly dies the death save in rare instances, for there will always be left-overs from the older order who persist in regarding beer as a handkerchief. But for the newly developed and more acutely critical theatre audience it is the clean, bright, robust, realistic and honorably moving sentiment of today's drama that is alone expedient.

One of the biggest successes of recent seasons is the Messrs. Lindsay's and Crouse's *Life With Father*, derived from the late Clarence Day's family chronicles. It illustrates in a measure what I mean. Though a minor item in the dramatic catalogue, it emphasizes the difference which has come over theatrical sentiment. All one has to do to appreciate that difference is to compare the emotional solicitation of such an exhibit as this with that of equally successful box-office exhibits of fifteen and twenty years ago. In that era, described in the more facetious barroom circles as the good old daze, audiences' softer emotions were generally invoked by a purely theatrical and largely factitious portraiture of human fowl, with any realistic collateral humor either run away from as if it were the pox or gingerly approached in terms of obviously hypothecated comedy relief. It was, to a considerable popular extent, the era of paraphrased Cinderellas come uniformly at eleven o'clock into three-hundred-dollar white dresses and the embraces of young millionaires from the other side of the railroad tracks, of delicate young virgins just out of French finishing schools loved platonically and from afar by their champagne-guzzling, race-track follower, roué guardians, of Pollyannas, both male and female, who spent half the evening arranging blooms in vases and the other half reciting the lyric of *Hearts and Flowers*, of mothers so indefatigably sweet that the lemonade stands in the back aisles of the theatres reaped a small fortune from the more intelligent portion of the audiences seeking a counter-taste, and of fathers no less paragons of all the virtues.

This arch-marmalade has, as I say, now disappeared from the stage except in the rarest of instances, and even then is never so sticky as once it was. In the frankly sentimental drama of today—and *Life With Father* is an illuminating example—the alloy of human fact and intrinsic humor is not overlooked. And the result is a drama that, for all its signal critical unimportance, is a hundred times more relatively worthy and a hundred times more estimably affecting than the antecedent moonlight and honeysuckle species.

Nevertheless, let us muse upon the apparently ingrained and persistent critical attitude toward sentiment in general. Surely one not given to a tutti-frutti philosophy of life, I am nevertheless often puzzled by some of my colleagues' arbitrary objection to it per se. What is so wrong about it?

The answer, of course, is nothing. But for some reason or other a liberal share of the critical fraternity seems to be professionally afraid of it. In private life the gentlemen, if I know anything at all about them after years of close friendship, are the most of them as sentimental fellows as you can find this side of a Dixie magnolia arbor. But once they don the first-night bib and tucker a change comes over them wondrous to behold. The quondam gentle brows become furrowed with Dostoievskian frowns. The baby-blue eyes become etched with thunder clouds. The warm hearts turn to stone. They become, in short, as hardboiled as so many Easter eggs.

Why?

Well, one reason may possibly be found in their apparent conviction that sentiment is something for a critic to be ashamed of, that tradition demands he be toughly realistic whether he feels like being toughly realistic or not, and that there is something about sentiment, however rational, honest and sound, that is just a little infra dignitatem to the completely adult mind. And a second reason may be discovered in their collateral theory that the way to pass oneself off for a brainy fellow is to exercise an aloof iconoclasm, a superior condescension and a general air of kindergarten Nietzscheism in the presence of even a field buttercup.

This latter-day business of sneering most dramatic sentiment out of countenance is the critical equivalent of the ancient vaudeville act in which a man vehemently informed another how he was going to put his wife in her place and then, when she was heard yelling for him, hang-dog went to obey her. The hardboiled protestations in the case of the critics similarly fool nobody, except the critics, who nevertheless frequently give themselves dead away.

For example:

The majority of them last season loftily waved aside the play, *Claudia*, because of its sentimental treatment. That any other treatment, in view of its theme, would have been illogical and that the sentiment had entire dramatic integrity, did not matter to them. It was sentimental and hence not for a moment to be critically condoned. On the other hand, many of the same critics fell hook, line and sinker for *Watch On The Rhine* which was every bit as sentimental but which, since it dealt with a man's urge to fight Hitlerism instead of a young girl's marriage problems, somehow allowed them to persuade themselves that it was not at all sentimental but rather pretty masculinely realistic. Miss Hellman was every bit as impressionable in her treatment of her theme as Miss Franken was in the treatment of hers. The sole difference was that the strength of their prejudice against Hitlerism obscured the issue, being too powerful to permit them to detect and resist the sentimentalism of the author, whereas their relative indifference to the problems of a young girl gave them plenty of time to concentrate on the sentimental approach of the second author.

Personal prejudice aside and viewing the plays as plays, still irrespective of philosophical sympathy with their theses, surely no plays could be more thoroughly sentimental than *There Shall Be No Night, Flight To The West* and *The Talley Method.* Yet merely because they have dealt good hands to the doctrines stoutly held by the majority of the critics, the latter have failed to perceive them as the basically sentimental affairs they have been. Evidently the way to fool the bravos into good notices this season will be, while keeping the rest of the plays largely intact, to make all the Peg o' My Hearts distraught refugees from the Gestapo and all the Little Lord Fauntleroys nephews of Winston Churchill.

Hate is simply sentimentality with its coat inside out. Let these critics remember that when in the future they assay the relative values of plays about men with swastikas on their arms and of plays about girls with bunches of roses in theirs.

VI

The Contribution of the Irish

If critics who write books were paid their present dispro-
portionately handsome royalties to ask questions rather
than to answer them—ah, rosy day!—I should begin this
chapter with the query: What has happened to the Irish
playwrights?, and should thereupon under the new dispensation promptly demand a raise. But the world being
what it is today, what with capitalism in the saddle and us
poor critical slaves still forced to work for our hire, I am,
alas, driven to pursue the inquiry. Baring myself to the waist
and mopping my brow, I accordingly go to work.

It was only a very short time ago that I, along with other
drama critics, stoutly believed and vociferously affirmed
that in the Irish playwrights, if anywhere, rested the hope
and glory of the contemporary theatre. And for that belief
and that affirmation there seemed to be abundant justification. Surely what imaginative and poetic life our stage enjoyed in more recent seasons was largely the gift of the
Irish. And equally surely it was the Irish in the antecedent
years who could usually be relied upon to bring to the
drama of our hungry theatre that blend of wonder and
humor and fancy and delicate rhythm that for long has been
their peculiar blessing.

But lately something seems to have happened. Except for O'Casey, whose *Purple Dust* is a happy exception, the quondam rich vein appears to have run dry. Carroll, who gave us *Shadow and Substance* and *The White Steed*, has collapsed utterly in both *Kindred* and *The Old Foolishness*. Ervine, who began so auspiciously with plays like *John Ferguson, Jane Clegg* and *Mixed Marriage*, has wound up with a succession of weak minor comedies, the one most recently exhibited here, *Boyd's Daughter*, being so shockingly inferior that it was hard to associate Ervine's name with it. Denis Johnston, whose *The Moon In The Yellow River* was a thing to treasure, has since turned out *The Bride and The Unicorn*, a garbled mythological fantasy so poor that it appealed for production only to a pretentious amateur group, and an infirm comedy, *The Golden Cuckoo*, which no one has found sufficient interest in to produce.

Dunsany has sometime since gone into a decline as precipitous and alarming as a ski-jump. Lennox Robinson, remembered for *Patriots, The Lost Leader, The White-Headed Boy*, etc., has in his later plays substituted garrulity for drama and in the process laid his audiences flat. George Birmingham, who negotiated the admirable satiric *General John Regan*, has not been heard of for years. Teresa Deevy wrote *Katie Roche*, whereupon her talent curled up on her. George Shiels has similarly fallen off; Brinsley MacNamara has written nothing since *Look At The Heffernans* to attract even a moment's notice; and their story is the story of the rest. The newer and younger playwrights, moreover, seem to have next to nothing to offer, as witness such shoddy comedy as the Farrell-Perry *Spring Meeting* of several seasons ago and such gimcrack drama as the Louis D'Alton *Tanyard Street* of last season.

This *Tanyard Street* (called *A Spanish Soldier* when

originally shown at the Abbey) may in a measure, I think, be taken as a gauge of some of the reasons which have worked toward the Irish drama's late enfeeblement, since it happens to be infected with many of the typical schizomycetes. About the only one, indeed, that is absent is the dyed purple passage or passages singsonging either the glory of the old Celtic saints and heroes or the rustlin' o' th' leaves and th' swishin' o' th' wathers about Mourna-na-Mourna whin th' spirit o' ould Mitch-na-Crounihanoughin steals like a skithy leprechaun out th' shadows o' th' glen o' Houl-na-Shilgalowiddlidonderry. All the others are there, getting in their dirty work.

First among them is the micro-organism of the church, or the bacterium tholoideum theologicum. While originally nonpathogenic in the case of a number of Irish dramatists, it has gradually of late proved itself rather virulent. Metaphor aside, the topic has been hashed and rehashed for so long and so often belabored that the dramatic juice has gone out of it. It frequently seems that when an Irish playwright can't think of anything else to embroider a play with he will drag in a churchman and pitch him and his credo against some opposing character, much as an American playwright in the same arid situation will often introduce a styptic spinster given to wisecracking repartee or an English playwright a male of indistinguishable gender given to the same thing in slightly more blasé, world-weary and refined accents. The Irish have apparently now rung all the changes possible on the subject of the church and the theme, whether central or subsidiary, wears a wan and tired look.

In the second place, we have the recent mechanical introduction into the plays of what for quick identification may be described as the Barry Fitzgerald character. It doesn't matter who plays it, whether it be Fitzgerald or

Laurence O'Brien or anybody else, it persistently remains largely the same character. Derived from the great O'Casey roles of Fluther and Joxer, it has been reduced and bastard-ized into a kind of Irish minstrel show end-man and has been arbitrarily incorporated into plays (vide *The Old Foolishness, Tanyard Street*, et al.) for comedy relief. You recognize it at once: the shiftless, ill-kempt mick, most often an amiable sponger, who is either constantly and wryly be-moaning the state of his liver and lights and the world about him in general or with irrepressible gab discoursing on the sad plight of Ireland today as opposed to the rare, brave, gallant Ireland of the time of the old gods. Now he may come on with only one shoe and his shirt-tail hanging out, now he may appear with a mysteriously acquired black eye but with a larky mien withal, and then he may show up hav-ing comic trouble adjusting his Sunday-go-to-meeting starched collar and his other pair of pants, but call him what they will it is always O'Casey's character borrowed and in-differently paraphrased. And with small exception it has come to be as dully stereotyped—even when the matchless Fitzgerald himself has been persuaded to play it—as the comic maidservant and the dry monotone detective of the routine American plays or the imperturbable manservant and the wise old duchess of the routine English, or for that matter the senescent boulevardier with an eye still for the girls and the discreet cabinet particulier waiter of the routine French.

Thirdly, we engage the chatty neighbor busybody, some-times male but more often female, who periodically in-trudes upon the action for no other reason than that the author has to fill out his play by fair means or foul and who contributes less than nothing to the development of the evening. This character (occasionally in more trying cir-

cumstances elaborated into a married couple) generally
bustles or flounces in, plumps down either at stage center or
at the dining-room table to one side, and in a brogue that
usually seems exaggeratedly brogueful for that particular
neighborhood, considering the speech of the other characters, launches into a theoretically hilarious rapid-fire con-
fabulation animadverting upon everything and everyone in
sight, intermittently, if female, embellishing the palaver
with Biblical quotations, all of them miscited.

The humorous high point in connection with this female
character comes when the play's central male figure, believing she has already left, enters the room inquiring if that
fat oul' hen has gone yit. If the character is male, it comes
when he pours the fourth increasingly copious spot o' liquor
out of his host's treasured bottle and, finding nothing more
in the bottle, gets up from the table, wobbles unsteadily to
his feet, elaborately adjusts his hat to his head, and starts
to make his departure, only to hesitate momentarily and
make certain there isn't a wee drop left that he may have
overlooked.

The mystic touch is No. 4. The mystic touch has come to
be pretty arbitrary in Irish plays. It seems that Irish playwrights think it is expected and demanded of them, even
when their plays would be better off without it and when
they themselves have no more mysticism in them than
Louis B. Mayer or a fiedelbrett. As a consequence, it is an
uncommon Irish play in the more contiguous years that at
one point or another has not vouchsafed us a little of the
eerie delicatessen. It may be something in the way of a holy
miracle, as in *Tanyard Street*, or a weird sense of the past
wrought by the moonlight, as in *The Old Foolishness*, or a
congress of ghosts out of the obdurate yesterdays, as in
Kindred, or anything else of the sort. But more often than

not, save in the better Irish plays of earlier seasons, the attempt at mysticism has been enveloped with a forced and illicit air. And more and more, its dubiousness easily penetrable, it seems to be incorporated into the plays with a studied commercial eye to much the same effect sought in inferior American plays, albeit less subtly, through the incorporation of such more earthy attestations as "God damn" and "son-of-a-bitch."

In the finer Irish plays the quality of mysticism is deeply impressive and genuinely moving and beautiful. But in the second- and third-rate plays it has come to be just a trifle ridiculous. The idea that every Irish writer is a bit of a mystic in his soul, an idea liberally encouraged and even boozily asseverated by the Irish writers themselves, is in the light of many of their latter day exhibits open to considerable suspicion. Self-convinced that they are veritable and authentic bierbrüder of Ireland's mythological deities and thirty-third degree lodge brothers of all the elves and gnomes and sprites, numerous otherwise possibly valid Celtic playwrights have cavorted in fields in which they have been psychically gringo, and their plays have accordingly and refractorily taken on the aspect of so many Hallowe'en pumpkins desperately hoping to pass themselves off for the ghosts of proud Finn, and Fergus, and Cathleen ni Houlihan, and the gentle Deirdre, and Mavourneen eternal.

Which brings us to item 5. In other words, the omnipresent young Irishman in conflict with his surroundings, the counterpart of the brash young radical ubiquitous in most of the bad American drawing-room plays of the last dozen years. This character has become a stencil of the more recent Irish drama. Customarily played by a tall, lanky, touseled haired young actor in unpressed tweeds and with ever a look on his face suggesting he got out of bed on the wrong side that morning and anticipates an imminent seizure of cramps, it is designated sometimes as a rebellious school-teacher, sometimes as a youth who has been out in the world and returns to the hide-bound village that was his home, sometimes as one who has served in the military and been wounded by the dastardly English, and at still others as one who is doomed to live out his life in the constricted community and who strains at the shackles that bind him. But whatever it and he be nominated, it and he are always pretty much the same. He is sure to be sore as hell about everything; he will in all likelihood be found to be in love with the female property of another; he will be certain to let loose soon or late with a contemptuous tirade against everything and everybody, including the female in the case; and in the end he will in all probability either leave the house in a dudgeon or, if the play be of slightly more sombre cast, be shot by the authorities while trying to escape, in which event he will be carried back into the house and prolong the agony by irrelevantly and at undue length assuring his oul' da and the female of his hopeless passion that the spirit of Ireland will never die.

A sixth specialty is the Canon. You can't get away from the Canon. At times and in the hands of some playwright like O'Casey or the Carroll of *Shadow and Substance* and *The White Steed* he turns out to be a rich and fruity delight, but in the hands of the general later run of Irish playwrights, including the hands of the more recent Carroll himself, he is as inveterate as the butler of contemporary English comedy or the Indian chief of the 10-20-30 stockade melodrama of the American last century. With negligible exception he always looks like the kind of actor who couldn't otherwise get a job unless someone revived one of the old E. S. Willard plays at a dollar top; he always comports him-

self as if he had just miraculously recovered from a bad
case of choleraic diarrhea; he frequently alternates his
stern counsel with a schnitzel of mellow and understanding
humor; and he occasionally is not averse to a covert sam-
pling of the biscuits of the household he is visiting—indeed,
a glass of good port is also not beyond his pseudo-hesitant
acceptance, bad for his rheumatism though it be, glory be t'
God.

Finally, there is the ingénue. Just why she is in four out
of every five of the later Irish plays, it is rather difficult to
make out, since she usually seems to have only the vaguest
connection with what is going on and appears to have been
written into the play simply because the author either had a
crush on some little lassie to whom he wanted to give a job
or was tired of always sitting around in the pub after his
other plays with the undeniably talented but haplessly old
and fat actresses in the companies. This ingénue, her exact
association with the other characters seldom very clearly
defined, uniformly wears the only fresh, clean-looking
dress in the play, has her trim legs, however poor and
squalid the setting, encased in the very latest thing in silk
stockings, and earns her weekly histrionic salary solely by
frisking breezily hither and yon about the stage and periodically varying the procedure either by bringing in or carrying out a dish of something or other, all to no discernible
purpose.

VII

The Business of Killing Cock Robin

Doubtless in no other field of dramatic writing is so much ingenuity called for as in the mystery, murder and detective play. The demands of an audience are stricter in the case of such a one than in the case of almost any other. A poor other kind of play will every once in a while succeed, but the murder mystery has to be pretty good or its goose is cooked. If a poor murder mystery has prospered in the last ten years, I do not know its name. I can, on the other hand, give you the names of several dozen that, failing to meet the audiences' standards, have been abruptly dispatched to the storehouse.

The hypercritical attitude of an audience toward this species of entertainment proceeds from two causes. First, the average customer of mystery plays, being an admirer of such things, is usually a big reader of books of the same sort and thus is not only something of an authority on the subject but is on to most of the tricks of the mystery trade and hence doubly hard to please. And secondly, whereas nervous suspense and surprise are not always essential to the enjoyment of another kind of play—as witness, for example, all sorts of successful plays like *Abe Lincoln In Illinois, The Man Who Came To Dinner, Life With Father, The Time Of*

76]

Your Life, etc.—they are as vitally a part of the mystery exhibit as vitamin B to a country doctor's therapeutical conversation. This nervous suspense and this surprise are
difficult to induce in a sophisticated audience, inasmuch as
you cannot effectively repeat the devices wherewith they
are inculcated, though you can repeat other devices on end
in other forms of drama and happily get away with them.
So, obviously, inventiveness must constantly be multiplied
by inventiveness.

In the other drama, you can rewrite time and again, say,
the scene in which the separated husband and wife are reunited at eleven o'clock by their lonely child—it has been
done successfully for fifty years and as recently as in *Susan
and God*—but try to repeat even once the scene in which a
character like Sherlock Holmes escapes from a room by
means of a lighted cigar butt and your audience will give
you the hoot. You can go on making money, if you are not a
mystery, murder or detective play writer, even with the
episode wherein a husband finally turns on his shrew of a
wife or wherein a blackmailing hussy shows up at a critical
moment in the hero's career, but you will go posthaste to
the junk-can if you try to get away a second time with hiding
your own particular Raffles in a grandfather's clock, or dis-
guising your own particular Bat from head to foot in black
swathings, or moving a colored light around a room to represent your own paraphrase of the protagonist of *The Unknown Purple.*

So severe, indeed, is the demand for convincing dramatic
ingenuity in the mystery play that mere novelty unaccom-
panied by such ingenuity fails to satisfy. Certainly there has
not been a more novel device than that in *Trick For Trick*
when one magician seeking to outwit another challenged
his guilt by asserting that the corpse of the murdered person

would be made to float from an outside room onto the stage, and when the challenge was duly made good. But, though the trick was admirably managed, it made no impression upon the audience because, while novel and inventive, it was not *dramatically* convincing.

To add to the problems of the mystery play fabricator, most of the hitherto tried and true devices have lately been laughed out of the theatre by audiences. The door that opens mysteriously without human aid, the sliding panel, the suit of armor that suddenly shows signs of life, the skeleton in or out of a closet, the sudden dousing of the lights, the scream in the dark, the hand slowly reaching from behind the door to turn off a switch, the rattle of the window blinds, the mysterious breaking of a window pane, the pocket flashlight in the dark, the loud-ticking clock in the empty room, the sinister shadow against the bedroom wall—all these and other devices like them have gone on the index expurgatorius. The dry-voiced detective with the slouch hat may still be relied upon once in a while, although his day is pretty well done; the body of the murdered man which surprisingly falls out of the cupboard has again been utilized recently by Owen Davis in *Mr. and Mrs. North* (he used it previously in *At 9:45*); and playwrights may still conceivably now and then get by with the business of obtaining a suspect's fingerprints by amiably handing him a glass of whiskey and soda or asking him to see if the piano is in tune. But woe betide the author who brings out again at this date the murderous desk paper-knife, or the bookcase that mysteriously parts in the middle, or the sinister butler, or the flash of lightning that reveals the corpse, or the old Conan Doyle trick of the long cigar ash that proves the smoker is telling the truth when he denies he just came in from the tennis court.

But more particular than in any other direction has an audience become in the matter of murder solutions. To court prompt failure these days all you have to do, for example, is to let your murder mystery down with the news that it wasn't murder after all but suicide. The authors of *Cue For Passion* found that out all too quickly only last season. Another sure road to the storehouse is finally placing the guilt on a character who has been too elaborately concealed during the evening. And still others are the news that the man died from heart disease just before the would-be murderer got in his dirty work, the revelation that the dead man in the securely locked and guarded room met his fate from a heavy chandelier tricked to fall on his head, the disclosure that a vengeful East Indian was the guilty party, or the dénouement that the deceased was killed by electric wires secreted in his dinner-table chair.

The riddling of alibis also calls for a steadily increasing callidity. The old exposures having to do with the clock that has been fixed, with the telephone conversation maneuvered from a remote point, or with the theatre ticket stubs for a show that is found not to have given a performance on that particular night because of the star's kidney trouble are no longer allowable. Nor are many such others as the trip to Boston on a train determined to have been canceled, or the getting off some other train at the 125th Street station, or the hypothetically injured right arm in a sling, or the revolver that has cleverly been imprinted with another's fingerprints.

Such old hokum has long since gone its way, and in its stead a new and more fertile and less theatrically stenciled chicane is demanded. As an illustration, take the final blowing-up of the alibi of the culprit in the aforenoted recent murder mystery, *Mr. and Mrs. North*. The murderer's alibi

here was that he had spent the hour of the crime at his
apartment broiling live lobsters for a party he was giving
that night. (He was that kind of bird.) His guests duly allowed they had had the lobster dishes and, as everyone
knows that broiling live lobsters is not done in a few minutes, the rascal seemed to be telling the truth. That is, until
a snoopy woman guest with some household experience of
her own suddenly recalled that the fellow was a tightwad
who had passed off on his guests American champagne carefully wrapped in napkins as the real thing, and that the lobster was of the canned variety.

Nothing very awfully exciting in that, we may readily
admit, but it nevertheless enjoyed the virtue of being recog-
nizably logical to an audience, and the further virtue, simple
and artless as it was, of being at least a welcome departure
from the stereotyped betrayal of the suspected party
through his inadvertence in having put on the wrong over-
coat, in having overlooked the fact that it was Washington's
birthday and that the bank was closed, or in being unmind-
ful that the murdered man had a few minutes before been
using a still running dictaphone.

Up until about ten or fifteen years ago, the idea of having
the man posing as the detective turn out to be the murderer
was good enough for any audience, but try it today and see
how far you get. Or try to make the suspected criminal believe that a phonograph turned on in an adjoining room is an
actual person speaking. Or, if you are a glutton for box-office
punishment, give your audiences any of the old stuff about
the dead man having accidentally fallen against the fire-
place andirons and broken his skull, or about it having been
the suspect's twin brother who did the killing, or about the
murderer having disguised himself in women's clothes, or
about the strange tropical plant that did the strangling. You

have to do a whole heap better than that nowadays if you expect any royalties.

So extreme in their prejudice against the old routine agnellotti have audiences become that more and more are sagacious playwrights abandoning the straight-out handling of murder mystery materials and resorting to either a humorous and farcical or a sardonic treatment. And with consequent much greater chances of success. Thus, a waggish approach as in the recent case of *Arsenic and Old Lace* is instrumental in accomplishing a box-office smash, whereas a straight approach as in the recent case of *Eight O'Clock Tuesday* promptly puts cobwebs on the box-office. The play with the culprit who acts and talks as if he had swallowed an old melodramatic green light stands little or no chance these days, as witness the failure of all such latter day exhibits as *Timber House, Arrest That Woman, Love From A Stranger, Black Limelight, Angel Island, Escape This Night, Come Across, The Woman Brown, Goodbye In The Night, Suspect, The Strangler Fig, Grey Farm,* et al. But the play in which the scoundrel has a paradoxical sense of humor, a debonair manner, or at least maybe a faint silver thread among the gilt of him, has one point in its favor even before the first curtain goes up on it. As witness, in turn, the greater relative acceptance of such exhibits as *Night Must Fall, The Amazing Dr. Clitterhouse, Kind Lady,* and the like.

Complexity in the solution of a murder mystery is another potential dose of red ink. There was a day in the theatre when playwrights still managed to get by with a final five minutes of explanation and elucidation so deliberately intricate and so rapidly rattled off that the audience, not being able to make head or tail of it, was persuaded either to take it all on the authors' say-so or to remit its judgment on the ground that it, the audience, probably hadn't been paying the necessary amount of strict and close attention to what had been going on. But today's audiences are no longer either so charitable or such gulls. If the solution is not perfectly clear and comprehensible they will show it on their faces when they leave the theatre, and the play itself will in all probability be leaving the theatre not long after them. The great success of *The Bat*, the biggest mystery play gold-mine that the Broadway theatre has known (it ran for 867 performances) was, so the late Avery Hopwood, one of its authors, confided to me, due to the scrupulous care which was exercised in this direction. When he and Mary Roberts Rinehart had finished the play, they found after studiously going over it that there were no less than five little points in the mystery that didn't fully jibe with their solution of it. Working back and forth—the job, he said, took them two solid months—they managed finally to make the whole thing absolutely water- and critic-proof. This, he took some humorous satisfaction in pointing out to me, was duly proved when I loftily allowed that my own lynx-eye had nevertheless spotted some fancy equivocation in the business of the projection of the figure of a bat by the automobile headlight and when he in turn put me in my place by taking me out that night and showing me how ridiculously simply, easily and convincingly the trick could be done.

VIII

The Business of Laughter

The theory that people go to the theatre primarily to laugh is widespread. Although it is a theory that must come as a considerable surprise to those who have gone in such rich box-office droves to the plays of writers like Eugene O'Neill, Robert Sherwood, Lillian Hellman and the like and to the graver presentations of such actors and actresses as Maurice Evans, Katharine Cornell and Helen Hayes, there is by and large nevertheless something in it. And the fact that there is something in it is hardly overlooked by the majority of the more bank-minded workers in the playhouse.

The history of our modern theatre shows that two of the three plays which have achieved the longest runs, to wit, *Abie's Irish Rose* and *Lightnin'* have been laugh shows, and that the third, *Tobacco Road,* was not without its very considerable vein of low humor. The record further proves that of the plays and shows which have achieved from six hundred to almost nine hundred performances fifteen out of twenty-three were laugh shows, and that all the rest, with but three exceptions, contained liberal doses of humor. (The reincarnation play, *The Ladder,* does not count, as its run of more than seven hundred performances was an artificial one financed by the author.) The record still further attests to the fact that of the third group of plays and shows representing runs of from five to six hundred performances sixteen out of twenty-one were full of fun, and that at least two of the remaining five had plenty of chuckles in them.

That laughter is rich ore and that the men who can mine it are destined for all kinds of reward is, true enough, peculiar not only to the theatre. It is true also of the movies, the book world, the comic strips, pleasure parks, cabarets, and numerous other things. But more than any of these—more, paradoxically, than even the so-called comic strips, many of which like *Tarzan, Superman, Dick Tracy, Flash Gordon, The Phantom* and *The Lone Ranger* are oddly on the melodramatic and unhumorous side—the theatre usually seems to be laughter's pet province. Even our serious playwrights, indeed, have occasionally profited on the side from a recognition and admission of the fact. Thus, O'Neill made a mint when he turned to humor in *Ah, Wilderness!* Sherwood, after *Waterloo Bridge*, did the same with *Reunion In Vienna*. And George Kelly made more out of *The Show-Off* than out of any three other of his more earnest plays.

Look at some of the other playmakers. Lynn Riggs was pretty hungry until he gave audiences *Russet Mantle*. Clare Boothe started out with an Ibsen frown in *Abide With Me*, failed to make a cent, and then turned to laugh shows and became rich. The Spewacks stopped crying into their soup with *Spring Song*, which failed miserably, and turning a thematic flip-flop brought home the bacon with *Boy Meets Girl*. Saroyan gets prizes and more money than he hitherto dreamed was in circulation with a *The Time Of Your Life* that tickles the trade's funny bone. Kaufman and Hart have made fortunes out of audiences' guffaws. And

Zoë Akins, after ten successive more or less vain stabs at the box-office with untipsy plays following her *Declassée,* let go with the boozy comedy, *The Greeks Had A Word For It,* and cleaned up.

Rachel Crothers has been successful at the box-office when she has set out to capture laughter by the tail and a failure when she has tried to give audiences something not designed for laughter. S. N. Behrman has prospered most greatly when he has been waggiest; certain of his purely witty, or what are called "smile," plays have not got nearly so far with the public. Philip Barry hasn't made a dime on such sober attempts as *John, Hotel Universe* and *Bright Star* but has gone big when he has peddled comic stuff to the crowd. George Abbott lived in a dingy two-by-four hole in the West Fifties when he put on such exhibits as *Those We Love, Four Walls, Heat Lightning* and *Lilly Turner* and was able to move to the St. Regis only when he put on *Three Men On A Horse, Boy Meets Girl, Room Service, Brother Rat* and *What A Life.* George M. Cohan has gathered in the coin with most of his frankly funny plays and lost it with most of his more serious ones like *Gambling, Whispering Friends* and *Pigeons and People.* It often seems to be that way.

Look at many of those who either have not learned or superiorly have not cared to learn the box-office lesson, some of them possessed of some serious talent. How big are the estates or bank accounts of Susan Glaspell, Elmer Rice, Paul Green, Sidney Howard, Hatcher Hughes, John Howard Lawson, Martin Flavin, Dan Totheroh, E. P. Conkle, Robert Ardrey, Robert Turney, Irwin Shaw, Leopold Atlas, Francis Faragoh, George O'Neil, Stanley Young, John Dos Passos, the Siftons, Lula Vollmer, Albert Bein,

Michael Gold, Paul Peters, Reginald Lawrence, Albert Maltz, George Sklar, Sophie Treadwell, and a lot of such others, God bless them?

(I insert the God-bless-them because this is not a chapter of dramatic criticism but rather simply a statistical record, and I am on the side of any writer, good or bad, who values his independence and integrity above the beckoning finger of potential mauve motor-cars, marble dunking pools, English butlers, and seven-dollar neckties.)

What have been the most successful single laugh-provoking scenes in the theatre's last few years? Opinions may vary, but I have an idea that the consensus would nominate the following as tops:

1. The scene at the end of the second act of *You Can't Take It With You* when the fireworks idiotically being manufactured in the crazy Sycamores' cellar explode and rock the house, with everybody rushing madly in all directions save Grandpa, who just says, "Well, well, well!"—and sits down.

2. The scene in *Hellzapoppin* involving the escape artist in a straitjacket who, it is announced, will extricate himself in two minutes by the clock and who is still found vainly trying to get out of it on the floor of the outer lobby when the show is over.

3. The scene in *The Time Of Your Life* in which Willie, the marble game maniac, spends the greater part of the evening trying to beat the machine and eventually, with a shout of triumph and upon the machine's bursting into colored lights and playing the *Star Spangled Banner,* wins six nickels.

4. The episode in *Love's Old Sweet Song* wherein the Okie who has been lazily and contentedly snoozing for hours on the rich woman's lawn suddenly sits erect and with the utmost indignation blames all that is wrong with the world on the moving pictures.

5. The scene in the same play in which a vendor of *Time* magazine by way of making a sale gravely recites the names of its three dozen or more editors, rolling the monikers on his tongue with infinite relish and repeating the more euphonious ones for the benefit of the aforementioned Okie's slattern wife.

6. The scene in the men's washroom in *Du Barry Was A Lady* wherein Bert Lahr, the attendant in the washroom who has just won a sweepstakes prize, elaborately instructs his dumb successor in the complex art of brushing off a client.

7. The episode in *Boy Meets Girl* in which the daffy Hollywood movie scenario writer, who allows he can't dictate to a stenographer because stenographers won't wear tights, subsequently engages in a protracted long-distance telephone conversation with one Jascha Simkovitch in Paris and when his scenario-writer partner objects to the use of his 'phone for such a purpose—"Certainly I object; I ain't gonna pay for your calls"—disgustedly returns, "All right, if that's the way you feel about it—here's your nickel!"

8. The scene in *Leave It To Me* in which Victor Moore, in the role of the American ambassador to Russia, timidly receives the diplomatic representatives of other nations but when the Nazi ambassador shows up kicks him instanter in the belly.

9. The conclusion of *The Man Who Came To Dinner* wherein the irascible women's club lecturer who has fractured a hip and who has installed himself in the Stanley home at length gets up from his wheel-chair and, to the rapt relief of the household, declares he is making his departure, only to slip on the icy porch steps, to break his

ankle, and to be carried back into the house again.

10. The scene in the dell in *Hooray For What?* in which Ed Wynn, attempting peacefully to read a book, is interrupted by a succession of anticking dogs.

11. The bit at the very end of *The Boys From Syracuse,* a musical version of *The Comedy Of Errors,* wherein Jimmy Savo, as one of the two dromios, pokes his head out of a door upon the stage delivery of the only line retained from the original play and whispers, "Shakespeare."

12. The scene in *The Primrose Path* in which the bawdy old grandmother of the dissolute household takes her young granddaughter on her lap and lewdly instructs her in the world's way of things—and then howls for more gin.

13. The scene in *The Male Animal* in which the two disconsolate males discourse alcoholically on the sex philosophy of animals and gradually work themselves up into a fighting mood to regain the women who have deserted them.

14. The second act curtain to *My Sister Eileen,* with the officers of the Brazilian navy going into action against the innocent girls from Columbus, Ohio, and winding up with all wriggling in a crazy conga line, the urchins of the Greenwich Village neighborhood facetiously hanging on to its tail.

It has often been the diversion of critics definitely to catalogue the machinery of laughter and to prove that time-honored hokum is at the bottom of even the laughs that seem superficially new. In these catalogues figure such basic motivations as the fall on the anus, the attempted articulation of a difficult word and the despairing substitution for it of a simple synonym, the use of a cuss word for a suddenly humorous shock, and the abrupt turning of the ignominious worm into a fellow of impudent and brave resolve. While it can not be denied that such old corn still operates luxuriantly—as witness the successful utilization of the devices named in, respectively, *Hellzapoppin, The Time Of Your Life, Margin For Error* and *Three Men On A Horse*—one finds that more and more the theatre is beginning to demand laughter of a fresher and more ingenious cut. It will still almost automatically reward with its audible glee buffoonery based upon the hokum of the drunk scooping the moisture off the bar back into his glass (*The Time Of Your Life*), the character waiting impatiently to get into the lavatory (*Call It A Day*), the dignified woman who gets tipsy (*You Can't Take It With You* and *Love's Old Sweet Song*), and even, Heaven forefend, the hefty colored maid who ambles about the stage gabbling about d' Cibil Waw (*Kiss The Boys Goodbye*). And it undoubtedly still, it seems, will pay out its money to chuckle lustily at comedians who come out wearing funny-looking hats (Ed Wynn); who find themselves, with knees quaking, mistaken for brave heroes (Al Jolson); who are made passionate love to by six-foot Amazons (Bobby Clark); and who gullibly are taken in by Weber and Fields gambling games (Abbott and Costello). But despite all this and just the same it is clearly observable that a change, at least in some measure, is due gradually to come about.

Most of the biggest laughs in the dramatic plays of the last six years have accordingly been found to depart from the old, safe hokum and to venture into a somewhat more vernal field, however here and there slightly. Instead of relying, as so frequently in the past, upon the externals of humor they have veered to the better humor that proceeds more intimately from situation, surroundings and character. Much of this better comedy in the recent theatre follows the Ring Lardner principle of accuracy of duplication of eccentric popular speech, and the laughter derived from it is healthier than that brewed by the old, forced lingo gag. The wisecrack, furthermore, is slowly on the way out, at least in non-musicals; its place is being taken by the humorous retort that springs not from paraphrased vaudeville sidewalk conversation but from the individuality of the mind of the character making it. If, by way of ironic answer, you point out that the wisecracking *The Man Who Came To Dinner* has nevertheless been one of the biggest successes in the recent theatre, the critical answer in turn is that the central character of that play is deliberately presented by the authors as being by nature an incessant wisecracker and that the character itself is derisively designed as the incarnation of the wisecrack. In this instance, accordingly, the wisecrack *is* the character and vice versa.

Life With Father, the outstanding comedy success of recent seasons, hasn't a wisecrack in it from beginning to end; the humor proceeds naturally from character. *Tobacco Road,* the outstanding dramatic success of the modern theatre, finds its ribald humor similarly proceeding from character. On the tombstone of vaudeville those who run may read the necrological inscription: "Who was that lady I seen you with that was no lady that was my wife."

IX

The Best of the Actresses

She hasn't, in the popularly accepted sense, looks; she lacks that theoretically necessary star acting attribute, height; she is wholly deficient in that quality which Hollywood calls glamour; her voice, by any old histrionic standard, is a small one; in her own person she is without what the critics call authority; she has a face that looks far from being a likely mirror of either the tragic or comic mask; and she is the best actress in the American theatre.

She has breasted other hurdles. Her well-meaning if somewhat too confiding mother publishes a book about her which makes her out to be a not always entirely loyal party in the matter of traffic with friends and associates, and often, to boot, something of a wilful and irritating person. Her otherwise charming husband encourages her into fruitless quarrels with the drama critics which she, as a dutiful wife, acrimoniously pursues. She every now and then speaks out in public on subjects removed from her own province, and gets her foot into it. She lends herself to advertising a commercial product on the radio. She fervently endorses bad plays written by persons close to her as pearls of dramatic art. Her publicity photographs would make Florenz

Ziegfeld turn over in his grave. And yet, in addition to being the best actress on the American stage, she is peculiarly
the most romantic and—to borrow that profaned Hollywood
term—glamourous.

Ladies and gentlemen, Miss Helen Hayes.

Only a very expert actress could have made out of the
dubious stage materials that are this Helen Hayes the leader
of her sex in her profession. It is that expert actress who has
acceptably metamorphosed a diminutive woman into the
royal Mary of Scotland, who has vividly turned the forty-
year-old mother of two children successively into a child of
eighteen, the tremulous girl-wife of Prince Albert and the
obese, seventy-eight-year-old Queen Victoria, who has been
now and convincingly a Viennese madel and then and
equally convincingly a young girl of Dixie, a Scottish spinster, and the dreamed Cleopatra of Bernard Shaw. It is this
expert actress, more, who has with equal skill at times played
everything from Shakespeare to Molnár, from Barrie to
George Abbott, from farce-comedy to melodrama and blank
verse. Her recent appearance as Viola in *Twelfth Night* only
again emphasizes the fact that if there is a better and more
versatile and more audience-warming actress in our theatre
she must be hiding not only her light but herself under a
bushel.

It isn't, surely, that Helen Hayes has not sometimes
failed. Her attempt at Portia was far from successful and
her sortie into the Irish drama of Liam O'Flaherty was
more than unfortunate for her. But it isn't that way generally. Even when she has appeared in such dreadful rubbish as *Ladies and Gentlemen*, which in all likelihood
would have dismayed the courage of almost any actress,
she has emerged with some honor to herself. She can usually
further glorify a genuinely fine play; she can add lustre and

interest to a middling one; she can even make superficially possible, at least while she is on the stage, a trashy one. She has proved that.

There are various things which have contributed to her rank, her box-office popularity, and her position in the theatrical community. Although, in that book about her, her mother takes considerable credit for having picked some of her earlier plays, it is pretty hard to believe that it hasn't been Helen Hayes herself who, since that period in her career, has exercised a generally shrewd personal judgment. Such slips in that judgment as the aforementioned *Ladies and Gentlemen*, for instance, are understandable, since the play was written in part by Charles MacArthur, her husband, and since their marriage has been and is well-known to be a love-match. But aside from such mistakes, deliberate though in all probability they have been, her knowledge of her own script needs most often has been accurate.

She has also been wise in her selection of managements, a matter in which certain of her rivals have not always shared her wisdom. Furthermore, the theatre being her religion, she has seen to it that the plays in which she appears, irrespective of their critical quality, have always the best supporting casts and the best productions possible. She doesn't allow her audiences to be cheated, whether in New York or in any thitherward city. She has become her own trade-mark.

There is still another reason, and one that accounts in great part for the affectionate regard in which the public holds her. I once expressed it thus, and I express it so again:

There is something about Helen Hayes that most of our other actresses of her age and experience—indeed, of even more than her age and experience—completely miss. It may be an inner warm womanliness; it may be a dramatic heart beating in a theatrical mind; it may be that little-girl spirit that has ever been a vital asset to the world's best actresses of whatever vintage; it may be a natural and ex officio sincerity that siphons itself into her stage person; it may be any one or ten of a dozen things. That it is, above them all, a genuine acting talent we of course know. But it is these other qualities, too, that must surely and so brilliantly differentiate and distinguish her from the rank and file of director puppets, greasepaint crooners, big chest-tone purveyors and superficially competent old warhorses of all ages who so often drive us out into the cold alley to warm up.

Who are Helen Hayes' chief rivals for first acting honors? The one most often mentioned in this connection is Katharine Cornell, but there are others: Lynn Fontanne, Ina Claire, Judith Anderson, Jane Cowl, Laurette Taylor, Ethel Barrymore, Grace George. Let us consider them.

Katharine Cornell, personally an infinitely more romantic figure of a woman, has many performances to her considerable credit, but most of them are much the same performance. For in the general run of things Miss Cornell offers less a characterization of a role than she offers herself. Most of the roles she plays are less different characters, whatever the dramatist and the program may seek to suggest, than they are Katharine Cornell in different situations and different costumes. Always an attractive stage figure, possessed of a fine and indubitably effective voice and with admirable carriage and poise, it nevertheless remains from the record that, whereas Helen Hayes definitely characterizes her various roles, Miss Cornell simply recharacterizes the fundamentally unvarying Katharine Cornell. It remains primarily Katharine Cornell as everything from Lucrece to Joan of Arc, from Elizabeth Barrett to Juliet, from Candida and Iris March and Jennifer Dubedat to Casanova's temptress and on through the heroines of *Age Of Innocence, Flowers Of the Forest, Alien Corn* and the rest. The Malay princess of *The Wingless Victory* is as surely Katharine Cornell in dark brown grease-paint and with bangles rattling from her wrists as the heroine of *The Letter* is the same Katharine Cornell in lighter makeup and minus the bangles. Miss Cornell, in short, is a first-rate actress of a single role. That one role she plays beautifully. But one role hardly constitutes a critical career.

Lynn Fontanne is a meritorious comédienne and in this category merits all the applause she regularly gets. But, although her performance in a more serious dramatic role in *There Shall Be No Night* was an excellent one, her adventures into a field removed from comedy, while not altogether negligible, have been not too happy. O'Neill's *Strange Interlude,* Chekhov's *The Sea Gull* and Dostoievski's *The Brothers Karamazov,* among others, have clearly betrayed her shortcomings. It is as a comédienne that she shines, and as a comédienne she is uniformly delightful. But there, unlike Miss Hayes, she seems for the major part to be pigeonholed.

As a comédienne, Ina Claire is and for some time has been Miss Fontanne's superior; in this restricted field she is the most proficient actress in our theatre—her most recent performance in *The Talley Method* again attested to the fact; but, like Miss Fontanne, the same pigeonhole confines her.

Ethel Barrymore, Laurette Taylor, Grace George, and even Jane Cowl are of the somewhat older acting order. All have now and again acquitted themselves handsomely—Miss Cowl's Juliet is accepted by many, including myself,

as the best we have had in the American theatre of our time
—but none of them, I believe, is today entirely the actress
she once was, and none of them, as we view the scene today, is Helen Hayes' transcendress. Miss Barrymore knows
all the tricks of the trade and surely, as late as *Whiteoaks*
and *The Corn Is Green,* has made grand use of all of them;
more, she miraculously retains much of that charm that
made her, in her younger days, the toast of the town. But
though she periodically comes through with a gleam of the
old glory, the career which started out and for some time
continued to be so rich in brilliant promise has latterly and
gradually seemed to fade with the evening star.

Miss Taylor, once one of the loveliest of the younger
actresses of her day, suffered something of an eclipse in her
later years, largely because of a misguided selection of
second-rate plays, and most recently seems to have con-
demned herself to obvious so-called character roles. Miss
Cowl has done little in the last half dozen years, and that
little with none of the flash and fire of her yesterdays. Miss
George is an excellent comédienne who runs Miss Claire a
photo-finish for top honors, but save for a very good performance of the beset spinster in the melodrama, *Kind
Lady,* has not indicated overly much in later years in the
way of straight dramatic acting, or at least what is commonly understood by that term.

There remains Judith Anderson who, to this mind, is in
this day and year Helen Hayes' closest contender. Although
she has got her full share of favorable critical notices, it
seems to me that Miss Anderson has never quite received
the general respect for her talents that is her due. In no role
that she has played—and the roles have been exceeding
various—has she failed to do herself justice. Her mother of
Christ two seasons ago was as gently beautiful a perform-

ance as our stage has seen. Her mother of Hamlet was superior Shakespearean acting. And from the far day of *The Dove* and *Behold, the Bridegroom* down through Pirandello and O'Neill (her performance in *Strange Interlude,* incidentally, cruelly showed up the deficiencies of Lynn Fontanne's) and on through such things as *Firebird, Come Of Age* and *The Old Maid* she has suggested in each instance her unusual imagination, her very considerable resource, and her genuine playing gift. If she ever has given a really poor performance, I have not seen it—and I have seen her in all the roles she has played since first she came into our theatre.

Just what it is that has kept real recognition from her, I do not know. Perhaps her protracted excursions to Hollywood have hurt her with the theatrical public, perhaps not. But whatever it is—it may be poor management, faulty consistent build-up, or something of that sort—it has to an appreciable degree denied her the public standing which her gifts have amply demonstrated she deserves.

Nevertheless, all things considered, the sheer black and white record as it stands gives the ballot, after a deep bow to Miss Anderson, to Helen Hayes. She has come a long way from the baby actress in a Lew Fields show of thirty-odd long years ago to the Viola of *Twelfth Night.* Nor has she trodden the easy path to fame. She has taken chances and failed. She has taken even more chances and succeeded. And always, from the very first, she has flown her theatre's flag high, and proudly, and challengingly. Her artistry has triumphed over great physical handicaps; she has created beauty out of what was not beauty; she has ridden the hard and rocky road to eminence in her profession. It has been said of her by experienced men of that profession that she knows more about acting in her little finger than most of her sisters know in their whole hands. I don't know about that. But summing it all up and giving several of those sisters of hers their full due, nevertheless maybe they are right about her. They seem to be. Or at least she persuades me that they are, and that is all I happen to be here concerned with.

So, gentlemen, on your feet. To Zuleika Dobson!

X

Yes, We Have No Bonanzas

Anyone even casually interested in the theatre must some-time since have observed a peculiar fact. That peculiar fact is the absence from the stage of even so much as a single authentic specimen of the handsome bonanza who in past years titillated the fancies of the lady customers to such a degree that he earned for himself the sobriquet of matinee idol.

You remember the lovely creature. Now he was a Mel-bourne MacDowell with the build of a lion and with a lion's mane of rippling locks who impressed the girls as one who could simultaneously love them into a dizzy faint and bounce off the premises any half dozen impertinently intrusive low icemen. Now, a little later on, he was William Faversham—or Favvy, as the girls in daring self-intimacy liked to know him—a tall, erect, slim, fashionable, rich Burgundy-voiced beaut who looked like a Laura Jean Libbey hero drawn by Henry Hutt, Howard Chandler Christy and Henry Raleigh working in rapt collaboration. Now he was a James K. Hackett, in appearance a barber glorified even beyond the dreams of shopgirls by some celestial Ziegfeld; or a Richard Bennett and a Harry Woodruff with curly blond hair so ravishing it made the ladies cry into their boxes of matinee caramels; or a Robert Hilliard and a Vincent Serrano, the former ever as immaculately polished as a shoe belabored by an Italian bootblack, the latter dark, elegant, modish to the last quarter-inch, and as orientally mysterious, in the girls' imagination, as a Turkish punk-stick. And then—for the stage was full of such agitating bijoux in those days—he might be anyone from a Chauncey Olcott, who on Thursday matinees converted the Irish maids and cooks in all the land into yearningly concupiscent eight-dollar-a-week Pompadours and Du Barrys, to a John Drew, who on the Wednesday and Saturday matinees inspired the maids' and cooks' mistresses to rush home at five-thirty and divorce their husbands instanter on grounds of unstarched collars, uncreased pants, and the comparative manners of Bowery bums.

What has happened to the American stage today? Why is there not visible anywhere on it one such Adonis to stimulate women into a mad gallop of box-office worship? Search as you may, you will be unable to discover a sole male figure in the tradition of a Henry Dixey, who once palpitated the fair sex out of all reason and self-control, or of a William Courtenay, whose merest pop of his oyster orbs floored 'em as far back as Row Y, or of a Lou Tellegen, who for some years got the girls from seventeen to seventy where they lived, or surely of a John Barrymore—Jack in those days—whose classic profile passionately wobbled even great-grandmothers.

It certainly cannot be that the male of the acting species in the aggregate has suddenly been deserted by a formerly beneficent God and has overnight become a gargoyle hideous enough to frighten the girls into white hair. There are among the species at the moment several who, though hardly in the running with such snifters of yesteryear as James O'Neill, Kyrle Bellew (there was an enchanter!), Frederic De Belleville, E. J. Morgan, Robert Downing, Hamilton Revelle and James Carew, or for that matter Bruce McRae, Cyril Scott, Edgar Selwyn, Frank Worthing and Charles Cherry, are surely not impossible eye-sores, whatever one's view of the quality of their performances. But just the same there is not one in the lot who can edify even ten dollars out of the girls as a matinee idol.

Philip Merivale, for example, has some of the external attributes of the matinee magnets of other years, yet he apparently doesn't dent the ladies in the least. And it is the same with Walter Abel, McKay Morris, Kent Smith and John Halliday. Victor Mature and Leif Erickson, two younger boys who in another era might conceivably have upset the equilibrium of the female customers, today seem to have little more effect upon their exotic emotions than a couple of tomato juice cocktails. Paul Muni and Burgess Meredith may appeal to the critics, but when it comes to the belles there is, aside from their performances, small magnetism of an extra-dramatic nature. And Fredric March, Franchot Tone and John Garfield, when they show up on the stage, find what feminine autograph seekers are waiting for them in the alley are composed mainly of Hollywood devotees.

And here we come to the first of several possible reasons for the decline and fall of the stage matinee idol. It isn't that some of the present approximately pretty fellows can't act. Some of the matinee divinities of the past couldn't act either, as witness Tellegen, Woodruff, Scott, and a number of others. It is, rather, that the matinee idol as an institution has been abandoned by the theatre and has been given over to the screen. If Muni, Tone, Mature and suchlike do not

get far with the feminine theatre crowd they are nonetheless trumps with the feminine picture crowd. And for a
second reason. The picture-going woman of today is a direct
mental and emotional descendant of the theatre-going
woman of yesterday. She is a fan for attractive male per-
sonalities, irrespective of the quality of their vehicles,
whereas the theatre-going woman of the present time has
grown up both mentally and emotionally to the point where
the quality of vehicles and the quality of actors as actors
supersede the mere physical allure of star hams. It is thus
that a Maurice Evans, who certainly would not win any
blue ribbons in beauty contests but who knows how to act
and selects sound drama to act it, draws infinitely more
women into a theatre than any dozen much more aphrodisi-
acal mimes you can name.

Consider the leading actors in plays that were successful last season, at the same time recalling the fact that
women are even more instrumental than men in making
the success of a play. The leading actor in the humorous
The Man Who Came To Dinner was Monty Woolley, whose
lush whiskers would hardly excite any girl under sixty into
abandoning her husband and running off with Monty to
Atlantic City. On the road, where the play was also successful, the role was played by Alexander Woollcott and
Clifton Webb, neither of whom is of a pulchritude to give
Tyrone Power or Clark Gable any tortured concern. The
New York leading man of *Life With Father* was Howard
Lindsay, the Middle Western was Percy Waram, and the
eastern road company's was Louis Calhern. Surely both
the first and second are considerably removed from the
matinee idol type, and while Calhern is on the prettier side
it remains that he has not drawn women into a theatre until
he got a job in the aforementioned sure-fire play.

Certainly no one will argue that Boris Karloff is the girls' dream prince, yet he helped to pack them in in *Arsenic and Old Lace*. Diminutive Ernest Truex is scarcely a lady-killer, yet the women delighted in him in *George Washington Slept Here*. No woman felt her heart jump over Richard Waring when he was playing in Eva Le Gallienne's company, in *At The Stroke Of Eight*, in *Come Across*, or in *The Man Who Killed Lincoln*; it took a vehicle like *The Corn Is Green* to make him interest her in the least. The success of *My Sister Eileen* was hardly predicated on the gorgeousness and sex appeal of Morris Carnovsky or any other male in the company. And assuredly bald-headed Paul Lukas in *Watch On The Rhine* hardly became the rave of the season because of his personal beauty.

Alfred Lunt certainly does not draw women into a theatre on the score of his looks or animal magnetism, nor does Eddie Dowling, yet both were enormously successful in, respectively, *There Shall Be No Night* and *The Time Of Your Life*. José Ferrer looks something like me, which is surely nothing to set a house on fire, yet he delighted the honeys with his antics in *Charley's Aunt*. And so with the rest.

On the other hand, consider the more or less feverful movie boys who in the last few seasons have tried their luck in this new theatre and failed to get anywhere with the girls in the audience. Fredric March was a dismal failure until he made himself up as an old man in *The American Way*, and even then didn't get far except with the critics. Paul Muni was a failure, save for the critics, in *Key Largo*; Lyle Talbot in *Separate Rooms* was popular only with the cut-rate ticket girls whose taste is strictly Hollywood; and Lee Tracy in *Every Man For Himself* was forced through lack of audiences to shut up shop after a few days.

Go on. John Garfield in *Heavenly Express*, Douglass Montgomery in *They Knew What They Wanted*, Russell Hardie in *Sea Dogs*, Richard Ainley in *Foreigners*, Edmond O'Brien in *Leave Her To Heaven*, and even Laurence Olivier, that peacherino, as Romeo all were shunted off the boards almost overnight. Beautiful Glen Langan went pronto to the storehouse in the case of *Glamour Preferred*, and likewise beautiful Donald Woods in *Quiet Please*. The somewhat older Ralph Morgan was a dreadful bust in *Fledgling*; Ralph Holmes got nary a feminine flicker in *Where Do We Go From Here?*; and John Beal has failed to attract the slightest attention in plays from *Soliloquy*, which lasted just two performances, to *Liberty Jones*, which ran a couple of weeks to no business and then had to close. And it has been much the same with such beauties as Francis Lederer, who got by in *No Time For Comedy* only on the score of the box-office pull of Katharine Cornell; Henry Fonda in *Blow Ye Winds*, which managed only thirty-six performances and to barely enough customers to fill a third of the house; Alexander Kirkland in several appearances; Derrick de Marney in *Young Mr. Disraeli*; Sidney Blackmer in *Stop Over*; Charles Bickford in *Casey Jones*; Frank Lawton in *I Am My Youth* (the girls wouldn't take him on even in the role of Percy Bysshe Shelley); and Vincent Price, when deserted by Helen Hayes, in *The Lady Has A Heart*, *Heartbreak House*, etc.

What is behind all this terrible state of affairs and what is the second reason behind the first reason? With my customary rare sapience, I'll tell you. The male matinee idol has been succeeded by the female matinee idol. The women who once swooned over actors are now doing their swooning over actresses. If you do not believe it, sweep an eye over the current scene.

Sweeping that eye, you will discover that Gertrude Lawrence presently herds in the matinee girls the way John Drew used to, and that Ethel Barrymore has taken in their matinee affections the place long ago occupied by one of the other gala males. You will see women crowding the matinees to applaud Katharine Cornell and Helen Hayes and Tallulah Bankhead and Katharine Hepburn as they in the past crowded them to bask in the effulgence of the he magnificoes herein previously mentioned. And you will behold them at the stage doors after the performances, their eyes aglisten with excitement, just the way they once lingered there for a glance at their masculine deities.

In the case of even the musical show it is no longer a Donald Brian or a Jack Buchanan who fetches the ladies; it is Ethel Merman and even Ethel Waters. And so far as the contemporary approximate male colossi go, it is not a Dennis King but a Beatrice Lillie.

The stage pretty boys have had almost as hard a time of it in the theatre as the Hollywood pretty boys. Leslie Howard, when last he made his appearance, could not draw enough customers to keep his play going for more than a very short run. Kenneth MacKenna, Rollo Peters, Oscar Shaw, Tonio Selwart, Walter Woolf King, George Baxter, Edward Crandall, Vernon Steele and other such physical matinee idol materials have either disappeared altogether or seem to have experienced great difficulty in getting jobs. The better looking an actor is, the harder, indeed, appears to be the going for him, as witness the case of a lengthy list embracing Raymond Hackett, George Metaxa, Phillips Holmes, Philip Huston, Philip Reed, James Rennie, Michael Whalen, Tullio Carminati, Robert Shayne, John B. Litel, Roland Drew, John Emery, Austin Fairman, Barry Thomson, Stephen Courtleigh, James MacColl, John Buckmaster,

Ben Lackland, and such others.

The truth of the matter seems to be that when the girls do not prefer their matinee idols to be actresses what wins them most greatly in the theatre are actors who are far from being Adonises. Since I myself am of the species of pulchritude that scares cats, to say nothing of small children and even policemen, I hope the aforesaid gentlemen will not be too deeply offended when I list them as not overwhelmingly lovely spectacles. So, then: the before mentioned Messrs. Lunt, Evans and Dowling, along with Raymond Massey, Noel Coward, Leslie Banks, Ray Bolger, Cedric Hardwicke, A. E. Matthews, Orson Welles, Frank Craven and their like. Indeed, also maybe even Jimmy Durante.

XI

The Musical Shows

A champion of the moving pictures may loudly deny that they suffer serious shortcomings in comparison with the stage, but there is at least one point in favor of the latter that he would, however reluctantly, have to admit. It concerns the musicals. The all-important and significant difference between a film musical show and a stage one is that when you fall hard for the third girl in the line from the left in a film musical you have no means of knowing if at that moment she is still alive or dead, which, even the champion must sadly confess, is rather disconcerting.

If ever any form of public entertainment depended upon realistic biology it is the musical show. More than any other it depends upon the spectator's positive awareness of the fact that he is in the immediate presence of living, appetizing and inviting femininity and that, if he had money in his pocket, if his hair were not getting thin, if his wife were away, and if the gods were just, he could go around to the stage-door and take a prime sample of it out to supper. For above everything else in it, a musical is first and last a girl show, and a girl show in which the girls are represented only in ersatz, as on the screen, cannot, however otherwise satisfactory, fulfil its principal function.

If, perchance, the aforesaid movie advocate scoffs at our third-girl-from-the-left argument, let him calmly reflect on his reaction to any old picture whose star he knows is dead. Can he get the same feeling from it that he gets from a picture whose admired one he knows is still alive? I leave the answer to his own honesty.

Romantic reaction to the photograph of a pretty girl is, of course, possible. In my boyhood, I used to collect cigarette pictures myself. But the time comes when the photograph doesn't suffice and when you have to see the girl herself or bust. That accounts for movie fans' desperate safaris in quest of a look at their idols in person. And it also explains why the greatest film musical ever made remains in the end a poor substitute for the flesh and blood stage show. You can't smell the perfume behind the ears of a lovely on the screen. She can't, even in your most fantastic imagination, spot you out in the audience as an exceptionally handsome fellow and wink at you. Of course, to be perfectly fair and give the screen its due, she can't slap your face either.

The American theatre, almost everyone agrees, is and for some years now has been the world's leader in the department of song and dance shows. Even long before the war there was no theatre abroad to match it. And not the least—not the least by a jugful—of its virtues has been and remains the superior odylic-force of its young women. If any lindbergh thinks that this is mere vile chauvinism, let him not overlook the attesting and corroborative fact that Alfonso, late king of Spain, tumbled precipitously for a couple of them, that the then Prince of Wales, now Duke of Windsor, found no less than seven of them his favorite dancing partners and supper companions, that his younger brother, the present Duke of Kent, was filled with a similar admiration, and that Adolf Hitler Himself not so long ago went publicly bereft over a brace of the Yankee vesuvii.

The song and dance and girl show is the alcoholic liquor of the playhouse. It makes people for the nonce oblivious of their cares and suffuses them with rosy dreams and illusions. It warbles their adversities out of their immediate consciousness and hoofs their woes into temporary limbo. And it laughs themselves out of themselves. The greatest performance of *King Lear* would fall flat on a night of deep worldly concern, but a show in which forty beautiful hussies kicked up their trim heels and in which a couple of comedians dejected themselves emphatically on their nether-cheeks would stand a pretty good chance. If theatrical entertainers at the front were ever to try to bemuse the soldiers with excerpts from the classic drama or even Clifford Odets the boys would indignantly cast aside their guns at once and would desert to the enemy, who they hoped would have enough sense to redraft Elsie Janis along with Claire Luce, Gracie Fields, Maurice Chevalier and others like them to make them forget their cooties.

Another point in favor of the stage musical as against the film musical is the censorship that operates in the instance of the movies. When, for example, such a show as *Du Barry Was A Lady* reaches the screen, no less than eight of its biggest stage laughs have to be deleted. And the same with many other stage musicals. Yet it has always seemed to the theatre that anything which makes a representative audience laugh immoderately cannot be considered either immoral or objectionable. But the movies may not comfortably indulge themselves in any such philosophy. On the screen, Rabelais must have a touch of Lloyd C. Douglas in him, and Boccaccio a liberal leaven of Fannie Hurst.

But for all that the stage musical must ever primarily remain the parent of the film musical. Cole Porter, Irving Berlin, Rodgers and Hart, Jerome Kern and the other stage composers and lyric writers have to be borrowed at heavy fees to contrive the Hollywood counterparts. And Fred Astaire, Carol Bruce, Eleanor Powell, Jeanette Macdonald, Fannie Brice, Al Jolson, Eddie Cantor, Grace Moore, Bert Lahr, W. C. Fields, Bob Hope, Mary Martin, Patsy Kelly, the Marx boys, the Ritz boys, Mary Boland, Desi Arnaz, Hugh Herbert, Charles Ruggles, Joe Penner and dozens upon dozens of the other film standbys have similarly had to be borrowed. Hollywood may be able to supply its own chorus girls, but with small exception it has to rely more or less upon the stage for the other main materials. And it usually does. Which is at least one point to its credit.

Who represent the high water marks in the later American musical show? The best clowns are Bobby Clark and Ed Wynn. The drollest comedian is Victor Moore. The best composer is Jerome Kern. The best of the lyric writers are Lorenz Hart and Ira Gershwin. The best looking girl is probably Marcy Wescott. The most attractive young dancer is Grace McDonald. The best male singer is Paul Robeson. The best female, Kitty Carlisle. The most imaginative costumers are Nat Karson and Raoul Du Bois. The best designer of scenery is Jo Mielziner. The funniest team is probably Abbott and Costello. The best dance director is George Balanchine. The best ballet dancer is Vera Zorina. The best blues singer is Ethel Waters. The most amusingly explosive zany is, by long odds, Jimmy Durante. The best quiet comique is Joe Cook. The best tap dancer is Bill Robinson. The best travesty hoofer is Ray Bolger. The prettiest colored girl is Joyce Beasley. The best colored woman singer is Anne Brown, with Ruby Elzy the runner-up. The most effective and charming recent importation in the way of a songstress is Carmen Miranda, and the best comédienne the English Beatrice Lillie. As for the men who write the books of the shows, top honors go to George S. Kaufman, Morrie Ryskind and Moss Hart.

Surveying not merely the moment but the landscape of the American musical show of our more modern times, who stand out as its prime figures? As composer, surely, Victor Herbert. As bookmaker, perhaps George Ade—with the above mentioned Kaufman and Ryskind in the case of *Of Thee I Sing* sitting securely alongside high on the throne. As comedians, Raymond Hitchcock and W. C. Fields. As acrobatic clown, Fred Stone. As pantomimic comedian, Bert Williams. As most effective popular singers, Blanche Ring and Marie Cahill. As scenic artist, Joseph Urban. As probably the most decorative young woman, Lotta Faust. As dancing girls, Marilyn Miller and Adele Astaire.

An essay might be written deploring the tendency of the later musical shows to be rather dirty, but I fear I am not the one to write it. They have been pretty dirty all right but they have at the same time also been very amusing, so that would leave me professorially with my shirt-tail out. I am prepared to write all the essays you wish—for, of course, the customary honoraria—disparaging shows that are dirty purely for dirt's sake, but when they skilfully extract good sound fun from what would otherwise be mere dirt you may keep your money in your pocket so far as I am concerned.

It isn't that I can't appreciate the feeling of some of my colleagues when they lament the decline of romance on our musical stage. There is something still to be said for the musical show that makes one think of holding vicarious

hands with the beautiful Princess Mirabella in the moonlight, the while a white swan is pulled by a stagehand across
the watery backdrop and the lovely girl herself sings softly
about looking for a man like yourself to love. And there is
also surely something to be said against shows which indiscriminately substitute for the Princess a lavatory attendant brushing off a client's backside. But nobody in late years
has invented a show in which the Princess has seemed other
than a coloratura pain in the neck and several fellows have
written shows in which the lavatory attendant or his equivalent has been mighty comical. So as between the two I'll
take the lavatory attendant or his equivalent with gratitude
and preserve the more tender emotions in my bosom until
such a time as Mirabella is her old self again.

But now, before I move an inch farther, I want to say
that the next time I go to a musical show and hear another
song about how sad it is that Paris is not what it used to
be I am going to start things. It isn't that Paris wasn't
salubrious. I lived there on and off over a period of many
years and some of the most charming days and nights of
my life were spent there. (I remember some of them with
a strange and deep affection.) But this professional Broadway nostalgia that miscellaneously pours itself out in song
offends not only my delicate sensibilities but also my esteem
for the verities. What is more, if another such show accompanies such a song with still another presumably heart-
breaking spectacle of can-can girls, apaches and senile
flower vendors and with a view of a gilt Eiffel Tower on
the backdrop, I'll bite the ushers.

As I've said, I don't want you to get me wrong. I have
had some delightful times in Paris—for that matter, I have
also had some pretty swell times in Boston and Newark—

and I am duly grateful. My point is rather that they always imply that Paris was the one and only city in the whole world that was a chip off the rim of Paradise and then, by way of convincing you of the fact, customarily describe it in terms of a combination booze parlor, bed-house, night-club and general honky-tonk. They may occasionally stick in an allusion to chestnut blossoms, the Seine, Sacré Coeur and the Bois de Boulogne—at which point the tune will provide the singer with an opportunity for a quavering gulp-note—but the essence of the picture will be the same. And if they think they can instil in me a wistful and overpowering homesickness by recalling to my memory, however lyrically, the red, fat bottoms of those Tabarin can-can dancers, the allure of a tourist Montmartre, the gigolos at the Ritz bar, the midinettes who hadn't had a bath for a week, the fancy women in the corridors of the Moulin Rouge, and the gang of American expatriates who hung around Maxim's, they have picked the wrong boy.

Many of our local lyric writers who cry into their stingers and sidecars over the passing of Paris very evidently knew it only in such of its aspects as these. They saw and see it not as the serene and beautiful city it was in spirit but as the Midway it was on the surface: a sideshow of promiscuous love affairs, cheap champagne, Latin Quarter shindigs, apéritif guzzlings, facile pickups, and the like. And though, as I have noted, they may try to conceal the fact with incorporations into their ditties of longing sighs for the moon over the Arc de Triomphe, the dawn over the gardens of the Tuileries and April in the Bois, the Paris they invite us to brew a tear for remains a Paris for which any decently romantic Parisian himself had only the profoundest contempt. There was another Paris, and a lovely one. But the passing of the Paris they describe can affect no one any more tenderly than the passing of, say, the Chicago of Mike McDonald.

One of the main critical stencils has it that musical show books are generally bad. The stencil is legitimate. The great majority of them are. Why they should so regularly be bad is something of a conundrum. The libretti of modern opera do not suffer any such acute pain; those of operetta are usually pretty good; and even the revue form is sometimes satisfactory. What may be the explanation? I have the sagacity to report that I don't know. But, like most persons who don't know what they are talking about, I venture to express an opinion anyway.

Perhaps one reason lies in a powerful conviction on the part of musical show bookmakers that they must periodically be funny, whether the immediate nature of their materials calls for comedy or not. We thus are made to endure arbitrary injections of strained humor which not only violate the mood that has been strugglingly maneuvered but which, being arbitrary, jar the ear beyond subsequent recapturings of that mood. This is particularly noticeable in the case of sentimental passages where a bogus sophistication and fear of accusation of softness impel the book writers to protect themselves and seek absolution in facetious and sardonic interruptions. The wittiest criticism of these donkeys is to be discovered in the old book of Victor Herbert's *The Fortune Teller*, with its character assiduously searching for a joke around which to build a musical show but happily never finding it.

A second possible reason is the arbitrary conviction that there must be a more or less definite plot. Such plots have wrecked many an otherwise passable show. If exhibits without music can be eminently satisfactory without any plot to speak of, why may not exhibits with music be doubly so? Yet were such practically plotless and worthily amusing plays as *March Hares, The Time Of Your Life, You Can't Take It With You* and the sort to be converted into musical shows the responsible asses would doubtless inject plots into them and monkeywrench the works.

A third conceivable reason is the almost impossible business of dovetailing lyrics often written independently with the aforesaid arbitrary plots, resulting not only in making the plots seem doubly silly but the lyrics, however good, appear to be designed for an entirely different show.

The really good musical show book should probably be written around the music and lyrics rather than the music and lyrics around the book. There are exceptions, to be sure, as, for just one example, *Show Boat*. But for each such exception you will find at least a half dozen exhibits like *Too Many Girls, Very Warm For May* and *Du Barry Was A Lady* which, largely written in the opposite manner, betray themselves as a whole.

On this whole, isn't it time someone got around to devising a slightly fresher form for the shows? It isn't, certainly, that some of them are not pretty good as they are, yet more and more one hears the customers saying, "Yes, they're pretty good, but they're usually much the same old thing and it would surely be fine to get something a little new for a change." The customers are correct. The drama has seen all kinds of new forms, but the musical show by and large has in later years been standing still.

Go to a musical comedy or even revue these days and you can in most instances accurately predict the complexion of the evening. In the case of the musical comedies, particularly, the general formula is surprisingly like that of the same species of entertainment so long as twenty or

thirty years ago. If today's second acts often open with some
kind of ballet number, so did the second acts of two and
three decades ago, as witness *The Blue Lagoon,* et al. If
today's comedian in *Du Barry Was A Lady* suffers humor-
ously from a sharp implement in his sitzer, so did the far
yesterday's, as witness Jefferson De Angelis in *The Tore-
ador,* et al. I needn't mention the changeless hokum of
lovers separated at ten o'clock, but if you somehow imagine
that, anyway, the present satirical approach is completely
modern I'll have to refer you 'way back to George Ade's
The Sultan Of Sulu, The Sho-Gun, and so on.

The inevitable comic song, usually spotted in today's
second acts, is as agedly routine as the course of the sun.
Even the risqué comic song. Years ago it was *What Did
Mrs. Rip Van Winkle Do While Rip Van Winkle Was
Away?*; today it is *But In The Morning, No.* The revue
opener with the girls reciting a confidential lyric harks back
to George M. Cohan's revue day. The youthful show with
football appendage, of which *Too Many Girls* is a recent
sample, has been with us all the past distance from *Leave
It To Jane* to *Good News.* The naming of the show-girl
duchesses after cheeses, as in *Du Barry Was A Lady,* was
old-hat back in the Weber and Fields Music Hall era; the
naming of the girls after various nations, as in *Two For The
Show,* was still older back in the 1893 Chicago World's
Fair *1492* spectacle era; and the naming them after different cities, as in three latter-day revues, was so stale by
1926 that it helped quickly to close Charlie Dillingham's
Oh, Please, just as naming the comedian something like
Stonewall Moskowitz helped still more quickly to close even
the great Ziegfeld's *Betsy* in the same season. But very evidently, judging from the success of the more recent shows,
the customers relish the old grist more than they like to

admit. Stonewall Moskowitz may be long dead, but Rodgers and Hart can seemingly still get away with the Duchess of Holstein-Kuhhof, Fred Allen with Meyer Lonsdale, Lindsay and Crouse with O'Reilly Duquesne, and Noel Coward with Elmer von Robespierre, God forbid.

For every such beautifully original musical show as *Of Thee I Sing*, for every such genuinely imaginative musical comedy as *Music In The Air*, and for every such fresh and delirious revue as *Hellzapoppin* we get a dozen exhibits in each category that follow the old tracks like so many freight cars. If it isn't the same old lover's duet, it's the same old clog dancer who does his stuff while they're shifting the scenes. If it isn't the interpolated straight ballet, it's either a heavily modernized paraphrase or a travesty of it. If it isn't the timid comedian finding himself in a critically dangerous situation (shades of Jimmie Powers, Francis Wilson and Frank Daniels!) it's the grand ballroom, the pavilion in the gardens, the yacht or country club, a salon in the palace, Germaine's boudoir, or the Ritz-Waldorf roof, with a string of green and yellow incandescent bulbs.

XII

The Theatrical Producers

Theatre critics habitually write about everyone connected with the theatre but the producers. They write about playwrights, actors, actresses, stage directors, scene designers, costume designers, dancers, pantomimists, chorus girls, other critics, and even the girl ushers if they happen to be good-looking. But the men who put up the money, or—more usually—get someone else to put it up for them, seem to get a break from them only when they die or go into bankruptcy, on both which occasions the critics work up a little sentimental reaction to them, rather belatedly.

By way of giving the poor, neglected fellows their day in type, I magnanimously devote this chapter to them. Aside from affording them a little gratification, it may also serve a collateral constructive purpose in acquainting theatrical hopefuls in the direction of playwriting and acting with the nature of the men they will have to deal with. I proceed to the biographical remarks alphabetically.

George Abbott does not drink or smoke, thus preserving his unimpaired energy for rumba dancing, which he engages in nightly for six or seven unflinching hours, and for the kind of direction which converts his stages into a cross between the Preakness and an intercollegiate hockey match. His success is chiefly with musical shows and farce-comedy, at which he is a foxy hand. When he tries that hand at the more elevated species of drama, it loses its cunning. Give him something in which three men rush madly about a hotel room tearing frantically at their neckties, the while the pants fall off one of them, and worrying how they can raise five dollars either to pay their bill, bet on a horse, back a play, waggle a movie deal or get control of a gold-mine, the while in turn they ejaculate "Nuts," "It stinks" or "How about calling up Jock Whitney?", and the next morning you are certain to read my colleagues' tributes to his remarkable genius, along with the news that the line of art-lovers at the box-office is a quarter of a mile long. But give him a play in which human emotions impel their possessors to sit down quietly once in a while and to speak their thoughts without once resorting to such facetiæ as "Sez you" or "I wonder what Lee Shubert is writing on the tablecloth at the Astor," and he gives the impression of being lost.

In the way of what is often too restrictedly called popular entertainment (for, after all, such a play as *Tobacco Road* has run much longer than Abbott's most successful runner, *Three Men On A Horse*, such a one as *The Children's Hour* longer than *Boy Meets Girl*, and such as *Rain, The Green Pastures* and *Street Scene* longer than *Brother Rat*)—in the way of this so-called popular entertainment Abbott at present has few rivals. But if someone like O'Neill or O'Casey were perchance to send him a script, he would be so puzzled and confused that you would probably find him that night doing the minuet under the impression that it was the conga.

Richard Aldrich, husband of Gertrude Lawrence, is a quiet, well-educated, reserved fellow who has not yet done enough individual producing for one to get a critical slant on him. His summer theatre at Dennis, Mass., seems to be his most active arena.

William A. Brady, on the other hand, has been in the business so long that he himself can hardly remember when he began. He is, naturally, a representative of the older theatrical and dramatic order, an order whose chief characteristic is a peculiar conviction that the theatre died on the day that the road couldn't assimilate more than seven companies of *A Trip To Chinatown* and that the drama is in the doldrums because there are no more Jules Eckert Goodmans writing masterpieces like *The Man Who Came Back*. Bill, a genuinely charming old boy, for some years has held the record for proclaiming the demise of the theatre. The statistics show that he has proclaimed it at least thirty times each season over a period of twenty-three out of twenty-six years. In the other three years his annual obituaries fell to a mere nineteen, due to the fact that one year he was laid up with a bad case of rheumatism, that in another he went to Europe and didn't want to spend money for the heavy cable charges, and that in the third he had produced a play which was embarrassingly packing his theatre to the roof, presumably with people who had given up going to the theatre.

The languid firm of Bushar and Tuerk is composed of George Bushar Markle, a wealthy Pennsylvania coal-mine owner, and Johnny Tuerk, who for years worked for the above mentioned M. Brady. Markle is a worldly and engaging fellow and Tuerk knows the managerial side of the theatre business, but save for their acceptance and production of O'Casey's *Within The Gates* their taste in and judgment of play manuscripts has been exceedingly bad. For one example, they rejected Carroll's *Shadow and Substance* in favor of the Goodmans' *Many Mansions*, thus simultaneously losing critical affection and their chemises instead of achieving the former and making a pot of money on the side.

Delos Chappell must be listed as a dilettante, although it is to his credit that he saw the considerable virtues in Robert Turney's excellent script, *Daughters Of Atreus* (subsequently, not to his credit, woefully botching it in production), as well as the appetizing humors in *Father Malachy's Miracle*. He indicates a measure of taste but is handicapped by a half-hearted approach to the theatre and by inexperience. If he were to apply himself singly and seriously to the job he might in time develop into a producer of some relative merit.

George M. Cohan has not been overly active in late years, and when he has gone in for production has confined himself mainly to plays of his own handiwork. There have been few men in the American theatre who have known more about its popular box-office phases, although his former uncommon knack of putting his knowledge into successful practice seems to have become greatly diminished in recent seasons. George Abbott stems from Cohan, but Abbott at his best misses something that the other and older George once contrived to get into his productions.

Cheryl Crawford was originally one of the Group Theatre crowd and withdrew to go it on her own. She has put on a brace of plays which, while defective and understandable failures, were not without traces of probity. What, if anything, she will do in the future remains to be seen.

Alfred De Liagre, Jr., is a society-minded young blade with voluptuous manners and of Chesterfieldian, nay, Menjouan address. Although he has not done much thus far in the way of producing, the few exhibits he has revealed have indicated some adeptness in casting, staging and direction. In *Yes, My Darling Daughter* he unearthed an amusing comedy, but otherwise his manuscript eye has done considerable blinking. His interests lie in the direction of the decidedly minor drama.

Eddie Dowling, who began as a musical show author and actor, has proved himself to be a better judge of reputable play manuscripts than nine-tenths of his fellow producers. He slips once in a while, but in even his slips, *Madame Capet* signally excepted, there has been detectable both some reason and some gesture toward quality. His greatest extra-theatrical activity is adopting babies. His dramatic prejudice is largely in favor of the Irish drama. Give him any script which opens with a Celt allowing in a rich brogue that the English are a bunch of lowlifes and he will not lay it down until he has read it through, even if it is so bad that he then throws it into the wastebasket. But despite his predilection for the Irish drama, he is hospitable to any other species that poses itself above the conventional Broadway standard, particularly if it reaches, however obliquely, toward a gentle faith in the glory of Heaven and a vigorous sentimental faith in the essential decency of mankind. He is himself a first-rate dramatic actor, to say nothing of an uncommonly understanding hand at production. A curious mixture all around, but one whose career bears close critical watching.

Vinton Freedley, who in his Harvard days was a Hasty Pudding luminary, devotes his vitality chiefly to musical shows, in which field he has been very successful. A fellow given to modish habiliments, a change of boutonnière at regular two-hour intervals, a country estate with a swimming pool and blue ribbon goats, and a charge account at the better converted speakeasies, he dips into the drama (minor) only at protracted intervals, and then only if the year's crop of chorus girls is not up to his demanded standard of oomph. His favorite histrionic artist is Fred Astaire; his favorite literatus, Ward Morehouse, theatrical chronicler to the New York *Sun;* and his favorite composer, Cole Porter, whom he rates but slightly lower than Johann Sebastian Bach.

John Golden began his career as a song writer, two of his greatest artistic triumphs being *Poor Butterfly* and *Goodbye, Girls, I'm Through.* Suffering a bad cold one day and finding that he could not whistle them to his proper satisfaction and connoisseur delight, he went into the producing business with the late Winchell Smith and made a haul out of such things as *The Fortune Hunter, Turn To The Right* and *Lightnin'.* With this rich treasure he went it solo after Smith's death. His announced policy is "Clean Plays Or Bust." Those he selects for presentation are directed primarily at the box-office and his aim in that direction has often proved faulty. Rachel Crothers, his best box-office bet, is his idea of a great dramatist. His heart is in the theatre and in his own way he sincerely tries to do the best by it, but his critical standards when it comes to drama are considerably less exalted than might be wished.

Max Gordon has done some creditable things in the way of production, both dramatic and musical, but Hollywood has lately contaminated his psyche and there is no telling where his theatrical future lies. He is now and then associated with other producers when he appears in the theatre, and in some instances with playwrights, usually George S. Kaufman and Moss Hart. He started out as a vaudeville office slave, then became a vaudeville booking agent. He really admires the better-grade drama, even if he does not always practise what his taste preaches.

Sam H. Grisman went about leasing one-quarter of all

the theatres in New York two years ago and gave most of them up about three months later. He has made big money out of *Tobacco Road* and has lost a lot of it on a series of exhibits which the critics have sent galloping to the store-house. His producing career is of such recent vintage that one cannot predict which turn, if any, it will take. At the moment, he may be set down as one of the coterie who have their eyes, monocles, and even strong binoculars sedulously trained on the ticket-till.

The temporarily suspended Group Theatre, with Harold Clurman as its generalissimo, demonstrated enterprise and some competence. It brought out Clifford Odets, Irwin Shaw and William Saroyan and was honestly interested in the development of the newer drama. Although it some-times failed of its own mark, its intentions were always honorable. It was, in short, a producing organization that represented something definitely valuable to the American theatre and its re-emergence is a consummation to be desired.

The Theatre Guild, on the other hand, which once did represent something valuable, has declined steadily year by year. At length tardily recognizing the fact, it not long ago called itself into worried meeting and vested its control in the persons of Lawrence Langner and Theresa Helburn, two of its six directors. These twain, properly appreciating that other and outside producers know more about plays than they do, have rested their heads largely in such others' laps, hoping thereby to give the Guild's long suffering sub-scribers a decent run for their money. The Guild went to pieces because it did not know a good play when it read one, because it cast its plays with indifferent actors, being unwilling to pay out much in the way of salaries, because several of its directors caught the Hollywood disease and tried to sit on two stools at the same time, and because many of the better playwrights and better actors grew sick of the whole set-up and refused to submit themselves longer to its amateurish didoes.

Jed Harris, once a potentially important talent, began sliding down the chute six years ago and has now buried himself in a Hollywood grave.

William Harris, Jr., a producer of quondam sagacity, has annually for the last five years announced some play or other, but does not seem to have got around to doing anything about any of them. What has befallen him, nobody knows.

Arthur Hopkins, once the authentic white hope of the American theatre, has disappointed his early champions, of whom I had the honor to be a vociferous one. He has permitted his own shortcomings to become confused in his mind with shortcomings of the theatre itself, and has wasted a lot of his energy in attributing to the latter the defects in himself. He was at one time the soundest judge of plays in the producing circle, and his productions of them were admirable. Then, suddenly, his acumen faded. In addition, he so unyieldingly adhered to his early principles of staging that his productions often became wholly and absurdly out of key with the plays themselves. He has a good dramatic head and he is never under any circumstances cheap, so it is possible he may one day again find himself. One hopes so, because down at the bottom of him there is a fine pride in the theatre.

Guthrie McClintic, husband and sponsor of Katharine Cornell, is often a skilful fellow when it comes to the production of the contemporary drama—his *Winterset*, for example, was a capital job—but his adventures with Shakespeare have grieved the judicious, if not many of the critics.

In the staging of the lesser drama, however, he indicates a nice combination of talent and showmanship, though there are times when one wishes he would forego the over-elaborate species of lighting favored by the late Belasco which periodically makes his stages resemble so many candy boxes with prettily colored little electric bulbs concealed in the gumdrops. His judgment of scripts is of the up-and-down variety. He will pick a relatively worthy script one day and the next a completely trashy one, sometimes even when both are the work of the same playwright, as witness Maxwell Anderson's above-mentioned *Winterset* along with *High Tor* on the one hand and Anderson's *The Star-Wagon* on the other.

Gilbert Miller esteems the fashionable life so highly that it is reported by his Hungarian crony, Alexander Ince, that he even breakfasts in a white tie and tails, with a white carnation in his lapel and two platinum cigarette cases studded with rubies in his rear trouser pockets. His productions are uniformly in the very best of physical taste and he himself is a director of uncommon perception and suavity. He is, however, seldom possessed of courage in dramatic production, preferring to play safe by buying plays only after he has seen them in other more venturesome men's productions. Thus he bought *Shadow and Substance* and *The White Steed* for future London presentation only after looking at Dowling's local presentations. Thus he has bought Hungarian plays, French plays and English plays only after he has seen them acted, and before sufficiently large paying audiences, in Budapest, Paris and London. He has done little or nothing to help and encourage the American drama. It is a pity, for with his financial resources, innate discrimination and adroit directorial hand he might do much.

Brock Pemberton, originally an associate of Arthur Hopkins, is personally a fellow of morals so cautious and circumspect that it is said he once deleted the adjective in the phrase "naked truth" in an article he had written for the New York *Times'* Sunday supplement and substituted "whole." Yet, paradoxically enough, the plays he produces are generally on the rough and saucy sex side. Farce-comedy in a G-string is the species of dramaturgy that fetches his fondest interest.

The Playwrights Company, composed of Maxwell Anderson, S. N. Behrman, Robert E. Sherwood and Elmer Rice, is an intelligent and estimable producing fraternity, and it has again now and then demonstrated that, when it comes to a play, the man who writes it generally knows considerably more about what should be done with it than almost anyone else. Its plays, however, nevertheless and alas, have themselves the most of them lacked something.

The Shuberts, aside from their musical shows and revues, serve chiefly as investors in other producers' scripts. Contrary to the fairly popular belief, they often indicate a nice discrimination in the matter of such scripts and have been part backers of some of the very best of them.

Herman Shumlin's most luxuriant admiration for a dramatist is reserved for Lillian Hellman, who has provided him with three big successes in *The Children's Hour, The Little Foxes* and *Watch On The Rhine*. He puts on few plays and his taste in more recent years has run mainly to serious and here and there even lugubrious themes. He is a good hand at casting and direction, though generally disposed to an almost funereal slowing down of tempo.

Rowland Stebbins is a Wall Street broker who employs Laurence Rivers as his theatrical alias. His luckiest strike was *The Green Pastures*. His pet playwright for some years was George Kelly. He has done little in the way of producing for some time now.

John C. Wilson's god, Führer and superman is Noel Coward. A graduate of Yale, he associated himself with Coward some years ago and has served not only as his American producer but as his general business factotum. A soft-spoken, carefully wardrobed, trimly alert and companionable fellow, he has done well by his boss. But beyond his boss nothing else in the theatre interests him very much.

Finally, Dwight Deere Wiman, also a dressy spark down to the freshest lapel bloom, who inherited a fancy Middle Western plow factory, who likes the metropolitan night life, and who has enjoyed a share of success in both the musical comedy and dramatic fields. In the latter, his excursions have been confined chiefly to pleasant little comedies of a sentimental nature. He is interested in the "amusement" phase of the theatre rather than in its higher and more elegant dramatic phase. His exhibits are for the most part staged attractively. Like Gilbert Miller, John C. Wilson, Vinton Freedley, Delos Chappell, Alfred De Liagre and Lawrence Langner at their opening nights, he invariably shows up at his own dressed to the ears and, also like them, visibly enjoys himself no end.

XIII

The Truth About First-Nights

There are two legends about New York's theatrical opening nights. The first, inculcated in the minds of the citizenry beyond the boundaries of Manhattan by half the syndicated columnar chitchatters, is that they are uniformly resplendent affairs with audiences made up entirely of gentlemen beside whom the Duke of Windsor looks like a hand-me-down and of ladies dressed like a simultaneous explosion in Revillon Frères', Wadley and Smythe's and Cartier's shopwindows. The second, inculcated in turn in the minds of the same citizenry by the other and more cynical half, is that they are uniformly drab affairs with audiences made up for the greater part of actors' agents, Tin Pan Alley cats, ticket speculators, herring restaurateurs and the like, most of them in pants that badly need pressing.

Both legends, I may solemnly affirm after thirty years of on-the-spot observation, investigation and research, are what is designated in the more recherché literary circles as boloney. The usual New York theatrical opening is factually no more like either of these set pictures of it than the opening of a can of beer is like the popping of a champagne bottle, or vice versa. The truth is that it either lies midway

[129

between the two or is indistinguishable from a second, tenth, or even fiftieth night.

The widespread idea that before a first-night the audience, dressed to the nose, dines en masse at the Colony and proceeds elegantly to the scene in Hispanos is as fabulous as that which imagines it assembles at Lindy's delicatessen in yesterday's shirt and moves on to the theatre in garbage wagons. And no less spurious is the theory that, in either case or in both together, the jury is possessed of a remarkably rich acumen in the matter of theatrical values. For if first-night applause were to be accepted as a symbol of worth, there would be hardly a play or show that would ever make less than half a million dollars.

As an experienced student of opening nights, I may report that—favorite star actors aside—the higher the potential quality of a play and dramatist the lower will usually be the social tone of the audience. In other words, the better the play from a critical point of view the less pictorial the first-night gathering. This is one of the outstanding peculiarities of the New York theatre, although I have never seen the fact stated in print. A Lillian Hellman opening thus two times out of three will be lucky (if that's the word) to spot more than a half dozen people in evening dress in the entire house. And so will the first-night of a play by almost any other writer given to poetic expression or any generally regarded as having a serious philosophy of life. The fluffier playwrights on the other hand, particularly if they be English and know their way around El Morocco, the Monte Carlo and other such rendezvous of café society, usually draw a plenitude of *Vogue* and *Town and Country* camera bait.

Because of the strained tardiness, inattention and distracting volubility of such overdressed and exhibitionist audiences, producers, composers and writers every once in a while employ wily means to keep their first-nights, whether dramatic or musical, free from them. Cole Porter, for example, being a personal, if critical, friend of many of their constituent elements, last season in the case of his *Panama Hattie* so arranged matters that the species of audience in point saw his show at a charity preview the night before the opening, thus safeguarding his exhibit's first-night. The late Charles Frohman in point of fact felt so strongly about this idiosyncratic first-night crowd that he once whimsically observed that all plays should open on their second nights.

There are certain producers who draw fashionable audiences irrespective of what plays they put on and certain others who do not. Thus, Gilbert Miller customarily gets a dressed house whereas the Shuberts do not. The first-night of a Guthrie McClintic, Alfred De Liagre, Vinton Freedley, Dwight Wiman or John C. Wilson is generally very much flossier than the first-night of a George Abbott, John Golden, Herman Shumlin, George M. Cohan or William A. Brady. Few persons, aside from some of the older dyed-in-the-wool subscribers, prink for the average Theatre Guild opening, and no one ever did for a Group Theatre opening. But in the case of almost any musical show costing over sixty thousand dollars to produce, and whatever the management, you will usually find a large percentage of the audience in their fanciest regimentals. It is the party spirit induced by musical shows that apparently turns the trick. And, conversely, it is the absence of party spirit in the instance of the more serious dramatists that does not.

The big motion picture openings differ from the theatre openings in that everybody always arbitrarily dresses, even if he has to hire a dinner suit for the occasion and borrow

a white shirt from the management. Certain movie managements, incidentally, are reported to lay in white shirts by
the gross for just this purpose, since they are firmly convinced that a dressed audience is vitally essential to the
proper metropolitan launching of a picture.

It is a further New York peculiarity that those numerous
attendants of a movie opening who do not dress for a
theatrical opening invariably show up at a film première
looking like clothes-horses. This is doubtless because, in
the case of the more serious theatre, an audience most often
goes to see and, in the case of any picture opening, to be
seen. I appreciate that this is no vernal remark, but I risk
it because it is so often asserted that it is the first-night
theatre audience that also goes to be seen, and because in
the majority of cases it is not true. But in the instance of
the film opening it is always true, and no one in turn appreciates it better than the film people themselves, who
encourage it with spotlights illuminating the arriving motor-
cars and taxicabs and the lobbies, and who keep discharging
a battery of cameras both within and without the theatres.

A cross-section of the average metropolitan theatrical
first-night audience may be visualized from a list of the
following more or less regulars:

The leading dramatic critics, about a dozen in number,
the married ones generally accompanied by their wives.
The moving picture company scouts, about six in number,
ditto. Two or three illustrators for the Sunday newspaper
theatrical supplements. The theatrical writers for the leading national newspaper syndicates, about four in number.
Mr. and Mrs. Ira Katzenberg, who haven't missed a first-
night in years and who have seats always reserved in the
first row. Herbert Bayard Swope, editor of the old *World*
and present chairman of the New York State Racing Com-

mission. Brock Pemberton, the theatrical producer. Jack Kriendler, of Jack and Charlie's "21." And such social figures as the William Rhinelander Stewarts (Mrs. Stewart, incidentally, being the audience's most beautiful adornment), the William Randolph Hearsts, Jr., Beth Leary, Marian Tiffany Saportas, Clara Belle Walsh, Elsa Maxwell (when in town), Mrs. Gilbert Miller, Condé Nast, Mr. and Mrs. Herbert Weston, Mr. and Mrs. John C. Wilson, Mrs. Julien Chaqueneau, and John Hay Whitney.

To continue. The society column writers, Maury Paul ("Cholly Knickerbocker") and Nancy Randolph. The newspaper columnists, Walter Winchell, Louis Sobol, Ward Morehouse and Dorothy Kilgallen. The composers, Irving Berlin (and wife), and Richard Rodgers (and wife). The radio theatre critics, Bide Dudley and Howard Barnes. When in town and with a free evening, Jo Davidson, the sculptor, and Al Smith. When not themselves acting, Tallulah Bankhead, Miriam Hopkins, Ruth Gordon, Ilka Chase, Raymond Massey, Grace George, Helen Menken, and Erin O'Brien-Moore. James Montgomery Flagg, the illustrator, Damon Runyon, Moss Hart, Major Bowes, Alexander Ince, and Louis Schurr and Sam Lyons, the actors' agents. Also the theatrical reporters, Zolotow of the *Times*, Pihodna of the *Herald Tribune*, Sylvester of the *Daily News*, and Rice of *PM*.

Further, Howard S. Cullman, the tycoon who backs plays, Frank Case, who operates the Algonquin Hotel, Billy Rose, Eleanor Holm, Jules Bache, Valentina, the fashionable dressmaker, Harry Kaufman, the Shuberts' producing associate, Dwight Deere Wiman, the producer, Max Lief, the theatrical dentist, and Dr. Leo Michel, the theatrical medico. Too, Jo Mielziner, the scene designer (and wife) and Donald Oenslager, ditto (and wife). Also, whenever

in New York, Joan Crawford, Charlie Chaplin, Mary Pick-
ford, Norma Shearer, Joan Bennett, Walter Wanger, Norma
Talmadge, Richard Barthelmess, Douglas Fairbanks, Jr.,
and Nicholas Schenck. When not playing, Clifton Webb,
invariably accompanied by his mother. Also, Franklin P.
Adams, Edna Ferber, Fannie Hurst, J. Robert Rubin, the
MGM counsel, Bennett Cerf, the publisher, Mrs. George
S. Kaufman, Mr. and Mrs. Paul Streger (he is the actors'
agent), and Margaret Case Harriman (who does profiles
for the *New Yorker*). And at every opening, without fail,
Jules Brulatour, the Eastman film mogul, and his wife, Hope
Hampton.

In conclusion, Robert E. Sherwood (and wife), Mrs.
James Farley, Jules Glaenzer, the jeweler, Tommy Manville (with blonde), Féfé Ferry, the night-club impresario,
Huntington Hartford, heir to the A. and P. fortune, Horace
Schmidlapp, wealthy playboy and play backer, Mrs. Margaret Pemberton, wife of the producer, Antoinette Perry,
play director, and William Seeman, wealthy wholesale
grocer, accompanied by his wife, Phyllis Haver, the former
motion picture star.

There, I think, you have a rough general picture of the
chief ingredients of the general first-night audience.

There are, to the initiated, several ways to tell from the
conduct of a first-night audience whether or not the play
is a success. It used to be the custom of Paul Armstrong and
Wilson Mizner on the opening nights of their plays periodically to wander up and down the aisles and observe the
seating posture of the customers. If they found the latter
leaning comfortably back against their chairs beyond the
first act, they said they knew they had a failure. If, on the
other hand, they could detect an inch or two between the

backs of the seats and the persons sitting in them, they
knew they had a success. It was their philosophy that if an
audience strained forward, however little, to hear a play,
you could tell it liked it, whereas if it had no use for it, it
would slump in its chairs. That may be one way, but there
are others.

If all the seats are still occupied at the curtain fall of an
opening night it may not necessarily indicate a success, but
you may usually spot a failure if even so few as a dozen
seats are found to be empty after the second act. And if so
few as a half dozen persons leave after the first act, the
odds are three to one that the storehouse will soon get the
play. In all the three decades that I have been going to the
theatre in my professional capacity as a critic, I have known
only one case when this was not true. That case was *Tobacco
Road*. Fully two dozen people left the theatre after the first
act on the opening night, offended by the play's realism;
yet *Tobacco Road* turned out to be the record hit of the
modern American theatre.

If the nearby barrooms are crowded between the acts
of a play, it pretty often means not that the play is dull and
a failure, as the uninitiated might imagine, but that it in
all likelihood has won the audience and shows promise of
being a success. If a play is stupid, the audience generally
waits until it is over before having a drink, or at least until
it decides to make its permanent departure from the scene.
But if the play is stimulating, the audience paradoxically
further stimulates its pleasure and interest with a rush for
a little extra dividend of stimulation out of the bottle.

Applause may be meaningless, as I have already noted,
but there is one generally infallible way to tell whether
or not a play is to an opening night audience's taste. If that

audience hurries to get out of the theatre, the play is a failure. If it leaves slowly and leisurely and just a little reluctantly, the play is good for a run. That is, in both cases, unless it is a very rainy or stormy night.

XIV

Note on the Road

Every now and again we read a newspaper piece, usually concocted by some devout disciple of Cesar Romero and Zasu Pitts, to the effect that some metropolis like Mobeetie, Texas, has not had a legitimate show in all of the last twenty years. This is supposed to prove conclusively and beyond peradventure that the road, once so prosperous, is dead theatrically, having been put into its grave by the movies. The circumstance that Mobeetie and thousands of towns like it never, even in the heyday of the hinterland theatre, had a legitimate show—to say nothing of a legitimate dramatic theatre—somehow seems to be cleverly overlooked.

There were, of course, small towns that enjoyed theatrical bookings years ago and that enjoy them no longer, but they weren't the Mobeeties or anything like them. They were for the most part the relatively more sizeable towns, and while it is true that many of them have been abandoned by touring companies there is a modest and gradually increasing percentage that indicates a renewed theatrical life. But that is not the point. The point is that when the statisticians emphasize the burgs' abandonment by the drama they seem to hint that in the old days the aforesaid

burgs revelled in companies merchanting the flower of
drama and acting, and that it is a tragic cultural loss which
has since befallen them.

The truth is that most of these towns, even in the full
bloom of bookings, got a pretty acescent grade of dramatic
and acting fare. If they got a decent play and a decent
actor more than twice a year at the outside, they were lucky.
What they ordinarily got, when they got anything, were
fourth companies of *A Trip To Chinatown*, fifth companies
of *Charley's Aunt*, cheap Hal Reid and Owen Davis melodramas, Creston Clarke in *Richelieu* and *A Fool's Revenge*
(and were they choucroute!), Edwin Arden in *The Eagle's
Nest* (its big cultural moment consisting in a mechanical
eagle filching a doll, substituting for the heroine's bairn,
off a hilltop), sixth companies of *Ben Hur* (with a single
chariot economically racing against itself), Primrose and
West minstrel shows, Selma Herman in *Siberia* (with local
newsboys howling off stage like wolves), seventh *Uncle
Tom's Cabins* (with a couple of cocker spaniels masquerading as bloodhounds), and maybe some prestidigitator like
Herrmann or Thurston. That they admired such dispensations no end is not to be denied. But that they, the theatre
as an institution, and the art of the drama suffered an ir-
reparable loss when these dispensations disappeared from
their midst, I allow myself frigidly to doubt.

If it has been a good thing for the American theatre and
its drama to have had its cheaper elements harshly weeded
out by the improved larger cities' criticism, it has been of
equal benefit to get rid of a great deal of the road and its
nefandous æsthetic. Let that portion of the country wallow
in the movies, where its bad taste is comfortably and satisfactorily met by bad taste and with that combined corrupted taste offering neither challenge nor damage to the

hitherward legitimate stage. The theatrical producers, true enough, are out some money, but the theatrical producers who made money out of that kind of road were no credit to their profession and can serve it infinitely better by being kept in the poorhouse.

Another thing. The German theatre in its greatest day of dramatic glory developed out of the impulse of not more than a dozen cities; the French theatre in its out of not more than three; the English theatre out of not more than three; the Russian theatre out of not more than two; and the Irish out of not more than one. When, therefore, the book-keepers lament that the American theatre is dead because three hundred art centers like Lostspring, Wyoming, Patchgrove, Wisconsin, and Tuscarora, New York, have not had an attraction since Nellie McHenry forty years ago played them in *M'liss*, no one need be unduly alarmed, save perhaps the local correspondents, on space rates, of *Variety*.

XV

In Confidence to the Stagestruck

Judging from the volume of communications deposited in the course of a year at the desks of the professional theatre critics, about one young woman out of every three in the nation firmly believes she has in her, if maybe not altogether the stage potentialities of a Sarah Bernhardt, at least those of a Katharine Cornell or, surely, a Katharine Hepburn. The letters the girls compose are largely of a piece. "Please," they urge, "tell me what I can do to become the actress I know I shall someday be, and do let me know how I should go about getting my first job."

Since these letters generally go unanswered—after all, popular opinion to the contrary, critics have plenty of work as it is, what with luncheon, dinner, cocktail, and supper engagements, to say nothing of an occasional play to review—I shall, as one of their number, employ this chapter to give the girls the information they desire. But I warn them. I shall give them none of the futile blarney they customarily get from the usual books published on the subject and from the articles they read in ladies' home magazines, theatrical publications, Sunday newspaper supplements, and the like. I'll tell them frankly what I have found

out from more than three decades of professional observation of the theatre, its adjuncts and its people. I venture to
say, furthermore, that they will learn more hard facts from
what I shall here set down, and facts that will benefit them
a deal more, than they have gleaned from almost anything
they have hitherto either comfortingly or discomfortingly
read or been told.

The first piece of advice that is usually ladled out to
them is the desirability of attendance at a dramatic school.
This counsel should be scrutinized very carefully. With a
few honorable exceptions, the average dramatic school
often does more harm than good to the aspiring young
actress. It tends to destroy individuality and to reduce per-
sonality, and to make its students so many peas in a pod.
Moreover, many of the head acting coaches in these schools
have themselves been failures in the theatre and thus are
poor guides as to what is what. And, still further, the schools'
judgment as to appropriate experimental plays for the students is generally pretty bad, since the talents of individual
students in a particular dramatic line often have to be either
overlooked or sacrificed in order that such plays may be
used as will satisfy the vanity of a sufficient number of paying pupils by giving them their platform chance.

Most of these schools operate on a class basis. That is,
they go in for group instead of individual training. Such
group training may in some instances have its points, but
more often it neglects the possible talent of the individual
in favor of the lack of talent of the many. It is true that
some competent actresses have come out of dramatic
schools, but it is also undoubtedly true that many more
potentially competent ones have been buried in them and
left to die forgotten.

The safest recommendation, therefore, is some such

private coach as, say, Frances Robinson-Duff, or, if she be available, Margaret Carrington, wife of Robert Edmond Jones, the scene designer, and sister of Walter Huston, the well-known actor. Both have excellent records; both have long proved their practical ability in the names of the eminent actors and actresses whom they have in one way or another helped to develop; and both, the latter in particular, know the theatre rather thoroughly. Mrs. Robinson-Duff also has classes and they are more intelligently conducted than most. But it is not of classes that I am writing. It is, to repeat, of individual, strictly personal tutelage. Mrs. Carrington, as she has been professionally known, was, incidentally, responsible among other things for the development of John Barrymore into the actor he in his heyday became and for the dramatic training of Walter Huston, Clare Eames, Lillian Gish, and many another who achieved success. And it was Mrs. Robinson-Duff who did much for Ina Claire, Katharine Hepburn, Jane Wyatt, et al.

Speaking generally, it is advisable for the beginner to avoid the schools and classes presided over by foreign directors, actors and actresses who in late years have descended upon the local scene in such large numbers. It is not, surely, that some of these are not worthy enough in their own way. It is, rather, that very often the species of direction and acting they represent is alien to the American stage and hence, however suitable to their own Germany, Russia, etc., of dubious value to the American aspirant.

The majority of the apprentice schools connected with the summer theatres are downright frauds, and should be avoided. They are frequently headed by coaches who either know next to nothing about direction and acting or, if they do, look upon their work as a soft off-season snap and loaf on their jobs; they often overcharge pupils outrageously;

and their standards are so commercially and calculatedly elastic that youngsters who have no conceivable talent are accepted by the wholesale if only they have the necessary money and who clutter up the schools at the expense of proper attention to the few serious students.

There are, however, a few exceptions. These are at least decently conducted; they give apprentices a fair fundamental, if necessarily all too sketchy, working understanding of everything from diction to stage deportment and from makeup to costume; they see to it that those students who indicate some talent occasionally get the opportunity to act in small roles with the several theatres' professional players; and they give the pupils the cautiously watered seeds of ambition. Among such have been the schools connected with the summer theatres at Cape May, New Jersey, Dennis, Massachusetts, and Stockbridge, Massachusetts.

We come to the question of jobs in the professional theatre. Inasmuch as every season there are at least three hundred young women for every available acting job, the situation is none too encouraging. At this moment, I know of fully thirty young actresses of already successful experience on the New York stage who seemingly can not get work, so where the chance for the beginner? But, anyway, hard as the going is, I may provide the novices with a dozen inside hints that may be of some assistance to them. Here they are, in all stark and possibly inconvenient truth:

1. The prettier a girl is, irrespective of talent, the easier it will be for her to get at least a hearing from producers, who, with certain exceptions, are after all human.

2. Waggling an acquaintance with a playwright can help a lot. Playwrights have frequently given chances to beginners whom producers and directors have brushed aside.

3. Get, by hook or crook, a personal introduction to this or that producer outside the theatre. You will then not have to sit in his outer office for hours on end before getting in to see him. He will see you ahead of the others and listen to your story. He may possibly also give you a reading.

4. Don't overdress when you apply for a job. It not only makes the poor girl in the outer office so sore that often she won't even telephone your name in, but if perchance you do get in to see the producer he'll know at once that you are not only an amateur but something of an idiot.

5. If a manager or producer scrutinizes your figure closely, don't jump to the conclusion that he is a wolf. He is simply doing what every audience you may ever play before also does. He is just making sure in advance of the audience's aesthetic comfort.

6. Dyed hair has lost many a girl the chance at a job. Whatever color your hair may be, leave it that way. And no red fingernails!

7. Don't at any time during an interview with a prospective employer mention your Shakespearean ambitions, express rapt admiration for Stanislavski, or announce what plays you did at dramatic school. They all do.

8. If you have a simple blue dress with a touch of red somewhere about it, wear it. Men like the combination and more girls in blue and red have got jobs than those in yellow, green, pink, brown, or any other color. It doesn't make sense, but from the record it is apparently true.

9. Don't say you are so eager to act you'd be glad to work for nothing. That is the sure raus-mit-'em cue.

10. Be yourself, whatever you are like, and don't try to make an impression by being someone other than your natural self. You won't fool a producer. He has already seen plenty of bad acting as it is.

11. If you have a Southern accent, get rid of it. Not one play in a hundred calls for an actress with a Southern accent.

12. Don't tell a producer that you just know you will succeed if only he will give you a chance to prove yourself. With all the chances in the world even such experienced actresses as Ethel Barrymore, Helen Hayes, Katharine Cornell, Laurette Taylor, Grace George and Ina Claire have occasionally failed.

I am, of course, presupposing in all this that the young applicant really has some talent for acting. Otherwise, if she follows the recommendations however closely, there is little eventual hope for her. But if she has that share of talent, they will, I assure her, serve her.

Here are some other things the girl applying for a role in a play should appreciate:

a. Remember that if another girl of no more experience than yourself gets the role it isn't necessarily any reflection on your ability. The role may call for a girl who looks like the other girl. Two very able young actresses of several years' professional dramatic experience recently applied for a role in a play being staged by George S. Kaufman. The one who arbitrarily got it, got it simply because she was two inches taller than the other, the particular role, because of the need for stage contrast, demanding a girl over five-three in height.

b. If a producer says he has nothing for you at present but that he will let you know when and if he has, don't invariably conclude that he is politely lying. He may be telling the truth. Any girl of ordinary sense can readily tell if she has made a good impression on a man, and it shouldn't be too difficult for the applicant to discern the honest attitude of the producer.

c. Do not rely upon letters of introduction. Nine times out of ten they irritate a producer or playwright, who gets all sorts of them during a season. Very frequently, furthermore, they never get farther than the attendant in his outer office.

d. Don't try tricks to get in to see a producer. Even when and if they work, they generally get you nowhere, since as soon as he catches on, the producer will be doubly annoyed. Of all such tricks I have heard of in the last four years—and I have heard of many—only one seems to have operated. That was in the reported case of Thelma Schnee who got in to see Herman Shumlin and finally landed a role in his *The Corn Is Green* through the circumstance that she found they were both living in the same apartment house and sent in word that she had been sent by a mutual acquaintance, the aforesaid mutual acquaintance turning out to be none other than the colored elevator man.

e. If a producer asks you what you think of the moving pictures, tell him that you detest them and wouldn't go to Hollywood on a bet, even if you are lying. Producers don't relish taking chances on promising young actresses being seized from under their noses, after they have started them on a stage career, by the picture people.

f. Finally, more aspiring young girls have wrecked their chances in the theatre by getting married in the early stages of their careers than you can shake a stick at. Marriage and a career may be compatible later on, but not in the beginning when interest and resolve should remain undivided. And, furthermore, a young girl who is married hardly, in the producers' correct imagination, serves any too well the eternal romantic fancy of the theatre's audiences.

XVI

In Confidence to the Arrivals

I make further bold to offer the appended suggestions to actresses who have arrived and who find themselves cast in romantic roles. During my many years of professional theatregoing, I have laid eyes on so many otherwise competent and engaging stage ladies, young and not so young, who in one way or another have intermittently invalidated the effect of their performances in such roles that it occurs to me a little impolite tectonic criticism may be in order.

1. Don't, if carrying a handkerchief, continue to hold the moist thing in your hand after dabbing your nose with it. Put it away somewhere. The sight of a mucousy rag, even—indeed, particularly—if it be of the most delicate lace fabric, is hardly conducive to a moonlit audience reaction.

2. Don't when sitting down, so cross your legs that the one is pressed so hard against the other that its calf takes on the spread aspect of a mutton chop afflicted with elephantiasis.

3. Don't use belladonna in the eyes. They will so overglisten in the earlier scenes that when the big romantic emotional moments come their artificially induced ecstasy will not only seem relatively dead but will give the impres-

sion of an express train that left the day before.

4. Don't let your director make you arbitrarily move about the stage too much by way of giving the play a semblance of increased movement and action. The most effective romantic actresses have always, without exception, been those who have been on the more sedative side. Nothing is less suggestive of a romantic woman than one whose vitality is over-emphasized. Poets do not chase after the Babe Didriksons of the world.

5. Don't list yourself among those numerous actresses who meditatively feel their faces with fingers or palms. The effect is less of charming abstraction than of exploring for pimples or other facial blemishes.

6. Don't display your posterior to the audience any more than is absolutely necessary. A posterior, however impressive otherwise and be it soever handsomely embellished by a couturière, is seldom associated in the fancy with cloud-born romance.

7. Don't, when you come to the love scenes, suddenly convert your voice from its previous normal and easy tone into a phony violoncello. Every man in the audience will think you are playing your lover-hero for a dupe.

8. Don't, save for purposes of comedy, shyly drop your eyes at any time. The last romantic heroines who could do that and get away with it romantically were Jane Austen's Bennet girls.

9. Don't, if called upon to appear in a riding habit, come into the drawing-room, as you customarily do, carrying your riding crop. You look like a damned fool. Leave it out in the hall. The hero doesn't come into the drawing-room carrying his walking stick, umbrella or golf clubs. And don't think that simply because you are in riding togs you have to be what is called breezy. You will seem an even

bigger damned fool. After a good hard ride you are a bit tired, or should be. If you aren't, you may be a meritorious athlete but you are certainly something of a romantic bore. And remember, as actresses seldom do, that after the good, hard ride your togs do not look as if they had just been delivered by Abercrombie and Fitch. Nothing is less romantically stimulating than a girl who always looks scrupulously neat at the wrong time, whatever it is.

10. If you are thirty-five or over, however relatively young you may still miraculously look, don't let them cast you in young women's roles. You can't successfully fool anybody. You may be critically admired for your acting gifts but you will remain romantically unconvincing and unpersuading. There is something about youth that age, save here and there in the austerity of the classic drama, can never catch and project.

11. Don't in a costume role, through your modern unfamiliarity with costume, make an audience disturbingly conscious of it, particularly in the matter of adjusting the voluminous skirt, walking up and down stairs, and sitting. There probably are not more than two actresses in the American theatre who can wear romantic old costumes and not seem absurdly awkward in them. This was attested to not so many years ago at a gala benefit show at the Metropolitan Opera House. There was offered a spectacular costume number in which figured a dozen or more celebrated American dramatic actresses along with the motion picture actress, Marion Davies. Of them all the only one who was properly pictorial and who did not seem a gawk was this Miss Davies. Why and how? Three days before the show she hired a carpenter to build her a duplicate of the flight of steps to be used in the number and, in costume, practised for hours walking up and down it. The result was that while

all the other actresses looked like suburban housewives, slightly in their cups, trying to crash the gate at a Beaux Arts ball, Miss Davies alone managed the proper costume mood. What our dramatic costume stage needs, apparently, are a lot of carpenters hired on the side some days before the curtain goes up.

12. Don't, after a great passionate, romantic love story, take your final curtain bows as if the evening's work had completely played you out. Your audience will take out of the theatre a very peculiar impression of the heroine you have created and, in view of your great exhaustion, a considerable humorous concern for the future amorous, romantic contentment of the hero.

13. Don't permit your management to list in the program the conventional credits for articles of your wearing apparel and accessories. The picture of a romantic heroine and a whole lot of stocking and garter manufacturers, brassière shops, shoe salesmen, corset and girdle entrepreneurs, beauty cream factories and dress shield merchants does not any too well jibe. No man wants to be told where the Princess Flavia gets her holeproof hose or her panties.

14. Don't give interviews to the press. I have in the last ten years read only one on the part of an actress of romantic roles that had any sense in it—it was Katharine Cornell's—and even an interview with good, hard, cold, realistic sense in it, as Miss Cornell in the same interview herself intelligently allowed, is the last thing in the world to add to the popular lustre of a romantic actress.

XVII

In Confidence to the Novice Playwrights

In a foregoing chapter I indited some confidential suggestions to the multitude of young women who aspire to jobs
on the stage. Inasmuch as it seems that the number of
young men who aspire to write plays is quite as great, if
indeed not greater, and inasmuch, further, as they seem to
be even more eager, judging from their voluminous epis-
tolary exercises, for advice on the subject, I dedicate myself to their enlightenment.

I shall not tell the counsel seekers how to write plays,
and for two reasons. In the first place, I am not myself a
playwright and hence no professor on the art, and in the
second place, that is the last thing which they, in their vast
self-assurance, seem to want to know about. So far as dramaturgy goes, they appear to have all the faith in the world in
themselves, for good or ill. But what they usually beseech
in their letters is, to repeat their most common query, "just
what it is that critics object to in plays and how best it can
be avoided."

It is, accordingly, that I take them at their wishful word
and herewith suggest to them how they may at least lessen
their chances of failure so far as the aforesaid critics are
concerned. And not only the critics, but, what is rather more

important, a very considerable share of the audiences.

For some reason or other, a great many novice play-wrights seem to be fetched by the notion of a mythological play. To their minds there is apparently something inordinately appealing about taking a number of the more familiar mythological characters, making them speak in an approximation to the modern lingo, and drawing from them some sort of analogy to modern customs, conditions or events. My advice is to lay off. Not one such play in a hundred stands much of a chance. Jean Giraudoux got away with a thirty-eighth paraphrase of the Amphitryon legend largely on the score of the Lunts' presence in the cast and Behrman's extremely wily adaptation, but many another contemporary experienced playwright—Denis Johnston for one example—has failed at the general business. It is safer to try some other theme.

The Christ theme, however, does not happen to be one of them. It has frequently been said that every young man with his heart set upon playwriting begins by writing either a play about the Saviour or one which ends with his hero's suicide. The Christ play commonly takes one of three forms. In the first, a modern character, sometimes a carpenter, sometimes a person described simply as A Stranger, is identified with the Saviour and duplicates in modern times and modern surroundings some of the Saviour's experiences. In the second, the scene is laid frankly in Biblical times and the Saviour, when not personified on the stage, is represented either by a light or an off-stage voice. In the third, the story, while following the Bible, is related in the modern idiom. Inasmuch as it takes an authentic poet or at the very least an expert showman-dramatist to do theatrical justice to the Christ story, most of these efforts are foredoomed to disaster.

Incidentally, the only new play on the subject seen in the American theatre in the last two decades that merited any critical notice was the Cowans' *Family Portrait,* and even that was hardly much of a success in the accepted theatrical sense. Maxwell Anderson's *Journey To Jerusalem,* in which Christ was seen as a boy on His way to the annual Passover feast, while original in so far as showing the Saviour as a youth went, failed dismally. Too much water has seemingly gone under the box-office since the days of *Ben Hur, The Servant In The House, The Passing Of The Third Floor Back,* and *The Fool.*

No more plays about the young girl who returns after a considerable absence, finds her father in difficulties, and goes about setting matters right! The reviewers and audiences are sick of them. They belong to the stage of twenty-five and thirty years ago. No more plays, either, about the young girl ward solicitously looked after by one or more dissolute old bachelors, one or all of whom were once in love with her mother! They also are out. And no more plays, if you please, about crooks who gradually see the error of their ways and decide to go straight; about wives who give their philandering husbands a dose of their own medicine, archly leaving the husbands in some final doubt, however, by cabbaging the last line from Henry Arthur Jones' *The Case Of Rebellious Susan;* or about the lovable old bone-head whom everybody takes advantage of but who muddles through and comes out on top at the end. Their day is done.

During the last year, at least sixteen of the unsolicited play manuscripts delivered at my atelier dealt either with the rehabilitation or the impossibility of the rehabilitation of prostitutes. This, of course, is one of the oldest of dramatic themes, and it has done valiant service in its time.

But its time, unless all signs fail, is now past. That is, if the prostitute is the chief character in the play. All the possible changes seem to have been rung on the idea; there is nothing left to say. There is a chance still if the character is not the dominant one in the play, as was proved by Saroyan in *The Time Of Your Life* and as will surely be proved again by O'Neill in *The Iceman Cometh,* but hardly otherwise.

Do not hope to sell reviewers and audiences the play in which a wife shows up the true character of the other woman, thus disillusioning her infatuated husband and winning him back to the family fireside. It is threadbare. Do not think you are going to get royalties on the play in which everything is finally smoothed out and set to rights by the Jewish character whom everyone has snubbed and looked down upon. They are all on to that hari-nuki and it doesn't any longer get you anywhere. And do not imagine that the first-night crowd is going to remove the horses from your carriage and enthusiastically draw you downtown if you give it the play in which the ghost of a young man killed in the war comes back in his old uniform and discourses however eloquently pro or con on the subject of war.

In the way of details, you will be taking a dangerous chance with the reviewers and also a liberal portion of the paying customers if you foolishly venture any of the following:

1. Having a character pause momentarily on each of his exits and exude a wisecrack.

2. Except perhaps in farce, having a woman character come down the stairs in her nightie.

3. Having a character play violently on the piano to heighten the nervous tension.

4. Incorporating into a play laid in the past references

to real persons and places by way of hoping to establish a convincing atmosphere.

5. Causing a character to become ill at the stomach and to rush off stage to relieve himself.

6. Bringing on for humorous effect a male character clad only in his underwear.

7. Causing the radiator steam pipes to set up an awful banging just as the characters settle down for a spell of rest and quiet.

8. Introducing almost any kind of wheeze about caviar.

9. Using unnecessary profanity.

10. Making a "society" character impeccably grammatical.

11. Save only on the rarest occasions, alluding sentimentally to Spring.

12. Unless you are absolutely certain of the casting, describing your heroine as a paragon of beauty.

13. Briefly dropping the curtain more than once during the course of a play to indicate a lapse of time.

14. Addressing a speech to the oil painting of someone hanging above the mantel.

15. Having a character return on the pretext of retrieving something he has left behind, usually deliberately.

16. Introducing a character who stutters.

17. Allowing a character to indulge in a succession of platitudes for comic effect.

18. Finally, out (double exclamation mark) with such paleogenetic rubber-stamps as the tag line "I wonder"; the wistful gaze out of a window; the turning on of a phonograph to liven up an otherwise dull scene with a little music; race horses which, instead of winning as the authors think the audience will anticipate, lose; drinking toasts; symbolic summer lightning; paraphrased Wilde epigrams;

French characters who employ such locutions as "ze" and "zis"; scenes in which a man and woman in a troubled situation lightly pretend to be gay and casual; and cynical bachelor characters.

The widely disseminated theory that plays about Lincoln seldom fail has caused all kinds of novice playwrights in the last three or four years to turn their hands to Great Emancipator dramas. It seems to be the idea of a considerable proportion of these hopefuls that all that is necessary to the negotiation of a very fine drama on the subject is to quote extensively from Lincoln's speeches. I am told it is a rare producer's office that at this moment has not at least a half dozen unsolicited plays about Abe still lying around waiting for the authors to send along the return postage. The best advice to the tyros is to sidestep the notion. John Drinkwater some seasons ago and Robert Sherwood more recently covered it sufficiently, at least for the time being. For a Lincoln play to succeed today, it will have to have double the imagination and skill of either Drinkwater's or Sherwood's, or triple that of E. P. Conkle's.

If you are contemplating writing a serious play with a trial scene in it, stop immediately. The critics and larger portion of the audiences are fed up on trial scenes. They are also fed up on plays about kept women, fights between Capital and Labor, the romance of the gypsy life, the amorous peccadilloes of Frenchmen, and last moments in death cells. Save your ink.

Allegories are dangerous. If you are something of a genuine poet you may get away with an allegorical play, but since in all probability you are not, it is better for you to resist the temptation.

The atheist hero has been done to death. Bluepencil him. The mercy killing idea is equally stale and you had best get it out of your playwriting head at once. The wise old grandmother with her liberal ideas on the sexual freedom of the younger generation has served her day and will not any longer get you anywhere with either the reviewers or the audiences. Paraphrases of the Robin Hood theme of the man who steals from one person to help another are good for snores, loud ones. The suddenly discovered codicil to the will that changes the situation went out of dramatic style many years ago, and the master and servant who change places for a night went out at the same time.

If you wish to chase the reviewers into the nearest barroom and a lot of the audience along with them, write a play in which a boy or girl is unjustly sent to a reform school and comes out sore as the devil and determined to get even with the world. Or if that does not appeal to you, give them a play about an actor and his actress wife and the way the latter wins back the vain old boy from the ingénue in the company. Some other good ideas in the way of filling the barroom are the play about the French Revolution, the play about the run-down business establishment developed into a whiz-bang concern through the enterprise of the young man in love with the owner's daughter (the owner having always deemed him a good-for-nothing loafer), and the one about Lord Byron.

Various other excellent ways to put the reviewers to sleep, get your audiences out of the theatre by the middle of the second acts, and lose the producers money are plays in which flashbacks are periodically employed to show the antecedent actions of the characters; in which the young Liberal son of a rich newspaper owner fights his father's paper because it hasn't been fair to the workers in the steel mill, one of whom is his sweetheart's poor, sick brother; and in which a scientist, big business man, inventor or statesman resolutely won't marry the woman he is crazy about until he finishes the big job he has in hand. Nor must there be overlooked the play about the youngsters whose parents do not understand them, the play about the all-patient, all-enduring mother who nobly bears her burden of trial and sorrow, the one about the proud and intolerant Aryan who is discovered to have had a grandfather named Goldfarb, or the one that sardonically essays to prove that a bawdy house and its inmates are essentially every bit as respectable as anything you could find on Park Avenue.

In conclusion and for extra measure, I suggest that when you sit down to your typewriters this evening and proceed to the composition of the Great American Drama you dismiss instanter the idea of dropping your final curtain on a humorous cuss-word, the dumbhead office-boy character, the machine (customarily represented on the stage by a fifteen-foot-high corrugated papier-mâché hat box) as a dire symbol of the present age, the sex-conscious bitter old maid, the dignified oldster who writes a hot sex book under a pseudonym, the character who suffers lapses of memory during which he is not accountable for his actions, the stern New England father given to Biblical admonitions, the California of the time of the gold rush, and the socialistically minded young banker's daughter.

*   *   *

Having recorded these hints as to what novice playwrights should not do in their quest of critics' and audiences' favor, I now presume to intimate to them some of the things they might do.

Let us first approach the matter of various themes.

No. 1, the Napoleon play, next to the play about Christ and the one about Lincoln a chief favorite of the aspirants.

Since Napoleon has already been pretty well done to death on the stage, both dramatic and musical, and since about the only hope, if any, is to approach the subject as it has not dramatically been approached before, I suggest that the ambitious tyro get hold of and read Filson Young's short story of many years ago treating of Bonaparte as a very young, romantic boy. There is an idea of sorts there—a rather charming idea—and it may possibly send the tyro's fancy off in a new and likely direction. At its worst, it would offer some diversion from the general stage spectacle of a five-foot-three actor with a Della Fox curl and with a sofa pillow under his belt meandering with dejected head through three or four acts, feeling his umbilicus through his vest, and comporting himself for the most part as if Madame Sans-Gêne had never existed, as if the Countess Walewska had been a hideous scarecrow, and as if the ghost of the Duc d'Enghien were ever assiduously worrying his coat-tails.

No. 2, the President play. For some reason, about the only Presidents of the United States most playwrights, young and old, ever seem to have heard of are Washington and Lincoln, with maybe here and there a hint of Jefferson and Andrew Jackson. Our drama has accordingly given us a surplusage of Georges and Abes, and to a sufficient degree Jeffs and Andys, and about all that the stage can do for them appears to have been done. So it might be a nutritious idea for the young playwright to forget his projected opus about one of them—you may be pretty sure it is already in the works—and fix his talents upon some other occupant of the White House. I can think of none better and none who offers more peptic dramatic material than Grover Cleveland. There, my boys, was and is a character for you ready-made for drama if ever there was one! Read

Paul Leicester Ford's *The Honorable Peter Stirling*, the tale
of the Buffalo days, for a starter; then study closely Grover's
career as chief executive of the nation; then go to work.
His story is literally bursting with stage materials: the fat
bachelor taking to wife the delicately beautiful Frances
Folsom in the White House; the garterless old white socks
falling down over his size-twelve brogans, cocked lazily on
his White House desk, as he challenges England to lay off
in Venezuela or, by God, the American navy will see to it
that she does (cheers from the gallery); the defeat and
re-election; the battle against cancer and the carrying on
with an artificial jaw made of vulcanized rubber; the whop-
ping fish stories, worthy of Saroyan's Kit Carson, with
which he was given to interrupting dull cabinet sessions,
to say nothing of too august foreign diplomats; the Falstaf-
fian jug of rum under the desk; the very great and very
lovable man beneath and above it all—what an opportunity!
I also offer a suggestion as to the casting of the role. There
would be no actor more ideally suited to it than Sydney
Greenstreet. So get busy.

No. 3, the play of married life. This one, as we commonly get it, pursues one of three courses. In the first,
trouble between the husband and wife is brought on
through the circumstance that either one or the other is
enamored of someone else. In the second, surroundings—
usually interpreted in terms of gin-swillers and wisecrack-
ers of indifferent morals—contrive to separate the pair, who
are ultimately reunited either by the husband's kicking the
gang out and taking his wife to the theoretically tranquil
countryside, or by their small daughter who is miserable
and lonely—the other school-children taunt her about having no mama and papa to look out for her, or by both. In
the third, either the husband is a drunkard and odious to

his wife or the wife develops into a shrew who drives the husband to seek sanctuary in the arms of some gentle, understanding woman or in Bali.

There are other variations, to be sure, but most of them follow more or less equally conventional tracks. Twenty-odd years ago, in a small manual called *A Book Without A Title*, I wrote a couple of paragraphs that may hint at a somewhat fresher and slightly more rational and realistic slant on the general theme of marital dissolution. I quote them:

> They could not understand why he married her, but the ironic little gods who have such matters in hand knew it was because she had a little way of swallowing before speaking, because she had a little way, when she came to him and saw him standing there with arms open to clasp her tight and kiss her, of sweeping her hat off and sailing it across the room, because she had a way of twining her little finger in his.
>
> They could not understand why he divorced her, but the ironic little gods who have such matters in hand knew it was because she had a little way of swallowing before speaking, because . . .

No. 4, the mystery play. Every one out of three beginning playwrights also seems to be busy on a mystery play. Most of them that the producers receive follow the established blueprint. Someone is murdered; a canny sleuth eventually tracks down the culprit; the culprit is duly punished. Why not, for a change, one in which the otherwise canny sleuth finds himself finally up a tree and defeated? There are plenty of unsolved murders in the police records and just as the public for long has entertained itself trying to figure out such mysteries as the Elwell and other cases so might it conceivably find a like entertainment in the instance of such a play.

There have been several plays dealing with so-called "perfect crimes"—A. A. Milne, of all people, wrote one of them—but they have been spoiled by the playwrights' arbitrary belief that the culprit, for public morality's sake, has to be rounded up eventually and made to pay. Even writers apart from the theatre have timidly subscribed to the conviction, as witness Austin Freeman. A play treating of a perfect crime without any such hesitation and moral qualm would be an interesting novelty.

No. 5, the detective farce. We have had any number of them in the last twenty-five years and some of them were funny enough, but I should like to see one in which the sleuth, a mighty brain in his own conceit, idiotically proves himself an even mightier one than he thought by deducing from the evidence that he himself is the guilty party and the man he has been looking for all evening. I do not know whether the idea has ever been employed before, but if perchance it has I am still prepared to laugh at it if it shows up again, so reserve me a seat, please.

No. 6, the comedy about two men and a girl, which is usually as basically old in its treatment as a horse and buggy doctor's treatment of lumbago, and as ineffectual. Let us have for a little new diversion some such play in which the girl's dilatory amorous shenanigans finally bore the two rivals stiff and in which they go out arm-in-arm to look up a couple of other less enervating and more charmingly companionable babies.

We turn to a contemplation of characters. Let the new, young playwrights break away from the stereotyped contemplation of so many of them. For example:

1. A college professor is not necessarily always an old fogy who wears glasses, whose wardrobe apparently consists of never more than one shiny black suit, and who comports himself like a man afraid of his own shadow. There are among the breed some pretty glandular boys and some pretty fetchingly lively ones, as the girls can tell you. Give them a break.

2. A great detective does not inevitably resemble an actor who looks like a road-company William Gillette. Pinkerton looked like a bartender at the old Hoffman House and William J. Burns like a prosperous Middle Western department store owner. The latter's son, Ray, who has taken over with his brother since their father died, looks, incidentally, like a younger and somewhat more comely Bert Lahr. In addition, detectives do not always talk like Brooklyn messenger boys. I know and have known a dozen of the good ones and most of them have spoken much better English than half the Wall Street brokers and poets I have met.

3. A bachelor of means and social position isn't always avidly sought after by women any more than a great stage beauty is always avidly sought after by men. Both know it is too much trouble and takes too much time and patience, so both intelligently and profitably lay off.

4. Nurses look attractive in their trim white costumes but they are not always tender, gently solicitous, and infinitely womanlike and understanding. Some of them are plenty tough; some of them would rather chew candy, gossip and make a play for the internes than hustle thermometers, bedpans and fresh linen; and a lot of them hate the sight of a man who has been too ill to shave for a few days.

5. Men given to drink are nevertheless sometimes very lovable fellows, and their wives adore them.

6. Refugees from the dictator countries are not necessarily all pitiable folk. There are any number of them who are downright objectionable and offensive.

7. Some young Negresses have just as high moral standards when it comes to sex as some young white girls. It is time playwrights appreciated the fact.

8. Young clergymen are not always trim, slim fellows who exercise a curious appeal to worldly women. A lot of them are far from attractive and would hardly appeal even to the least Polish chambermaid.

9. Philosophers are not always counterparts of inmates of the Old Actors' Home. Some of them even look like George Santayana.

10. An Irishman, American or Australian may be just as passionate a lover as a Frenchman, Italian or Spaniard. So can the old zucchini.

11. A rich society girl is not necessarily less desirable as a wife than a poor girl of plain people, and don't fool yourself.

12. Some Communists dress just as well as Capitalists and have infinitely better manners, much as we don't like to admit it. But playwrights shouldn't cheat.

Let these, further, be rigorously avoided:

1. Bankers who invariably dress like and resemble Grover Whalen considerably more than they do J. P. Morgan, Tom Lamont or Harvey Gibson.

2. Detectives who, whatever the weather, wear raincoats, address every woman as "sister," always take three cigars out of the box when it is proffered them, are customarily accompanied by an assistant who is the acme of stupidity, and on no less than two of their exits vouchsafe the parting shot, "I'll be seein' you."

3. Urban sirens who, their automobiles breaking down during rainstorms, are forced to spend the night at a farm-

house and who, though they have only a small handbag with them, subsequently appear in a rich variety of costumes leading up to a gorgeous pink negligée, the spectacle of whom in which gives the yokel juvenile such a palpitation of the libido that he breaks off his engagement to his rural intended then and there, causing his old mother to denounce the siren as a wanton and—her arm around her—to comfort the little rural one with the words: "Now don't you worry, child, everything'll come out all right, everything'll come out all right—it's God's will."

4. Members of pre-war house-parties on the Riviera including the tippling, good-looking young waster whom Lady Diana cannot get out of her mind; the elderly but vivacious Duchess who likes her glass of port and, recollecting her past with romantic sighs, lightly condones the anatomical transgressions of young Lady Sybil; and the oldish husbands who clutter up the scene drinking whiskeys and soda, talking about tomorrow's golf, and pachycephalously assuring their wayward wives they've never seen them look so spry. "It must be the good old Mediterranean climate," they sagely allow.

5. Ghosts. Particularly ghosts in modern dress who speak in the pompously measured tones of lower East Side lawyers and look as if they had died from swallowing overdoses of talcum powder.

6. Conventionally unsympathetic characters arbitrarily made sympathetic by playwrights obviously proud of their great originality.

7. Plump female Negro servants who beam good-naturedly all over the place and indulge in such Lew Dockstader locutions as "Is you-all gwine stay to home to dinnah dis heah ebenin'?"

8. Newspaper reporters of the newer theatrical dispensation who don't drink, who take their hats off in the room, who talk the way the New York *Times* editorials read, who dress like Anthony Drexel Biddle, and who, in an interview with even a most complex and abstruse statistician, never lower themselves into taking notes.

9. Illiterate bums in plays by blank verse dramatists who are privileged such stuff as "There, eftsoons, beyond the sheen of countless myrmidons in argent armor, glistening like the translucent Sabian sword upon the plains of Deteropolæ, beyond the effulgent vision of phoenixes unending, awaits a nobler dream, a dream of Thracian grandeur set like a Gregorian liturgy to the organ of the sighing stars."

10. Characters so cast against type by way of avoiding banality that a waterfront longshoreman looks like Beverley Nichols and an author like Beverley Nichols like a waterfront longshoreman.

11. Female characters presented as very reservoirs of spirituality who indicate their unworldliness and piety by closing their eyes when anyone else is speaking to them and by opening them as wide as a barn-door when they themselves are addressing others.

12. Poets who under no circumstances ever resemble Robinson Jeffers, Robert Frost, Archibald MacLeish, Louis Untermeyer or even Edgar A. Guest and who, were they to show up at a meeting of the Poetry Society, would be mistaken for tubercular Armenian rug peddlers and would be kicked out on their fannys.

13. Women who in the remote past have sinned once and who are pursued by a Nemesis for the rest of their lives.

14. Sir Neville Mountjoy-Frothingham, M.P.

15. Pablo, a peon.

We turn now to adaptations of foreign plays.

1. Do not think you stand a better chance with American audiences if you transplant the locale of a French play, say, from Rambouillet to Roslyn, Long Island, and change the names of the characters from Henri de Bourneville and Germaine Dalcroix to Henry Brown and Geraldine Daly. In most cases you can't do it any more successfully than you could transfer the locale and people of some American play like *The Time Of Your Life* to France. The thing, even at its best and most skilful, seldom sounds right and the play becomes bastardized and not a little ridiculous.

2. If you do not know the language of the play's country thoroughly, do not attempt an adaptation. You will give yourself, to say nothing of the play itself, away at intervals of every five minutes. And don't work from a rough translation made by someone else. That will make matters even worse.

3. Always keep in mind that what makes a play successful in one country may be the very thing that makes it unsuccessful in another. Playwrights and producers have lost all kinds of money by overlooking the fact.

We approach the subject of dramatizations of stories and novels.

There should be available and alimental plays, I believe, in the following:

1. Max Beerbohm's *Zuleika Dobson*. If adroitly dramatized and properly cast, the play should prove a delight.

2. André Malraux's *Man's Fate*. A stirring drama might result.

3. No less than three of the short novels written by Lilith Benda for the old *Smart Set* magazine, excellent themes and perfectly suited to the drama—particularly the story of the girl whose father resembled the late Diamond Jim Brady, to the disgust of her fastidious lover, and the one about the hesitant twain brought amorously together by the singing of drunken French sailors in an adjoining supper room in a country inn.

4. Maxim Gorky's *Twenty-six Men and A Girl*, a tale of the tragedy of men when their one glimpse of beauty, purity and illusion is taken from them.

5. George Birmingham's *The Lost Tribes*, a comedy about a wealthy American woman's fatuous attempt to galvanize a village in Ireland. But it would probably be a difficult job for anyone but an Irishman.

6. A dramatization of Rabelais' *Works*, with Rabelais himself somehow worked into it. I herewith put in an order for six seats.

7. Henri Béraud's *The Martyrdom Of A Fat Man*, juicy farce-comedy materials.

8. The novel, *Latitude Of Love*, which contains the essence of a droll comedy.

9. Finally, to go far afield and believe it or not, I have a feeling a funny play might be evolved from the old silent movie called *Convention City*. The story is an original one and with a rich old George Ade flavor. And, so far as I can remember, no one has yet written a play about the imbecilities of business conventions. The scene of the story is Atlantic City. I do not recall the author's name.

XVIII

In Confidence to the Producers

When Mencken and I were editing magazines together it was one of our practices arbitrarily to accept for publication any manuscript that had been sternly rejected by more than three editors of other magazines. If a script had been rejected by only two or three, we occasionally read it before buying it, just to make sure. But if it had been turned down by from four to six or a dozen we felt perfectly safe in buying it unread, save perhaps only for a cursory once-over to see that the commas were in their proper places and that there weren't too many of them, which nearly always is a sign that the author is either a female schoolteacher or a male of the belletristic species who too scrupulously polishes up otherwise unscrupulous literary performances.

It was our somewhat impertinent theory that most of the other magazines of the time had become at once editorially rule-bound and woefully stereotyped and that, accordingly, stories and articles which they would not for a moment consider were just our dish. And I think I simply repeat history when I say that our theory worked successfully in practice for a period of something like thirteen years.

All this is by way of getting to the point of what I would

do if I were a theatrical producer. Just as we had a graded
list of magazine editors whose rejections counted so many
points in favor of a manuscript—and some otherwise very
highly respected editors were on it—so would I prepare
myself a list of other producers and act accordingly. For
the records of the theatre indicate pretty clearly that you
can very often gauge not only the critical quality but even
the commercial potentiality of a play by the character and
number of producers who have contemptuously declined to
have anything to do with it. What is more, I would not hesitate to invest some of my money in plays which the producers, even when they do accept them, regard as having
but a small chance of success.

If you think all this is mere smart-aleckism, here are
some sample testimonials to my contention:

Exactly twenty-seven producers rejected *The Barretts
Of Wimpole Street*, that big critical and box-office success,
before Guthrie McClintic finally put it on.

Four producers, including Gilbert Miller, turned down
the recent critical and commercial hit, *The Corn Is Green*,
before Herman Shumlin decided to give it a chance.

At least four producers spurned Elmer Rice's *Street
Scene*, which ran for six hundred and one performances in
New York alone, before the author succeeded in persuading
William A. Brady to do it, the aforesaid William A. Brady
being the producer who gave up his rights to the enormously prosperous melodrama, *Broadway*, in the belief that
it was not any good.

Edgar Selwyn, who had the first chance at Eugene
O'Neill's *Anna Christie*, spurned it as a poor play that
would offend audiences and would never go in the theatre.

The Shuberts wanted to close *Shadow and Substance*
after its week's tryout in Pittsburgh, insisting it could be

nothing but a rank failure. It subsequently was one of the hits of the season.

The Group Theatre, which announced that it was crazy to get hold of a good play, abruptly rejected Saroyan's *The Time Of Your Life*, which Eddie Dowling then promptly accepted and not only saw it win both the Critics' Circle and Pulitzer prizes but enjoy long runs both in New York and on the road.

When *Rain*, one of the biggest successes of the modern American theatre, was tried out in Philadelphia, the late and deeply lamented Sam Harris was so discouraged about it that he was willing to dispose of a quarter interest in it for twenty-five hundred dollars. It subsequently made a fortune. (Incidentally, Mencken and I published Maugham's novelette, *Miss Thompson,* from which it was dramatized, upon its rejection by the editors of exactly fourteen other magazines. Incidentally and further, it sold out our magazine the day after it hit the newsstands.)

Rose Franken's *Another Language,* which ran for four hundred and thirty-three New York performances, had been turned down all over town until Arthur Beckhard, an amateur, decided to give it a tryout in a little summer theatre.

Three Men On A Horse, which made all kinds of money, was rejected by several producers, even George Abbott, who touched it up and finally produced it for Alex Yokel, not believing overly much in it.

Within The Law, which coined money, was abandoned as hopeless by William A. Brady after its Chicago tryout.

Death Takes A Holiday, another money-maker, was viewed with disfavor—"You can't have Death as the central character in any play that hopes for success"—by eight producers to whom it was submitted by Adrienne Morrison, who wanted her daughter, Joan Bennett, to play the role of Grazia, which she should have done.

The Theatre Guild put on Eugene O'Neill's *Strange Interlude* with dire financial misgivings. You know the box-office smash it turned out to be.

If it had not been for the late John D. Williams, O'Neill's *Beyond The Horizon* would not have been produced, as no Broadway producer of the period would have been interested in it. It ran out the season and won the Pulitzer prize.

It took the actors Richard Mansfield and Arnold Daly, the latter a former office-boy of Charles Frohman's, to do Bernard Shaw first in America, the producers having utterly no use for him.

One might go on endlessly, but enough examples have been cited to show the way the wind often blows.

We come to plays I would not under any circumstances take a financial gamble on if I were a producer.

First, as I have intimated in the previous chapter, ghost plays. Or at least serious plays in which ghosts are represented on the stage in person. Nine out of every ten such serious plays are foredoomed to failure, since the critics understandably cannot dissociate from burlesque the physical presence of actors as spooks. The moment a dramatic critic these days hears that a grim new drama is coming along with a ghost or two in it, he makes a date for that evening with a girl over in Newark. The classics aside, he appreciates not only that ghosts are usually the last resort of a solemn playwright who can't think of any more inventive device for his play and who in despair puts them into it with an oh-the-hell-I'll-take-a-chance attitude, but that when the ghosts finally show up on the stage they generally seem like nothing so much as embarrassed actors at a dress rehearsal.

The chief concern of unimaginative playwrights who rely upon ghosts to implement their dramatic action, to say nothing of the playwrights' abashed stage directors, is, once they have confected their ghosts, to work like the devil trying to figure out a way to make them as little like ghosts as possible. This makes for some woebegone monkeyshines. Stage ghosts, as in the old days, are seldom any longer privileged their old white sheets or, if female, their robes of pale gauze, but are metamorphosed into creatures that no more resemble ghosts than Mayor LaGuardia resembles Tilly Losch. The new stage fashion, it seems, is to deny at least visually that they are ghosts and to present them in the realistic bodies of actors dressed in the latest creations by Finchley or Bergdorf-Goodman, smoking Racquet Club cigarettes which they light with the dernier cri in patented igniters and, when not speaking, either reading the latest James Hilton novel or listening to Orson Welles on the radio. It has all got to be so confusing that the only way one can any longer distinguish between the living and dead characters on a stage is to note the somewhat greater apathy of the actors playing the supposedly alive ones.

Secondly, plays in which a sex-starved woman married to a hopeless invalid or cripple finds a sudden release from her anatomical famishment in a passing young man, whereupon her hitherto glum face is instantaneously pervaded by a new, youthful glow.

Thirdly, plays in which a young Left-winger in a brown suit, blue shirt with a tie flying out and with rumpled hair enters the heroine's drawing-room and tells her and everyone else around that they are mere parasites.

Fourthly, plays dealing with Hollywood sex life, however truthfully and however good.

Fifthly, any play one of whose important situations is

developed through something suddenly heard over the radio.

Sixthly, the play which thinks to give a conventional plot an unconventional and important air by making the husband or lover a scientist of one sort or another and embroidering the dialogue with scientific allusions.

Seventhly, any play containing a symbolical thunderstorm, or a frumpy heroine who in the last act shows up looking like Lillian Russell, or a group of young people sitting around fingering tennis rackets, or a separated married couple who meet in later years and conclude that, after all, they mean more to each other than anyone else, or, finally, a racehorse.

Eighthly, Biblical plays that draw modern analogies. Or, in point of fact, any Biblical plays.

Ninthly, biographical plays about celebrated poets, authors or composers.

And in the tenth place, plays in which a timid little man eventually outwits and triumphs over a lot of tough mugs.

A favorite conviction of the majority of producers is that you can not tell anything about a play manuscript merely from a reading of it and that you have to get a glimpse of it in actual production before you know what you have got. This, I have the impudence to observe, is the sheerest nonsense. I certainly am no exceptional fellow but it seems to me one of the simplest things in the world to tell a good play from the reading of it in script form, and even a far simpler one to tell a bad play. The producer who can't tell whether a play is good from a script reading doubtless also can't tell whether a book is good from a reading of it. There is no mystery to it. Anyone with any slightest sense of theatrical values should be able readily to recognize the values or lack of values in a script.

I hope that I may not appear too offensively bumptious if I offer myself in this direct connection as a test-tube. And I am, recall, no experienced theatrical producer but merely an average dramatic critic. Well then, six months before the production of *Strange Interlude,* which I had read in manuscript, I published a critical article saying that, despite the grave and worried doubts over its excessive length, it was certain to be a box-office sensation. I read both *Shadow and Substance* and *The White Steed* in script and five months before they were produced announced both as potential prize-winners. After reading Saroyan's *The Time Of Your Life,* I printed an article boosting it fully seven months before its production. It should be noted here that Eddie Dowling, who, as I have previously noted, apparently knows much more about manuscript values than the majority of his producing colleagues, accepted the three plays mentioned as soon as they were submitted to him. He is one of the very few producers who does not believe in the bosh of not being able to tell a good play when he reads it.

I read the manuscript of Tennessee Williams' *Battle Of Angels,* which Bennett Cerf, the publisher, and the Theatre Guild were wild about and privately expressed the opinion to Cerf that it was very bad. The play subsequently had to be closed for extensive rewriting after a brief Boston tryout. Maurine Watkins some years back gave me the script of her *Chicago* and I promptly sat down and blew the trumpet for it in a magazine article. I told Saroyan to throw his *The Hero Of The World* and *Story Of A Soldier* into the wastebasket; he didn't do it and tried them out in the summer theatres; they are in the wastebasket now.

More seeming brag. O'Neill sent me the script of *Ah, Wilderness!,* which he appeared to have some qualms about inasmuch as it was such a departure from his accepted style and manner. I was enthusiastic about it and told him, as he will substantiate, that it was absolutely certain of both critical and commercial success. Incidentally, in the earlier days, it was your humble waterboy who, admiring the plays in script, sent *Anna Christie* first to Selwyn and then to Arthur Hopkins, and persuaded Williams to read *Beyond The Horizon*, O'Neill's first full-length play.

More immodesty still. I have read Saroyan's *Across The Board On Tomorrow Morning* and if he will carefully edit and expand it—it presently would run only an hour—he will, I believe, get an available play out of it. Sean O'Casey's short play, *The End Of The Beginning*, still unproduced, would prove to be as hilarious a one-acter as our theatre has ever seen. O'Casey's newest play, *Purple Dust*, announced for production as these lines are set down, is—as I wrote a year ago after reading it—beautiful writing and generally superior drama, for O'Casey after all is Ireland's greatest living playwright, but it is much too fine a work to make any real money at the popular box-office.

Still more deplorable ostentation. I read Robert Turney's *Daughters Of Atreus*, whooped it up as a worthy job, and predicted it would be favorably received by the critics but could never be financially successful. See the subsequent records. I urged Paul Vincent Carroll after reading the scripts of both *Kindred* and *The Old Foolishness* not to let any producer see them, as they were both impossibly bad. He allowed them to be produced by Edward Choate and John Golden respectively—producers who esteemed them highly—and both were immediate critical and box-office failures that severely damaged Carroll's standing.

I have read O'Neill's *The Iceman Cometh* and say confidently that, when ultimately it is produced, it is bound to be a great success and will win the Critics' Circle award as the best play of its year.

I could go on, but those sarcastic bean-shooters of yours are becoming altogether too stinging for comfort.

XIX

Ersatz Profundity

When it comes to confident and sometimes even arrogant misinformation, the world of the theatre usually outstrips all competitors. Provided only there be a minimum of truth and fact in a theory, theatre folk will accept it as fully as if it were God's Word, a United States Treasury certificate, or their best girl's affirmation that she can't understand what in the world other women see in whoever the agitating man is they see it in.

For a first example, they believe and endlessly repeat the philosophy that "a young actress can't play Juliet and when she gets older and is able to play it she is too old for the role." Buncombe! Mary Anderson played Juliet and was a sensation when she was seventeen years old. Fanny Kemble repeated the trick at nineteen. Julia Arthur, in point of fact, played Juliet with the Daniel Bandmann Shakespeare repertoire company and, according to report, played her extremely well at fourteen. Elisabeth Bergner was just twenty-five when she made her success in the role. Turn to the older actresses. Jane Cowl made an admirable Juliet at thirty-six. Julia Marlowe was still a lovely Juliet at forty, having made her initial appearance in the role at twenty-three. Helena Modjeska's Juliet began when she was thirty-three and continued successfully until she was forty; she played it at that age to Edwin Booth's Romeo. Florence Roberts was an effective Juliet at forty-one; Eleanor Robson won plaudits in the role in her very late thirties; and Katharine Cornell got by sufficiently in it at forty.

"No actor can ever fail as Hamlet" is a second familiar conviction. Dozens of actors have failed as Hamlet, some of them being such ignominious hams that audiences and critics have bestowed the collateral eggs upon them. Only a short time ago Leslie Howard failed signally in the role. Walter Hampden certainly made a pretty general poor impression in the part. In older days Barry Sullivan was reported a mess in the role, with E. L. Davenport not so very much better. George Jones, according to Professor Odell, acted Hamlet "to the accompaniment of laughter, jeers, ridicule and confusion." Charles Coghlan was a failure; so was Charles Fechter; Frederick Paulding was a dreadful miscarriage; and the celebrated John McCullough was a stinkerissimo superbissimo.

Having heard for countless years the old saying that critics "are those who have failed in literature and art" and that especially a dramatic critic, though he does not hesitate to criticize others' plays, could not himself write even a tenth-way decent one on a bet, theatre folk have in turn for the same countless years swallowed the indictment whole, not without considerable evident gustatory relish. Yet what is the truth? So many dramatic critics have written successful plays that to list their full number would be a reading bore. Without going back too far and confining ourselves to more modern times, here are just a few. Bernard Shaw, the best drama critic of his period, needs no further introduction. William Archer, a papa in the critical craft, became tired of reviewing a lot of second-rate melodramas and, for his own and everybody else's pleasure, wrote the first-rate *The Green Goddess*. Charles H. Hoyt wrote at least half a dozen farces that became famous. Bronson Howard, taking up playwriting, did a great deal to change the course of American playwriting. C. M. S. McLellan wrote not only *Leah Kleschna*, one of the outstanding dramas in the theatre of its day, but also *The Belle Of New York*, one of the most successful musical show books in the history of the American theatre.

Franklin Fyles and his *The Girl I Left Behind Me*, which opened the Empire Theatre, are still vividly remembered. Charles Frederic Nirdlinger wrote *Pompadour, The World and His Wife* and *The First Lady Of The Land*. Robert de Flers became one of the most esteemed of French comedy craftsmen. St. John Ervine has written *John Ferguson, Jane Clegg, The First Mrs. Fraser, Anthony and Anna, Robert's Wife*, etc. Harold Brighouse, critic for the Manchester *Guardian*, turned out several prosperous comedies. Paul M. Potter, critic on the old New York *Herald*, not only made the highly successful dramatizations of *Under Two Flags, Trilby* and *The Honor Of The Family* but wrote a number of original successes, among them *The City Directory, The Ugly Duckling, The American Minister, Our Country Cousins, The Pacific Mail, The Schoolgirl* and *The Conquerors*. André Obey's *Noah, Lucrece*, etc., are readily re-called. Walter Prichard Eaton did pretty well in the case of *Queen Victoria*. Nym Crinkle had a hand in the enor-mously popular *The Great Diamond Robbery*, played for years by Madame Janauschek. Channing Pollock wrote three or four hits. Robert Sherwood, don't overlook, was a magazine drama critic before he took up playwriting. Ren-nold Wolf, of the old *Morning Telegraph*, confected a number of successful revues, among them a Ziegfeld *Follies* or two. And so on.

The theatre impressibles are further persuaded that it is better to name a play with one of the early letters in the alphabet so it will rate a position well up toward the top of the theatrical advertising boxes. There, it will quickly be seen by prospective ticket buyers and thus stand a much better chance of customers than one whose title begins with one of the last letters in the alphabet and which will therefore be advertised and lost at the bottom of the boxes. *What A Life*, which was advertised at the very tail-end of the boxes, ran for more than a year. *Tovarich* was a great success, and so was *Stage Door*. *Tonight At 8:30*, *You Can't Take It With You* (Y is only one peg above Z), *Yes, My Darling Daughter* (also with a Y), *Room Service*, *Three Men On A Horse*, *The Man Who Came To Dinner*, *Susan and God*, *Winterset*, *Shadow and Substance*, *Whiteoaks*, *Victoria Regina*, *The Little Foxes*, *Watch On The Rhine* and *The Philadelphia Story*, all well down in the alphabet, have been among the hits of recent seasons. Among the greatest successes in American showshop history, incidentally, are *Tobacco Road*, which ran for seven years, *The Bat*, *The First Year*, *Seventh Heaven*, *Peg o' My Heart*, *The Children's Hour*, *Rain*, *The Green Pastures*, *The Student Prince*, *Street Scene*, *Show Boat*, *The Show-Off*, *Sally*, *Strictly Dishonorable*, *The Music Master*, *The Boomerang*, *Sunny*, *Personal Appearance*, and *Sailor, Beware!*

But the sausageheads are dogged. They are also firmly of the faith that a star actress takes a great chance with her public by appearing in an unsympathetic and unpleasant role. Chrystal Herne made her biggest hit as the nasty female in *Craig's Wife*, just as Tallulah Bankhead more recently has made hers in an equally ugly role in *The Little*

Foxes. Nazimova in *Mourning Becomes Electra,* Fay Bainter as the nuisance wife in *Dodsworth,* Pauline Lord in *Ethan Frome,* Mary Morris in *Double Door,* Nance O'Neil in *Night In The House,* Florence Reed in *The Shanghai Gesture* and Helen Westley in *The Primrose Path* pleased their customers enormously.

Oh well and good, persist the theatrical foxes, but there is one truth that remains a truth and anybody who argues it is not is a jackass. No playwright can ever deliberately fool an audience and get away with it at the box-office. George Cohan fooled audiences in *Seven Keys To Baldpate* and got rich. Then he fooled them all over again in *The Tavern* and got richer. Sacha Guitry has bamboozled them very profitably a couple of times. And at least a third of the old mystery playmakers made what money they did by treating audiences as come-ons and suckers.

XX

The Public Taste

Now that another theatrical season is in full swing, you will again be hearing a lot from the critics about taste. Taste is the critics' oyster. When they haven't anything in particular to write about, which is pretty often, you may lay a safe wager that taste will be, as per heretofore, the ticket.

It seems, according to these critics, who get quite worked up about it, that most other people's taste isn't at all what it should be. It's low, they say, which is a grievous tragedy for the theatre. How can anyone hope for a really fine theatre in the presence of such a disastrous state of affairs? How can the drama really ever get anywhere when most folk so sadly lack discrimination and æsthetic refinement? It's schrecklich.

As one who, like themselves, also earns a living practising the critical hocus-pocus, I have the traitorous honor to tell them that for the most part they are whining through their snoods. Perhaps in specific, isolated instances the theatre public's taste isn't all it might be, but in the general run of things it is just as respectable as many of the critics'. In some cases, indeed, considerably more so. What is more, some of the very things the critics denounce as evidences

[183

of popular bad taste are supportable as quite seemly for any taste. And what is still more, many of their arguments against bad taste are wholly without foundation, and rather silly.

The Elizabethan theatre which gave us Shakespeare and which was one of the greatest in history was made up largely of audiences whose taste, by present critical standards, was deplorable. To pleasure them and keep them in their seats you had to give them murder stories spilling over with blood, bad puns, comic drunks, thunderous belchings, women idiotically masquerading as men, low clowns, dirty jokes, false whiskers, frequent fallings on rears, resounding slapsticks, and most of the other things that made the Minsky brothers of our own time rich, before the police with their supposedly good taste interfered with them. Shakespeare, as everyone knows, is often as full of bad taste as Al Woods, bless him, ever was. The famous Commedia dell'Arte, which the critics are forever affectionately harking back to with tears in their eyes, was made by audiences whose relish of improvised low hokum was boundless. And the celebrated English theatre of the Restoration had to rely for its prosperity upon giving its customers more sex stuff—and sexier—than Mae West ever thought of peddling.

The drama even at its best, in short, has often been chock-a-block with bad taste. It has had to be in order to live and thrive.

But the notion that low taste is the exclusive privilege and attribute of the rag and bobtail is as dubious as the notion that the self-constituted elect, including the professional critics, are creatures of an impeccable æsthetic. I have often told the story of a large dinner given to me, on a visit to London, by those illustrious critics William

Archer, translator of Ibsen, and Arthur Bingham Walkley, who was instrumental in bringing the finer French drama to England. When speech-making time came, they asked me to stand up and tell them about the theatre in America. I duly stood up and began to expatiate on O'Neill, the Theatre Guild and other such grave topics. But I didn't get beyond the second sentence when both of them shouted: "To hell with all that; what we want to hear about is the Ziegfeld *Follies!*"

Thomas Hardy, the great English novelist, as I have also already recorded, seldom patronized the theatre save a good hot song and dance show with some low comedians in it was on tap. Georg Brandes, the celebrated Danish critic, became literally sick at the stomach the first time he went to a classic drama and thereafter resolutely confined himself on the occasions he went to the theatre to the bawdier species of entertainment. Woodrow Wilson, that immaculate intellect, preferred a vaudeville show to the finest play on the stage of his day. James Huneker, the best of American critics of the arts, after his first low burlesque show let out such a yell of delight that the cops thought he was being held up by Henry Krehbiel. Give William Lyon Phelps, who nearing eighty asseverates he can't stand musical girl-shows, a play in which anyone, preferably a banker, is found mysteriously murdered and he can contain his excited pleasure only with the greatest difficulty. And it is the same with a lot of other such hypothetically austere magnificoes, yesterday, today, and doubtless tomorrow.

Consider, for instance, if you want a laugh, the very dramatic critics who are currently taking pot-shots at your lack of taste and fondness for the lower elements in entertainment. What about them? I know them well and I hope they will forgive me if I give you the lowdown on them.

Brooks Atkinson, critic for the New York *Times*, who indites profound tributes to Thoreau and Emerson and who devotes long Sunday columns to the celebration of the dramatic art of Molière and Chekhov, falls into the aisle roaring with glee and bursts his suspenders in the presence of Bert Lahr, Bobby Clark and Jack Haley. And any trick dog act gets him where he lives. Richard Watts, Jr., of the *Herald Tribune*, can't resist a Garbo or Deanna Durbin movie, however bad, is crazy about baseball games, and spends long hours every night playing the match game, which consists in guessing how many matches the other fellow has concealed in his hand. John Mason Brown, of the *World-Telegram*, who never fails to quote Matthew Arnold in his reviews and who lectures on Marlowe, Sainte-Beuve and the Greek drama, amuses himself no end playing his small son Preston's toy saxophone, and Sidney Whipple, until recently of the *World-Telegram*, delights in doing soft-shoe dances, at which he is an expert, and has as his ambition the acting some day of the role of the rich drunk in Saroyan's *The Time Of Your Life*. He also has a great time playing jazz on the piano.

John Anderson, of the *Journal-American*, another of your solemn advisers on the higher culture, is a hand-ball fiend, admires himself in the role of Sisyphus and spends months of the year rolling huge stones up and down hills, and once had a hand in fashioning a detective show called *The Fatal Alibi*. Richard Lockridge, of the *Sun*, has also enjoyed himself no end in helping to confect a mystery play, *Mr. and Mrs. North*, a dramatization of his and his wife's mystery novel, *The Norths Meet Murder*, and further takes enormous delight in reading almost every detective story that comes along. Burns Mantle, of the *Daily News*, a pious number on the question of taste, is an enthusiastic venerator of the Hay diet, a golf maniac, a reader of such literature as *How To Win Friends and Influence People*, and a fellow who has a grand social time talking to the old ladies who make up women's clubs, after he has lectured to them. And George Jean Nathan, who has written and published twenty-four books of criticism eloquently arguing for an increase in good taste, likes low burlesque shows, the lower the better, Chinese blues singers, Gypsy Rose Lee and other such strip-teasers, and playing *Ach, Du Lieber Augustin* with a fork on wine and water glasses.

So don't be too discouraged when the arbiters tell you that you ought to hang your head in disgrace for not going to Shakespeare every night and sometimes preferring Ed Wynn. If, for instance, they tell you you should be ashamed of yourself for liking the saxophone, that degraded instrument, answer them that what was good enough for the Paris Conservatory and Richard Strauss and what is still good enough for Leopold Stokowski and even Preston Brown is maybe good enough for you. If they tell you that melodrama is an inferior form of drama and that you should not like it as much as you unquestionably do, ask them if *Hamlet* and *Macbeth* are not melodrama, if the aforementioned William Archer, the best known and most dignified English dramatic critic of his day, didn't take prime delight in composing the aforementioned successful one called *The Green Goddess*, if the classic Greek drama isn't full of melodrama, and if Hauptmann, Wedekind, D'Annunzio, O'Neill, Hellman and other such modern dramatists whom they admire have been loath to write it? (*"Do I contradict myself? Very well, I contradict myself."*—Walt Whitman.)

When a number of the critics continue to disparage you on the ground that you like mystery and detective plays, novels and stories, give them the elevated nose. If such eminent artists as Balzac (*A Gondreville Mystery*), De Quincey (*The Avenger*), Dickens (*The Mystery Of Edwin Drood*), Robert Louis Stevenson (*New Arabian Nights*), Henry James (*Sir Edmund Orme*), Joseph Conrad (*The Secret Agent*), Thomas Bailey Aldrich (*The Stillwater Tragedy*), G. K. Chesterton (*Father Brown*), Edgar Allan Poe and various others have seen fit to write them, why shouldn't you see fit to see them in dramatization or read them? If they have been all right for novelists like Hugh Walpole and Aldous Huxley, members of Parliament like A. P. Herbert, and lawyers like Melville Davisson Post to spend their writing efforts on, why aren't they all right for you?

Popular music is another of the critics' itches. You should, it appears, not waste your time on such trash and should occupy yourself instead with Mozart, Chopin and other such masters. Aside from the fact that many of the popular tunes that fetch you are stolen directly and bodily from such masters, as has been amply proved by musical sleuths like Sigmund Spaeth, the critics' notion that all popular tunes are bad music only attests to their ignorance of music. Dozens upon dozens of the popular melodies are good enough music for almost anyone. Lehar's *The Merry Widow* waltz, Victor Herbert's *Kiss Me Again*, Kern's *They Wouldn't Believe Me*, Kalmann's *Stradivari* and *Dance With Me Into Paradise*, De Koven's *Brown October Ale* and *O Promise Me*, Luders' *Heidelberg, Dear Heidelberg*, Gershwin's *The Man I Love*, and other such tunes past and present as *Make Believe*, *Gypsy Love Song*, *Ol' Man River*, *Egern On The Tegernsee*, *You Are My Heart Alone* and *A Kiss In The Dark* need no apologies from anyone.

It also seems that you are a miserable theatrical lowbrow because you are often inclined toward the sentimental.

You should, it appears, be more realistic. Well, you are in good company. Much like you in this respect are such low-brow writers as Schnitzler, Maeterlinck, Yeats, Sudermann, Rostand, Barrie, Sierra, Bahr, Hofmannsthal and Synge.

But the point by and large is that your low taste is and has been responsible for the purely commercial theatre and the retarding of the better drama. Well, your low taste has made Eugene O'Neill a millionaire and has provided a fat income for such other of our more aspiring playwrights as S. N. Behrman, Robert Sherwood, John Steinbeck, William Saroyan, Lillian Hellman and Maxwell Anderson, to say nothing of having done pretty well by such as George Kaufman, Moss Hart, Sidney Kingsley, Thornton Wilder, Elmer Rice, George Kelly, Clifford Odets, Rose Franken and Du Bose Heyward.

Your taste, however low, nevertheless in the last two seasons was instrumental in dispatching quickly to the store-house at least three-fourths of the trashier plays, which should give your critics something to think about. Your low taste further endorsed such critically endorsed plays in that period as *The Man Who Came To Dinner, Life With Father, The Time Of Your Life, Juno and The Paycock, The Male Animal, Ladies In Retirement, There Shall Be No Night*, the Maurice Evans Shakespearean presentations, *The Corn Is Green, My Sister Eileen, Native Son, Watch On The Rhine, Arsenic and Old Lace* and *The Doctor's Dilemma*, along with such musical exhibits as *Du Barry Was A Lady, Louisiana Purchase, Too Many Girls, Pins and Needles, Panama Hattie, Cabin In The Sky*, etc., which should similarly give your fault-finders something to think about.

To continue, your low taste past and present has guaranteed as among the longest runs in our later-day theatre plays like the following: *Tobacco Road, You Can't Take It With You, The First Year, The Children's Hour, Dead End, Boy Meets Girl, Rain, The Green Pastures, Broadway, Street Scene, The Show-Off* and *Victoria Regina,* almost all of them lauded by the critics as very tony stuff, which should give those selfsame critics of you even more to think about. And when it comes to your bad taste in musical shows, let them reflect that you also by your patronage established the record long runs of such of their favorite musicals as *Irene, Show Boat, The Student Prince, Sally, Good News, Blackbirds, Sunny, The Vagabond King* and *Shuffle Along.*

Critics who live in glass houses shouldn't throw stones. The day has come, according to the classic *Variety,* when even Richard Zeisler, manager, and Frank Reidelsberger, orchestra leader, of a burlesque theatre in St. Louis, by name the Garrick—the former a Justice of the Peace and the latter a police magistrate—carry on all their conversations in Latin.

XXI

The Critical Taste

The vagaries of the critical taste have, on the other hand, been responsible for some peculiar aberrations in both the esteem and disesteem of numerous plays in the modern theatre. To begin with plays that have been underestimated, there is, for a first example, the Irish George Birmingham's *General John Regan.* If there was a more entertaining satirical comedy of its theatrical day and hour, I do not know of it, yet on its presentation here it received such a cool critical reception that it passed from view in short order. Moreover, when some years later George Tyler revived it, it never, because of an even more intense critical apathy, got nearer to New York than Pittsburgh, where it opened and closed almost simultaneously. Yet Birmingham's lightly sardonic fable about a great hero who never existed remains in the memories of those whose ears do not wiggle when they laugh one of the humorous treats of its particular, or for that matter any subsequent, period.

Teresa Deevy's *Katie Roche*, of more recent vintage, is another example of what strikes me as local critical underestimation. A delicate psychological story of a young woman—the kind of play Pirandello might possibly have

[191

written had he been a Celt—it was hailed by various English critics as being everything from "a truly great play" to "one of the finest of modern dramas," which strikes me in turn as heavily exaggerated overestimation. It is nothing approaching that. But it surely is not the completely negligible work that the local critics unanimously nominated it and that audiences so acquiescently stayed away from that it was withdrawn after a few days. While it may not be great shakes as drama, it presents so shrewd an understanding of its subject matter that off-handedly to dismiss it, as it was dismissed, as mere foggy boredom is to register oneself a guest in the Hôtel des Ânes, that capacious inn.

Ashley Dukes' *The Man With A Load Of Mischief*, W. J. Turner's *The Man Who Ate The Popomack*, and at least half the comedies of Vincent Lawrence got a poor critical deal. Dukes' play is one of the most polished and amusing of later-day English comedies, as Turner's is one of the drollest and most original, yet both were greeted with thumbs down from the front of the local house, the majority of the critics no less guilty of the condemnatory pantomime than the paying customers. And as for Lawrence, who unless I am mistaken indicated one of the slickest talents for sharp light comedy writing discernible hereabout in the Twenties, the poor fellow was treated so cavalierly that he hied himself in disgust to Hollywood, where God knows what has happened to him.

Eugene O'Neill's *Moon Of The Caribbees*, one of the most beautifully contrived "mood" plays in American dramatic literature, while it has not, true, been overlooked by the critics, has nevertheless pretty generally, it seems to me, been simply patted on the head lightly and sent on its way. Yet it remains one of the finest things its author has done and not to esteem it as such merely because it happens to be in the short form is to be guilty of appraising art chiefly according to size and bulk. In other words, what we engage in such a case is the same critical antic which in one breath admits that art knows no hard and fast rules and in the next says that a one-act play however excellent is ipso facto not quite so important as a full length play however deficient.

It is this point of view which was also responsible, at least in part, for the gross underestimation of Saroyan's *My Heart's In The Highlands*. Not only was it condescendingly waved aside in some critical quarters because it ran less than the standardized theatrical time but in many more was it minimized on the whole. Yet no more beautifully imaginative play has come the way of our stage in some seasons.

Elmer Rice's *The Left Bank*, Ben Hecht's long ago *The Egoist*, and George M. Cohan's *Pigeons and People* are still further examples of the critical depreciation of which I speak. The first was a bitingly accurate picture of American expatriates on the other side of the Seine and here and there suggestive of Sinclair Lewis' very best reporting. The second, which the critics of the period would have none of, was as waggish a sex comedy as you could find along the Paris boulevards, and with a second act as witty in its amorous truth as Sacha Guitry at his best. And the third was as skilful a tour de force in sheer playmaking as the local stage has revealed. Yet all three suffered critical dismissal.

Zoë Akins' *A Texas Nightingale*, a thoroughly amusing study of an opera singer and the best of her full-length plays, got a critical reception so chilly that it soon expired, whereas her greatly inferior *Declassée* was so warmly embraced that it ran on and on. Karl Schönherr's *The Children's Tragedy*, one of the most moving dramas on its general subject matter written in the Central Europe of its time, received such careless critical attention that it lasted only a few days. And Hermann Bahr's *The Master*, that observant scrutiny of love and jealousy and what they can do to a man of otherwise hard intelligence—like *The Children's Tragedy* produced by the courageous Arnold Daly —was also so slighted and slurred that it quickly closed.

The Rapp-Thurman *Harlem*, a closely caught picture of Negro life in New York, was not altogether a theatrical failure but even so its virtues eluded many of the professional theatrical commentators, who contented themselves in allowing that it was fairly diverting stuff and let it go at that. Hugh Stange's *Veneer*, the simply but very effectively written tragedy of a young girl seeking her dream in New York, was so neglected that it speedily passed from the scene, and Molnár's *The Glass Slipper*, one of his two best plays, was so misprized that it, too, disappeared long before its due time.

These are only a few of the plays whose merits have gone critically unappreciated and which have missed the rewards that were their right. Rita Wellman's *The Gentile Wife* was another. Lennox Robinson's gay comedy, *The White-Headed Boy*, though it was properly esteemed in a few quarters, must be statistically set down as still another. Harry Wagstaff Gribble's *Revolt*, which was at least fifty percent valuable, was another still. And Chesterton's delightful *Magic*, Dorrance Davis' *A Lady In Love*, Ballard's *Young America*, Bowers' *Where Do We Go From Here?*, and, to step to a higher rung on the dramatic ladder, Brieux's admirable *Les Hannetons* were deplorable others.

When, on the other hand, it comes to plays that have

been overestimated and touted far beyond their merits, we engage a spectacle even more prismatic.

As a starter, consider, for example, Martin Flavin's *Children Of The Moon*. Here was a third-rate dunk into psychological drama that for some reason beyond the comprehension was hailed by the critics of the day as something of a masterwork and its author not only as a very remarkable fellow indeed but a shining white sail on the glorious horizon of American drama. The imbecility of any such appraisal was made manifest in Flavin's subsequent writings, to say nothing of in their own gradual misgivings about *Children Of The Moon*, which several years later they began to regard with ill-concealed symptoms of skepticism.

John Howard Lawson's *Processional* tricked those critics who knew nothing of the German experiments in Expressionist drama into the conviction that it was a highly novel and original piece of work, and even today it is still looked upon in some critical quarters as a milestone in American dramatic writing. What it was and remains is merely a rather interesting borrowed stunt. The Kaufman-Connelly fantastic comedy, *Beggar On Horseback*, was similarly accepted as very original stuff, whereas it was actually a paraphrase of a popular German comedy of several years before.

Probably no exhibit of our time has been more greatly overpraised than Clifford Odets' *Waiting For Lefty*, despite the fact that its relatively short length might have been thought to militate against it in the academic critical mind. That it had some force and drive there is no gainsaying, but that it got within hailing distance of anything approaching distinguished dramatic writing is hard to believe. It, too, was a stunt, and a good one, but it was hardly more than that. To a certain extent, the same thing may be said of

Irwin Shaw's *Bury The Dead*, which the critics swallowed
whole as a pâté of endocrinous art.

Sidney Howard's *They Knew What They Wanted* must
make those who originally saw in it something rare and
revolutionary in American drama hide under the table in
embarrassment. Even at first glance it should readily have
been spotted as merely a workmanlike paraphrase of somewhat earlier popular Central European drama. Looking at
it again when it was recently revived only made one further
conscious of the absurdity of the esteem in which its first
critics held it. It was and continues to be negligible stuff.

Because it was less chintzy than its author's previous
plays, A. A. Milne's *The Truth About Blayds* mechanically
persuaded its critics that it must be taken with considerable
seriousness, which was the way they took it. It was fairish
minor entertainment, but nothing beyond that. In its case,
we once again encountered the silly critical conviction that
there is an arbitrary virtue in relative sobriety even when
practised by one who is much better gifted in grimace.

John Drinkwater's *Abraham Lincoln* and T. S. Eliot's
Murder In The Cathedral certainly did not deserve the full
measure of praise which many meted out to them. The
former naturally and easily extracted the theatrical effect
implicit in its material but its stark literality reflected small
credit upon its author, who seemed little more than a
Charlie McCarthy sitting on the lap of history. A slice of
the latter's second act managed a certain eloquence, but
the rest of the drama, fore and aft, was rather on the high-
school literary side and, save for a few minutes toward the
end, was so self-conscious that the impression was of its
author talking to himself, with considerable admiration, in
a mirror.

Robert Sherwood's *Idiot's Delight*, while shrewdly

negotiated popular drama, hypnotized the more susceptible critics into accepting it as superior profundity. Philip Barry's *Hotel Universe*, a schoolboy excursion into metaphysics, was actually welcomed by certain critics as Big Meat and made the subject of grave essays. Marc Connelly's *The Wisdom Tooth*, a second-rate fantasy, was affectionately slobbered over by the teetotaler sentimentality that would cry into its beer if it drank. And Balderston's *Berkeley Square*, a box-office chronological stunt, was greeted as something very elegant in both a philosophical and poetically imaginative direction.

The list grows. Thornton Wilder's *Our Town*, a pleasant little dramatic experiment, got the beer-weepers out in large numbers and drew such gulping overpraise from their soft palates as had not been heard hereabout since Lee Fong down in Mott Street stopped using veal in his chicken chop-suey. Edward Sheldon's *Salvation Nell*, a good box-office melodrama, overwhelmed the critical professors of its day to such a degree that they announced it to be the great American drama and Sheldon the most remarkable genius who had appeared on the American scene since Thomas A. Edison and Frankie Bailey. And when it came to the psychological and sociological dramas of Augustus Thomas, that fraud,—but that is much too old and stale a story.

Let us in conclusion jump on our fiery mule and fly off briefly in all directions.

Bruno Frank's charmingly contrived *Twelve Thousand*, set against an American Revolutionary War background and ably played by Basil Sydney and Mary Ellis, was superciliously sniffed into limbo. Maurice Donnay's exceptionally amusing, to say nothing of deliciously written, paraphrase of *Lysistrata*, adeptly translated by William A. Drake, has

never attracted enough critical curiosity to stimulate the
interest of a professional producer. Jim Tully's *Black Boy*
got not even a half-way fair break from the critics, yet it
contained some observation on the Negro that was better
than good and several dramatic episodes of uncommon
virtue. Tom Barry's *The Upstart*, because of its cold critical
reception, was quickly junked, yet it had in it some humorous and novel sauces. And why has one of Sacha Guitry's
drollest comedies, *The Illusionist*, never been allowed to get
beyond a try-out performance in Washington, where the
critics elaborately derogated it?

Pinero's *The Wife Without A Smile*, his most skilful
comedy, was voted a critical failure in local circles. Robert
Sherwood's *The Road To Rome*, which indulged itself in
the old trick of employing modern slang in an ancient situation and which the author himself intelligently deprecated,
got a fine reception from the critics and was a big success.
And Kate Parsons' *The Commodore Marries*, one of the
most recreative comedies in a dog's age, was accepted only
half-heartedly by the critics and lived for but forty performances.

It doesn't make sense.

XXII

Beauty and the Box-Office

When all is said and done, there are not many things in the theatre or motion pictures that can beat the box-office value of good-looking women, and if they have sex appeal to boot you may pretty well dust off the S.R.O. sign. It is as true today, moreover, as it was yesterday. People did not go to hear Lillian Russell sing or act, because there were dozens of women who could sing or act twenty times better; they went to look at her. Nor do people go in these later days to see Hedy Lamarr because of any tremendous histrionic virtuosity; they go to get a kick out of her beauty. It has often been that way and it will probably continue to be that way so long as men are constituted as they are.

A pretty girl may, in Irving Berlin's song, be like a melody but for every fellow who yells "For God's sake, sing!" there are a hundred who are perfectly satisfied just quietly to look and permit their imaginations either a celestial or an earthy flight. And the entrepreneurs who appreciate the fact and cater to it usually wear diamonds. George Lederer's bank account was thus largely the result of such savouries as Belva Don Kersley, Virginia Earle, Edna Wallace, Mabelle Gilman, Lotta Faust, Polly Chase,

[199

Christine Blessing, Viola Carlstedt, Nina Randall, Irene
Bishop, Edna May and Vashti Earle, among others. Ziegfeld's fame and collateral were generated by Lillian Lor-
raine, Martha Mansfield, Marion Davies, Justine Johnstone,
Gladys Glad, and two dozen other such love-drops. Earl
Carroll's "Through these portals pass the most beautiful
girls in the world," whatever debate there may have been
on the superlative, filled his theatre season after season. . . .
A thousand men will go to see Veronica Lake on the screen
for one who will gallop to enjoy the art of Madame Ous-
penskaya.

Without looks, Maxine Elliott, who could not act for
German occupation francs, would have played to houses
peopled only by the ushers and a sour press-agent. And
much the same with a lot of other such relishes as Lily
Langtry, Lantelme (that eye-walloper), Yvonne Printemps
(the French are more honest in the matter than we sometimes are), Elsie Ferguson, and so on. Without looks,
furthermore, where would three-fourths of the successful
movie actresses be today? How far would Barbara La Marr,
Alma Rubens, Constance Talmadge, Mary Miles Minter
and Blanche Sweet have got in the past; just how far would
such as Jean Harlow, Mary Astor and Dolores Del Rio have
got a little later; and where today would be Vivien Leigh,
Rosalind Russell, Madeleine Carroll, Merle Oberon, Paulette Goddard and similar plums?

All this is by way of getting to two points. Point 1 is
that the films are presently stenciling the looks of their
young women to the box-office danger point, and Point 2
is that the stage is rapidly seizing the lead by pursuing a
wiser course. And Point 3, if you wish to go on and add it
to the point list for extra good measure, is that, accordingly,
the theatre is today showing the more genuinely good-

looking girls, or at least girls who more greatly appeal to the romantic male, and that this fact is proved by the avidity with which the movie people try to grab them if they can. That, true enough, they spoil the stage girls' natural loveliness the moment they get them to Hollywood does not alter the fact that it was the natural beauty of the girls on the stage that first fetched and floored them.

I certainly do not mean to say that there are still no good-looking women on the screen. There are. But the great majority of candidates for looks honors are at the first opportunity foolishly and ignorantly put through a beauty mill which turns most of them out looking so much alike that you can hardly distinguish one from another. It is only the handful who have stubbornly resisted being put through the mill who have retained any real looks worth talking about. After the average young girl out there gets out of the doctoring hands of the studio makeup experts, hair-doers and dresser-uppers she looks exactly like the girl who was made over before her, and that girl in turn looked exactly like twenty or thirty who preceded her out of the transformation can.

A year or so ago, a very pretty young stage actress was corralled by the movies and taken to Hollywood. Her father, a sapient fellow, saw to it as a precaution that her contract should specify that they could not change the color of her hair, the shape of her teeth, or anything else of the sort that Hollywood customarily and arbitrarily does. As a result, she made a ten times greater romantic impression on the screen than the half dozen girls who had gone out at approximately the same time and had had their looks monkeyed with by the pulchritude professors. Her name, for the record, is Gene Tierney. Incidentally, her father also stipulated in the contract that they could not change her name. It was thus an additional relief to get a good, plain, simple Gene Tierney instead of something like Gloria Tremaine or Graciosa Tuileries.

In the preparation of this chapter, I bought eight different movie magazines and I swear on a stack of Bibles I had to read and re-read the names of at least fifteen of the newer and younger screen actresses to make sure they were not all one and the same girl. They had all been manufactured with the same hair dye, hair-do, China teeth, shaved eyebrows, false eyelashes, grins, and swim suits until the net impression was like seeing the same girl reflected fifteen times in one of those many-sided Crystal Palace mirrors.

This is another reason why I, like many others, have a difficult time of it when I venture to go to the movies. Very often in the case of the run-of-the-mill pictures it is all I can do to get the characters straightened out half-way well enough to get the hang of the plot. I have now got to the point where I can faintly distinguish between the hero with the little mustache and the villain with the little mustache—even between the both of them and the latter's younger henchmen with the little mustaches—but bless me if I can tell the ingénue from her maid or the maid from the ingénue's girl-friends, or often for that matter any of them from the leading lady. So after the first twenty minutes I usually conclude that maybe I have had too many drinks, give it up as a bad job, and go around the corner to a newsreel in which, anyway, there is no mistaking Hitler for Winston Churchill or Mrs. Roosevelt for Gloria Vanderbilt.

Nor is this, as intimated, true mainly of the newer and younger film girls. Now that the already more than sufficiently beautiful Joan Bennett has been metamorphosed from blonde to brunette to look like Hedy Lamarr, now that you have to look twice (in both directions) to make certain whether it is Madeleine Carroll, June Knight or Alice Faye in Warner Baxter's, Ronald Colman's or Don Ameche's boudoir, and now that you go crazy trying to figure out whether you are not in a theatre looking at some picture star playing in another, the situation is even more ludicrously confusing.

Under the circumstances, it is a relief to go to the theatre, where you can at least be certain that the girl you are looking at is the one you think you are looking at. Whatever the quality of the play or show, it is a considerable satisfaction not to be all balled up in distinguishing such a pretty girl as Diana Barrymore from such another pretty one as Marcy Wescott, or such a looker as Betsy Blair, Dorothy McGuire or Sylvia Weld from such another as Katherine Wiman, Joan Tetzel or Grace McDonald, even though, alas, the latter's brief excursion to Hollywood a year ago contrived to change her bonny brown hair to a Paramount yellow.

Reflect what Hollywood has done to young women's natural loveliness. It altered Frances Langford's beautiful dark hair to a pinkish auburn, which no more suited her dark complexion than a red necktie would suit a fellow with a carrot-top. It let the resolutely independent Hepburn alone, Dei gratia, but it took its temporary toll of Ginger Rogers by dyeing her blonde hair black, of Nancy Kelly by modeling her into a bogus facial sophistication, of Claudette Colbert by hennaing her dome, of the already wholly ornamental Vivien Leigh, believe it or not, by unnecessarily painting an underlip on her, of Patricia Morison by too greatly reducing her, and of Jane Wyman by putting artificial eyelashes on her long enough to serve as whiskbrooms.

It further so enameled Jean Arthur that it robbed her of most of her natural expression, sex-appealed Mary Martin entirely out of character, and removed all the original fresh, rustic beauty of Virginia Bruce and substituted for it the aspect of a synthetic Gaiety girl. It still further short-bobbed Sylvia Sidney's attractive long dark brown hair, so intensified Adrienne Ames' naturally exotic look that the poor girl could hardly recognize herself in a mirror, padded the beautifully slim and appealing Loretta Young with idiotic maternal bosoms, and asininely put greasepaint wrinkles on Marsha Hunt's lovely young face so she would look old enough to be cast in old women character parts. It even put a phony wax Grecian nose on Jinx Falkenburg!

One might go on endlessly. There is, for example, Karen Morley, a promising screen actress, who was ruined by being made over to approximate the look of Garbo. There is Ida Lupino who was almost wrecked as an actress by being altered to resemble Toby Wing and Betty Grable, naturally of a wholly different type, and who made a hit and got back some position only after she finally put her foot down and said no more of such makeup and hair-dyeing nonsense. There is the case of Jean Harlow's young stand-in who, after Miss Harlow died, was used to finish the picture on which the star had been working and who had sometime before been made over to look so much like her that nobody could tell the difference, not even some of the executives who had equipped themselves for the occasion with binoculars. And there are at the moment three or four girls who have been given the moniker Brenda whom you can't tell apart even with help of a squad of Pinkerton detectives and the girls' parents, brothers, sisters, uncles, aunts, and old mammys. Then, too, there is the former stage girl, Harriette Lake, whom Hollywood has altered into a creature named Ann Sothern and who looks no more like the original, natural and engaging Harriette than I look like Groucho Marx, or maybe I had more accurately say Ben Turpin.

It is the great asset of the stage that a pretty young actress may make herself up in the manner which she correctly thinks and knows to be most suitable to her, and not have to trust her share of beauty to so-called experts whose expertness seemingly consists in reducing all pretty girls to a common denominator, calculated to drive discriminating men to drink, celibacy, or some place like Sandusky, Ohio, where whatever the girls may look like they at least all look different. The theatre, unlike the screen, would not for a minute think of taking an attractive, dark, young Latin actress like, say, Rita Hayworth (née Cansino), putting a scarlet wig on her, and casting her, at least tentatively, to match the title of something called *Strawberry Blonde*. Nor would it, even at its dumbest, think of trying to make one of its newer and younger actresses look the very image of Katharine Cornell or Helen Hayes. Were it to do so, it appreciates, as the movies do not, that not only would it ruin the young actress in question but make her in addition a laughing-stock, and—in double addition— slam the door on the box-office. One of the biggest remaining virtues of the dramatic stage is that every woman on it doesn't look exactly like either Joan Crawford or Carole Lombard.

XXIII

The Movies in Love

Some many years ago after the second act of a play by
Owen Johnson about a girl who emerged unsullied and
spotless from the amorous temptations of the New York
gay life—it was called *The Salamander*—I asked the late
Paul Armstrong, himself a playwright, what he thought of
it. "That," he ironically replied, "is what she wrote home
to her mother."

It seems to me that at least three-fourths of today's
motion pictures involving the love life of young women
remain similarly little more than missives to mama. And in
this, now that so much dramatic water has passed under
the bridge since the distant era of Johnson's play and plays
like it, we have, I think, one of the chief differentiating char-
acteristics of the films and the theatre.

It was not always that way. In the days before the
Messrs. Hays and Breen took over the morals of the movies,
the screen frequently treated its male and female characters
to a considerable sexual realism. But with the advent of
the Hays-Breen censorship there came about a gradually
cumulative change that, with negligible exception, has contrived to picture most film characters in their amorous re-

actions to each other as practically indistinguishable from little children dressed up in their parents' clothes and playing house. So great is the burden of innocence, restraint and respectability that the movies have been made to bear that today even the hitherto humorous hokum of slapping a lady on the bustle is out. And even the delicately insinuating asterisks implicit in fadeouts, so long a favorite device of saying something by emphatically saying nothing, are often frowned upon. Apparently it will not be long, if things keep up in this manner, before the only intimate screen relationships privileged to men and women will be a tender glance, arbitrarily leveled no lower than the chin, a hand held for a moment on that old familiar marble seat in the moonlight, a strictly curtailed kiss, and matrimony before the first reel.

The relative intelligence of such entertainment mediums as the cinema and the theatre is thus no better to be appreciated than in a contemplation of the way in which they approach, among other things, this subject of men and women in love. The theatre, often even at its trashiest, is forthright and honest in its approach; the screen, often even at its best, is evasive and dishonest. Among the rubbishy plays produced in the theatre last season were such as *Suzanna and The Elders, Beverly Hills* and *Glamour Preferred*. Yet, though all were rank failures, they treated of sex more frankly and more truthfully than any three of the best pictures that were exhibited in the same space of time.

Censorship aside, the American movie mind in the aggregate seems inclined to view sex mainly in single-track perspective. The subtle ramifications that the theatre allows to it, even the perfectly artless ramifications, are seldom vouchsafed to it on the screen, and then only when some wily foreign director like Lubitsch is allowed a peculiarly free rein. Take a single illustrative example. The drama well understands that a woman will confide in a man if she deeply loves him or, on the other hand, has absolutely no personal interest in him. The movies stoutly believe and practise the belief that a woman will confide in a man only if she deeply loves him, but never if she thinks that her love is not reciprocated and under no conceivable circumstance unless she has a personal interest in him.

Love, that despair of benedicks and boon of bachelors, offers some strange diagnoses in the name of film entertainment. When the screen does not borrow a play directly from the theatre and fashions its own material independently, it generally seems to recognize only three treatments of the topic: 1. A man and woman meet, fall in love, quarrel, fight and separate, come together again, love, and marry; 2. A man and woman meet, quarrel, fight and separate, fall in love with each other while separated, come together again, and marry; or 3. A man and woman meet, fall in love, quarrel, fight and separate, and eventually marry someone else.

I do not say that such situations may not be common and true enough. What I do say is that they are obviously far from being the only situations and that, even so, there is a lot more to them than the bare movie outlines suggest.

In the theatre's catalogue of more understanding plays we have men marrying women out of hate rather than love, women choosing men they love less passionately than other men, men tortured into insanity by the women closest to them, women transgressing for the sheer amusement of transgression, and men losing the love of their wives not because they are failures in the world but because they are successes. We have old men and young girls finding permanent happiness in marriage, young boys and young girls finding only misery in it and divorce, women murdering the men they most ardently love, men drawn into happy marriages by rank female schemers, holy men choosing sex above the church, and adolescents driven to suicide by sex. And we have, further, the naked emotions and naked re-actions of all the rare gallery of characters of dramatists like Ibsen, Strindberg, Wedekind, Brieux, Tolstoi, Haupt-mann, d'Annunzio, Bergström, Björnson, Chekhov, Gorki, Echegaray and Hervieu. I ask a question. Could or would —censorship again wholly aside—the Hollywood mind con-ceive of such things, uncorrupted, on the screen? Could or would the Hollywood mind, in Mary Colum's fine phrase, distinguish between love in all its complexities and lechery in all its simplicity?

It is all well and good to say that the screen must con-sider its great, heterogeneous audience. But that is not the point. For even when it goes liberal and arty and makes a gesture of catering to a more restricted audience it almost equally betrays its intellectual and emotional hesitations, doubts, shortcomings, and lack of philosophical experience. Not one single such Hollywood-made picture in the last half dozen years has been half so honest in its depiction of the relations of men and women as, say, even some such other-wise woefully inferior stage play as *Kindred, Christmas Eve* or *The Happiest Days.* And not one single such picture in the last twelve has seemed other than juvenile to any thea-tregoer who in the same period has absorbed the story of men and women as presented to him in even third-rate stage plays like, for example, *The Laughing Woman, The Puritan* and *Granite.* Or, to put it more bluntly, in even such tenth-rate ones as *De Luxe, Mulatto, On Stage* and *White Man.*

Furthermore, when it comes to the screen's arguing in

terms of its great, heterogeneous audience which has to be taken into consideration, the answer, at least critically, is liverwurst. The honest sex play, *Tobacco Road*, ran for more than seven solid years in New York to paying audiences—an all-time record in our theatre; and it has been played by various companies, also to paying business, all over America. But nevertheless observe what Hollywood did to it!

The movies are best when they throw aside all posturing and devote themselves very simply to purely sentimental, as opposed to sexual, love. And the drama is quite often worst when it does the same thing. D. W. Griffith's enormous success was due largely to the fact that his heroes and heroines firmly believed, and practised the belief, that babies are brought by the stork. The lowbrow who believed otherwise was always the Griffith villain.

The movie public, perhaps not so entirely dumb as many of the Hollywood executives privately like to make it out, has by its patronage long hinted its conviction that sex as Hollywood treats it is silly and has accordingly fallen back for its greater film satisfaction upon the purely sentimental approach. The sex actresses thus come and go, whereas the sentimental ones enjoy an extended life. The Mary Pickfords and Marguerite Clarks outran in popularity the Theda Baras, Olga Petrovas and Pola Negris. After them, the Janet Gaynors and Norma Shearers outdistanced all the hot potatoes but the exceptional Harlow, even the Joan Crawfords and Myrna Loys having to come clean in order to safeguard their public and their jobs. And today, with the Mae Wests in the discard and the Ann Sheridans going up and quickly down like skyrockets, it is the Deanna Durbins who are the box-office cards. In the theatre it is largely otherwise. With the sole exception of Helen Hayes, the most popularly admired are such frequent sex role actresses as Cornell, Fontanne, Lawrence, Anderson, Nazimova, Bankhead and Claire.

One often wonders, with the movies as they are, what a little girl brought up on them as a diversion diet may conceivably grow up to believe. I dare to venture a general guess:

1. That as the future father of one's child one should under no circumstances select a man who dresses well and speaks impeccable English, as these are infallible signs that something is wrong with his character.

2. That one of the surest ways to capture a mate is to bide your time until someone shows up with a wounded forehead and then bandage it for him, in gratitude and affectionate return for which he will soon thereafter propose matrimony.

3. That if a woman in an evening gown sits on a chaise-longue she should keep her eyes fixed resolutely on the lamp beside it, since if the lamp goes out she will in all likelihood presently become the mother of a child.

4. That no man on a Western ranch who has a small black mustache can be trusted for a minute.

5. That any bachelor apartment which rents for more than fifty dollars a month is a hell-hole of iniquity.

6. That a drink in a night-club is inevitably the first symptom of spiritual and moral decay.

7. That marriage is the one permanent solution of all one's difficulties.

8. That to be kissed by a man who has had so much as one Martini cocktail is as horrific and loathsome an experience as being bitten by a rattlesnake.

9. That one should beware the man with exceptionally good manners, as he is in all probability a dirty hypocrite.

10. That it is extremely dangerous to talk with a stranger on a train or bus unless he is the star of the picture.

11. That all bachelors, save they be old and fat, are wolves in sheeps' clothing, and should be avoided like the plague.

12. That it is all right for a girl to accept a lift in an automobile that costs under six hundred dollars, but that Rolls-Royces, Hispanos or any other expensive makes spell her doom.

13. That if you fail to close your eyes ecstatically when a man kisses you he will naturally and correctly assume that you are an old hand at the business, and will disesteem you as a wanton.

14. That any woman with a bathroom a bit on the fancy side is no lady.

15. That any woman who calls on your mama and who is very expensively dressed probably has a past. If she has a pet Pomeranian with her, you can bet your bottom penny on it.

16. That no decent man ever suggests that a lady have supper with him. Luncheon or dinner yes, but not supper.

17. That a beautiful bedspread intimates that the lady who sleeps under it isn't one.

18. That a Frenchman of title, if not given to comedy, is likely to be a dissolute rapscallion, but that an Englishman of title is nearly always to be trusted implicitly, he is so clean and upstanding.

and

19. That a man never falls passionately in love with a woman unless she has mammary glands the size of watermelons.

XXIV

The Cult of the Fatted Calf

What I am about to say will probably result in the denunciation of me as an obnoxious philistine, fit only for the company of half-wits and admirers of the art of Sir Walter Besant. However and nevertheless, I risk the indignation and say it. It is this. I offer you all but a relatively small portion of the modern art of the ballet for one American nickel. The remaining collop I'll keep for myself and, as for the considerable rest, if you haven't the nickel handy it is yours on the cuff.

I don't suppose this commercial transaction would be of any particular public interest if it were not for one fact. And that fact is the enormously increased American interest in the ballet during the last few years, not only in New York but in many other cities. Only in Australia, peculiary enough, where a single ballet troupe not long ago enjoyed an unprecedented run of eight months in the three or four leading cities, has a greater increase in curiosity been manifested.

What leads me to my spuriously generous offer is the conviction that much of the modern ballet is a hybrid that is gradually getting to be less and less real ballet and more

[213

and more a freak form that vouchsafes all the beauty and grace of a one-armed Ubangi toying with a squab. There are exceptions, true enough, but the majority of the exhibits that I have honored with my attention impress me as being little more than very bad short plays, most of them with a minimum of sense, performed by mute actors suffering from incipient attacks of arthragra but doggedly determined that the show must go on.

In some instances, indeed, the nonsense has reached such a point that dancing in any genuine sense has been practically eliminated and has been supplanted by something that looks to any intelligent layman like a cross between an invisible doctor testing the cast's knee reflexes and the plebes' drill ground at the Culver Military Academy. William Saroyan's *The Great American Goof* is a case in point. Not only is there no dancing in it worthy of the name, that is, outside a hospital ball for arteriosclerosis patients, but American speech has intermittently been provided the hoofers who, being foreigners, speak it like so many chipped Berlitz Russian and Swedish records. Supplement all this with scenery projected by colored magic-lantern slides which periodically act like jitterbugs and mingle an intended factory scene with a previous Ritz salon, or whatever it is meant to be, and you begin to get a faint idea that if you lay out that nickel I was talking about you will get the bad end of the bargain.

If, furthermore, you imagine that the aberrant Saroyan has been picked upon as a too easy horrible example your imagination needs looking into by a psychoveterinarian. There are a dozen boys and girls whose exhibits come pretty close to matching his, and another dozen who run him an even race.

Take a look, for instance, at something called *Mechani-*

cal Ballet, by Adolph Bolm. Originally manufactured for the movies, it may be acceptable Hollywood but in any other place where bloom æsthetics on however modest a scale it is likely to impress the beholder as a paraphrase of Eugene O'Neill's *Dynamo* concocted by the Minsky family and performed by their uncles, cousins and nieces, in tights. It is possible that a stage full of characters called Dynamos, Gears, Pistons and Fly Wheels all jumping up and down to an accompaniment of bangs and clangs from the orchestra may be art in the minds of the more frenzied balletomaniacs, but to any slightly more realistic mind it seems to be merely a lot of obstreperous imbecility.

Or turn to the number called *Dark Elegies*. This one is the brain-child of Antony Tudor and consists in an effort to combine choreography with Gustav Mahler's song cycle, *Kindertotenlieder*. Inasmuch as Mahler composed his music after the death of a particularly beloved child and inasmuch, further, as it reflects his deep and intimate sorrow, the idea of accompanying it with a troupe of kickers and posturers comes about as close to the obscene and ridiculous as is humanly imaginable. The only analogous mixtures I can think of would be *Uncle Tom's Cabin* with whites in the Negro roles and Negroes in the white or a ballet founded on the *Internationale* and danced by a stageful of Republican senators.

Or, still again, for another example out of the humbug carload cast your eye upon something called *Hear Ye! Hear Ye!* Fabricated by a Miss Ruth Page with the connivance of Nicholas Remisov, this one seeks to dance a murder trial into a ballet. After flashing a number of tabloid scareheads on the curtain—"Murder In A Night-Club," "Who Is Guilty?" etc.—we are vouchsafed a court-room with judge on bench, jury in box, and a gross of wooden dummies representing

the public in the spectators' seats. Attorneys for the prose-
cution and defense get busy and then a series of flashbacks
show seriatim the shooting of a male hoofer by his female
dancing partner, the shooting of the same hoofer by a
chorus girl, and the shooting of the selfsame hoofer by his
male partner, each of the pot-shots being equally fatal. After
each murder the jury proclaims the particular shooter guilty.
At the conclusion, it turns out that a stray maniac did the
dirty work, and the lawyers shake hands.

Now, gentlemen, I ask you! If such stuff, whatever the
music and choreography, is appropriate ballet material, I
resignedly await the day when we shall be treated to a
ballet danced to the annual report of the Commissioner of
Street Cleaning or choreography visited upon Jan Valtin's
home life.

The more recent urge to Americanize the ballet has
been responsible for some curios that outcurio almost anything this side of a believe-it-or-not museum. We have had
everything from ballets showing roadside gas station operators imitating Nijinsky, as in the exhibit by the late American Lyric Theatre, to ballets displaying Russian dancers or
their equivalents cavorting in far western ghost mining
towns. Where the fatuity will stop, no one can tell. The
time may not be distant when they will be laying the scene
of *Scheherazade* in Columbus, Ohio, and when they will be
having *Hommage aux Belles Viennoises* danced by the Four
Inkspots.

The Messrs. Cole Porter and Gerald Murphy, otherwise
honorable, have a lot to answer for. It was they who, nineteen years ago, inaugurated this sort of absurdity. Their
job was called *Within the Quota* and was the first ballet
with an American theme set to music by an American composer. I take the liberty of quoting the plot of the master-

piece as it has been succinctly recorded for posterity by that eminent antiquarian, Mr. Cyril W. Beaumont:

"An immigrant lands in America and before him pass, against a giant reproduction of an American daily newspaper, a cavalcade of American types—part real, part mythical—with which he is already familiar through visits to the cinema. His pleasure in these types is interrupted by a figure who assumes in turn the character of Social Reformer, Revenue Agent, Uplifter, and Sheriff. Finally the immigrant makes the acquaintance of the World's Sweetheart with the inevitable result, which brings the ballet to its conclusion."

That one is thrown in for extra good measure with the others, and all for the same nickel.

XXV

The Naturalist Movement

The strip-tease art, which in the last five years has assumed a popularity previously not equalled even by virtuosi of the musical saw and professors of the Sawing A Woman In Two illusion, is hardly the latter day phenomenon that most folk think it is. It was born forty-six years ago, and its mother—or rather grandmother—was a French baggage named Charmion. This Charmion subsequently toured the vaudeville houses throughout America for at least a dozen seasons and was during the period their star sensational attraction.

Although somewhat different from the act of her heirs and assigns, Charmion's performance was founded on the same general principle. That principle, as almost everyone now knows, is the gradual coy divestment of articles of feminine apparel to a sensuous musical accompaniment, and to the theoretical enormous stimulation of the masculine libido. But whereas the ladies presently do their divesting on a stage or some other such platform, Charmion did hers on a trapeze.

I remember her act well, child though I then was. (My father took me to see her no less than four times under the

218]

pretense that what interested him on the particular vaudeville bill was a trio of Swiss yodelers.) I say I remember
her well, and if you think to insult me by allowing that a
small boy's memory is not entirely to be trusted, I herewith
prove it to your satisfaction, inch by inch.

A small dark hussy, Mlle. Charmion, clad in a long
black satin cloak and with a large feathered black hat on
her head, emerged elegantly from the wings. Bowing gra-
ciously and flashing her teeth in a provocative smile, she
approached a lowered trapeze, deposited herself daintily
upon it, and was raised aloft. The stage was darkened; a
spotlight was centered on the beauty; and slowly the orchestra began to play.

Punctuating her process of déshabillé with many a cute
oo-la-la or winking tres-chic-n'est-çe-pas?, our siren now
first took off her hat and dropped it to the stage below. Then
followed her cloak, and our little pigeon was beheld in a
dress of black silk, and with long black gloves. The gloves
were discarded one by one, then off came the bodice of the
dress, then off came the skirt. Mademoiselle was now in a
long covering of pink petticoat, surmounted by an ample
pink something or other. The latter was next in line for
removal and was succeeded by the petticoat.

What one then observed was our Lorelei still in very
sufficient black net underthings, black net stockings, and
black satin slippers. The slippers were now the first to go,
and after them came the net underthings—to the disap-
pointment of the audience (doubtless including my father)
revealing Mlle. Charmion in still more net underthings,
albeit not quite so comprehensive.

By way of prolonging the terrible suspense, our temptress now maddeningly drew forth a small lace kerchief
from her bodice and with a saucy gesture cast it aside. She

thereupon added insult to injury by slowly adjusting a hair-pin in her coiffure. But wait! One by one now off came the stockings, revealing a pink silk garter above each. Pause! And then, tantalizingly unfastening one of the garters, our Circe tossed it into the audience—and the lights went out and the act, with the person of our heroine still concealed in enough black net underwear to dress a whole present-day musical show chorus, was over.

Nevertheless, that was the birth of stripteasedom. True enough, any such evasion in strip-tease circles today would be sufficient to cause a mutiny in the United States navy, but we patriots need have no fear.

Since Charmion's day, the diaperphobe business has made great progress, and progress is the word. Not only have more and more remaining bodily concealments grad-ually been dispensed with in the name of the art, but the art itself has become a veritable industry. Despite the oc-casional interference by divers municipal authorities, by the police and by assorted moralists in mufti, the strip-tease has thrived in burlesque, which is its current chief home, in musical shows, in night-clubs, in pleasure parks, honkytonks and carnivals, and, Will Hays or no Will Hays, even to a degree in the movies.

The most widely advertised of the later-day strippers is Gypsy Rose Lee (*née* Rose Louise Hovick), although Gypsy some time ago informed me she was, to quote her exactly, sick as all hell of the God damn business and rarin' to do something else. The daughter of a Pacific coast news-paper man, Gypsy invented what has come to be recog-nized as the modern strip-tease routine: the languorous removal seriatim of everything that the law allows, plus the suggested removal of that, too, just as the *naturaliste* undu-lates into the wings and out of sight of the audience. It was Gypsy also, who, if the records are accurate, first employed a purple spotlight to heighten the pseudo-Oriental atmosphere of her strip surroundings.

The other big shots in the exposing sorority are Ann Corio and Margie Hart. The former, whose name has erroneously been reported to have been derived from "anchor" as a tribute to the large burlesque sailor trade, is celebrated from coast to coast, has been at the game for a considerable time, was safely and respectably married to the same Irish husband for years, and draws the largest crowds in burlesque. Miss Hart, who is the best looker among the strippers, is of more recent vintage but has gained rapidly in popularity.

Less illustrious than any of these but familiar to addicts to the art are all kinds of other girls of all creeds, nationalities and color, including Chinese, Japanese, Irish, Danish, Swedish, French, Polynesian, Norwegian, Negro, and Bronx. There is, for example, the blonde Irish Della Carroll who for some years has displayed her talent and epidermis not only in burlesque, but in night-clubs both here and in London. There is Sen Lee, a Tahitian belle, known best to the night-club floor-show trade; and Noel Carter, English-American, who some months ago graduated directly from a Broadway burlesque stage to the fashionable Monte Carlo night-club on New York's east side; and little Babette, family name Bernhardt, who bills herself as "The Tiniest Tease" and is something of an odzookens with the Middle Western connoisseurs; and Zorine, hardly to be confused with Zorina, who goes in for arty embellishments, calls her act *Sacrifice To The Sun God*, and duly and devoutly sacrifices to that deity everything but her G-string.

Also catering to the omnivorous trade are such artistes as Mary Blaine, a pert baggage who cracks funny jokes while baring her anatomy to the cognoscenti in Dave Rosen's *Streamlined Follies* at the pleasure parks; the Latin Grace Carlos who features what she calls a teasing-tassel dance; the corpulent Margaret Gibson who kids Miss Carlos by doing much the same thing with a travesty slant; the blondissimo Alyn Payne who modestly permits herself to be billed as "The Versatile Venus" but whose versatility in song and monologue is considerably less impressive than her shape; and Peaches Strange, June St. Clair, Marcia Eloise and Linda Powers, genealogy unknown to this statistician and historian, who may be relied upon to pop the eyes of burlesque house Corinthians at least four times daily.

And I have skimmed only the surface. There are literally hundreds of other such houris with an allergy to clothing whom the strip industry has put more or less in the chips. Sherry Britton and the Chinese Noel Toy, for example, who pleasure the night-club trade; Maria Voe, who sheds a beaded costume bead by bead; Mariane Miller, who peels to the accompaniment of a hooch dance that knocks out the eyes of jack-tars even seated as far back in the burlesque theatres as row double-Z; Annette Cliff and Stella Miles, who substitute broad grins for the more usual far-away dreamy look while baring themselves to the breeze; Marie Cord, who lets go with a lusty soprano in the process of exfoliation; and the little Japanese Sue Loi, a newcomer to the sorority, who looks scared to death at the mere prospect of taking off even her hat. To say nothing of the experienced Georgia Sothern, who doesn't look at all scared of anything and goes to it on all cylinders; Elaine Park, erstwhile show-girl who won a recent strip contest at the National in Detroit and thus was graduated instanter into the professional ranks; and Trixie La Monte, Margie

White, Florence Leeper, Donna Rogers, Doris Hudson, Sandra Lee and Rita Green, who even at the moment you are fascinatedly reading this are probably catching their deaths of colds by denuding themselves hourly somewhere or other in the Republic.

The highest salaried of all the burlesque strippers is Ann Corio, who draws down from seven hundred to eight hundred dollars a week. Miss Corio, however, is a girl with loftier ambitions and during the hot weather months periodically takes time off to appear in dramatic plays on the summer theatre circuit, courageously sacrificing her bank account and the applause of marines for her histrionic art and the applause of Connecticut and New Jersey society. Next to Miss Corio comes Margie Hart in the matter of reimbursement. Miss Hart, I am informed, rates as high as six hundred doughnuts weekly for revealing herself in puris naturalibus, and who am I to say she does not richly earn it?

While she was active in the industry, Gypsy Rose Lee topped both these ladies when it came to the mazuma, getting as high as two thousand a week, and sometimes more. But, as has been intimated, Miss Gypsy has latterly sought other means of expression, the cinema and belles lettres among them, and may no longer be considered strictly a member of the moulting aviary.

The weekly rewards of the other apostles of birthday clothes vary. Some of those who offer themselves to the pleasure park trade get as little as twenty-five dollars for five shows daily, including Sunday; the night-club doffers draw anywhere from fifty dollars to two hundred; and some of the lesser burlesque baldies are lucky if they get fifty. In certain jitney burlesque joints and cabarets the star stripper is backed by a chorus line of six subsidiary strippers who get about twenty dollars a week for their exertions, when they get it.

Just what it is that makes one girl conspicuously successful in the strip-tease business and another not has baffled the experts, especially since both girls do exactly the same thing, that is, slowly take off their clothes. Yet the problem doesn't seem so difficult of solution. It isn't a matter of excellence of figure, as some maintain, since Gypsy Rose Lee herself once confided that her own figure was far from the kind adapted to the strip-tease. And some of the other girls who have triumphed at the box-office similarly haven't enjoyed such shapes as have girls who have failed. Nor is it a variation of the strip-tease itself, as has been noted, since the strip-tease, wherever you find it, is much of a piece. And certainly it isn't beauty of face, as some of the most prosperous exponents of the art do not compare in looks with some of the least prosperous.

What it is, to judge from a punditical investigation over a considerable area, is manner pure and simple. One girl has it and another hasn't it. It consists in a relative delicacy of suggestion, in the trick of assumed modesty, in an appearance of disembodying the purely physical. I have seen dozens of strippers of the brazen school and not one of them, for all the applause of the hounds in the audience, has ever ultimately got much of anywhere. But those who have mastered the technique of sly innuendo, of factitious shyness, and of seeming to be publicly in the privacy of their own boudoirs, have gone places.

Toujours la femme.

XXVI

Burlesque

Aside from the aforementioned strip-tease, which has become the chief magnet of burlesque, what is the general complexion of that entertainment culture? I present you with a literal outline of one of its today's typical and most popular passages:

The drop-curtain shows an expanse of desert with on it the Sphinx and the Pyramids.

Enter red-nosed comedian in ragged brown suit three sizes too large for him and derby three sizes too small.

COMEDIAN (*surveying drop-curtain*): "They musta forgot the Camel ad. Say, look what's coming! A juicy piece!"

Enter girl in revealing black gauze. She shakes her middle.

COMEDIAN: "Um. A piece proposal." (*He moves to put his hands on her. She coyly withdraws.*) "Um. A piece doo resistance. What's your name, broad?"

GIRL: "I—am—Cleopatra."

COMEDIAN: "If you're Cleopatra, I'm Mark Anthony. Looka (*indicating a bourgeois section of his anatomy*), that's the mark."

GIRL: "You're too cocky."

COMEDIAN: "You said it, Cleo! But what you doing here, kid?"

GIRL: "I was lonely. My tomb was cold and gloomy."

COMEDIAN: "I'll whitewash it for you like new. Come along, show it to me, babe."

They exit. Comedian reappears instantly.

COMEDIAN (*jiggling about with extravagant ego*): "Me, Mark Anthony, I saw, I came, I conquered. Oh boy, oh boy, oh boy!"

XXVII

Silk Hats and White Rabbits

To begin a chapter at this advanced date with the sentence that starts off, "There are two kinds of people," is one of the surest ways of committing reader-interest suicide. Yet I'll risk it.

So:

There are two kinds of people: those who are pushovers for the tricks of professional prestidigitators and stage magicians and those who prefer to buy vanadium-mine stocks. The second category of virgins does not interest me. But, when it comes to the first, I am a member-goat of long and honorable standing and this despite the fact that I have never fallen for the economy of a reversible necktie or a two pants suit of which the coat hypothetically doesn't outshine the other pair of pants.

Just to make things with the reader worse, I now amplify the first part of that "There are two kinds of people" with still another "There are two kinds of people."

So:

There are two kinds of people: those who are completely mystified by the tricks and those who offensively spoil the fun by saying they know how they are done.

[227

Here, I have the honor to confess that I belong simultaneously to both groups. That is, although I know how most of the tricks are done, I nevertheless find myself mystified by the consummate skill with which the professors do them.

Of these professors who have been on American view in the last fifty years, five stand out. First, there was Herrmann, or The Great Herrmann as he billed himself. Second, came Kellar. Third, was Ching Ling Foo. Fourth, came Thurston. And now, with all these others gone, there is Dante. But what, I hear you ask, of Houdini? Houdini was not strictly a magician, though he occasionally varied his act with feats of legerdemain. He was primarily what he dubbed himself: an "escape artist." His acclaim rested not on pulling rabbits out of hats and the like, but on extricating himself from handcuffs, strait-jackets and tied sacks, which is quite another art form. Also, there was, among various others, a professor named Carter but, though he confidently heralded himself as Carter the Great, he—like the others—was small-time.

Herrmann, who was the most impressive of all the gentlemen of his ancient and august order, offered as his pièce de résistance the so-called levitation trick. The illusion consisted in placing a woman (Adelaide Herrmann, his wife) flat on a table, covering her with a cloth, pronouncing the cabalistic words "chop suey" in pig-Latin, and causing her to float about rigidly in the circumambient ether. It never failed to induce a profound awe, the awe—as De Wolf Hopper, who never had any respect for tricks and bought vanadium-mine stocks instead, used to say—being awegmented when Herrmann moved a hoop around the figure to show there were no wires holding it up.

Although all Herrmann's successors repeated the trick and although Dante still does, it has long been considered à la provençale, as almost everybody is privy to the fact that the hoop actually does not go around the figure but is cleverly reversed at the half distance point, that the figure reposes on a steel frame shaped like a curved letter N* (which permits the hoop a deceptively circular movement), and that the woman isn't there at all, having at the very start been projected under cover of the manipulated cloth through a back trap and her place taken by a delicate collapsible wire frame outlining her shape.

Kellar's particular meal-ticket was a disappearance act called *The Mystery Of The Princess Karma.* The Princess Karma was a pretty Irish girl named Sally McQuinn who, dressed up like a box of Turkish nougat, was seated in a heavy chair on a small platform similarly embellished like an Armenian delicatessen store, who was covered with a cloth, and who at the shot of a pistol, the smoke from which was amplified by that from a dozen large punk sticks, disappeared in what under the circumstances was perhaps rather excessively described as "the full view of the audience." It went big for some years. Then suddenly it, too, became old-hat, although it is often repeated under one or another name even today.

It became old-hat because there presently appeared comedians in vaudeville theatres all over the country who, as part of their acts, burlesqued the illusion. The result was that it was not very long before even the youngest bonbon seller at the back of the house was hep to the secret that still another collapsible frame covered the shape of the Princess immediately she sat down, that the apparently solid front of the chair slid abruptly downward on spring hinges, that the Princess was dejected under the stage through a trap-door, and that when the magician thereupon

* Or by a so-called "goose-neck" shaped like a U.

pulled aside the cloth the concealed wire frame collapsed inside it.

The Chinaman Ching Ling Foo, who wore dragon-embroidered robes voluminous enough to enfold within them not only the Dionne quintuplets but Dr. Dafoe to boot, relied for his biggest bait on the materialization from no-where—except possibly from the whole *Follies* wardrobe embellishing his person—of graduated pans and fishbowls, all of them unbelievably filled, by releasing a spring in their false bottoms or on their mirror sides, with water.

Thurston's top trick was also a water act, and probably the best that has ever been shown. The illusion here consisted of a stage peopled by assistants in Japanese costume, among whom Thurston, similarly clad, passed with a wand. From whatever his wand touched, whether a parasol, a fan or a person's ear or foot, a stream of water flowed. And at the conclusion of the act, such a stream shot up from his own wand. This one bamboozled your present quidnunc for several years and interfered seriously with his sleep. Then, one day, being a friend of the late Fred Moore, who managed the theatre in Atlantic City where Thurston was playing, he prevailed upon Fred to let him in on the tor-turing secret.

Being magnanimously solicitous of his nocturnal repose and future well-being, this Fred escorted your quidnunc to the cellar under the stage and there your quidnunc was privileged to observe such an intricate network of small water pipes as he had not laid eyes on since he was last in that palace near Salzburg in the Tyrol wherein a long ago eccentric ruler of the domain had installed a similar plexus for the purpose of playing damp practical jokes on his guests.

The rest you have guessed. Tiny rubber hoses leading

from the network, attached to everything and everybody on the stage and operated by assistants at the water-taps below, deftly put the business into operation. It was wonderful all the same.

We come now to the latest of the Cagliostros, Signor Dante. Born plain Harry A. Jansen in Denmark and long an associate of Thurston, this Dante presents as his specialities two illusions. One is called *Television,* described as "the visible transportation of a human being, or how to be in two places at the same time." The other is called *Stratosphere,* described in turn as "the world's newest and fastest illusion; Dante's latest original sensation; greater than the Hindu Rope trick and positively the last word in modern stagecraft." (That "greater than the Hindu Rope trick," incidentally, calls for a bit of explanation from our finegoateed friend, since in the program of his show he expresses his belief that there isn't any such trick and offers ten thousand dollars for a performance of it.)

The *Television* illusion shows a blonde assistant seated in a cabinet. Only her head is visible. Slowly the lights fade out and as her head fades out with them her head gradually comes into view in an adjoining cabinet. This is a paraphrase of an old-time illusion given the necessary touch of modernity by the employment of the word television. Sometimes it is done with doubles: two girls made up to look exactly like each other. Sometimes it is maneuvered with a dummy head, modelled and made up to resemble the girl's head. And sometimes, in the older days and under another name, it was done with a lightning trapdoor switch. Which device, if any, Dante uses, I do not know and, as Fred Moore is dead, there is no one left to take me back stage or under stage to find out.

The effect of the *Stratosphere* illusion is of a precipitantly dropped tall open-wicker basket containing three people, the disappearance of the trio, and their almost instantaneous appearance in the auditorium of the theatre. This, too, is an ancient one under a modern label. A black velvet or black cloth backdrop, an instantaneously operated black shade in the front of the basket which makes the audience think that it can see the backdrop through the basket and that the basket is hence empty, and the employment of a trio of doubles hidden in the rear of the auditorium have usually composed the shenanigan.

The chief thing that impresses itself upon the follower of the magical art is the paucity of novelty. With the sole exception of the *Sawing A Woman In Two* act, which Dante claims to have perfected, there has not to my knowledge been a really new illusion shown hereabout in the last twenty years. And the sawing a woman in half has also been stale and knowledgeable stuff for at least ten years, as pretty nearly everybody has for some time now been in on the secret that it is one curled-up girl's feet and ankles at the left end of the sawed hollow box and another curled-up girl's head at the right end. The *Headless Woman* illusion which has lately been a feature of odditoriums and sideshows is at least thirty years old. But even the people who sneer that almost everything "is done with mirrors" seem to be willing to overlook that so is the headless woman.

The magician's lot nevertheless and generally is no longer the happy one it once was. Various things have conspired to reduce the mystery that once cloaked him, even though still, like Dante, he affect devilish black mustachios, a satanic goatee, sinister black eyebrows, and drape his person in Mephistophelean black cape. Trouble first began for him some years ago when the *Scientific American* every now and then printed explanations of some of his pet tricks. It grew when *Popular Mechanics* took up the practice. And it increased tenfold when more recently publishers began to get out fat books, many of them all-revelatory, about his craft and when there began to open up countless little so-called novelty shops with tricks for sale at small prices. It has got to be so, indeed, that some of these minor tricks—they sell for from fifteen cents up—are more mystifying than some of the magicians' expensive illusions. The Scotch purse trick, for instance, is one. If you can get a coin out of it without knowing the secret, you are something of a magical genius. Worse for the stage magicians, many of these cheap little tricks employ in miniature exactly the same hocus-pocus devices used for their bigger stage counterparts.

It is thus that when today an average audience sees a stage magico pull a large bouquet of flowers out of a handkerchief he knows from his own purchasing experience that the bouquet is made of expanding feather flowers that may easily be compressed in one's palm. He also knows that the silk hat has a false bottom; that the coin has got into the smallest of the nest of six tightly bound boxes through a slot poked down into it from the back and there-upon quickly withdrawn; that the apparently solid steel bar with the steel rings at either end can be unscrewed not at the ends, as seems remotely possible, but toward the inno-cent middle; and that a plate of glass may rapidly be con-verted into a serviceable trick mirror by a small gully con-taining quicksilver.

He has also for some time been on to the secret that coffee may be made to flow inexhaustibly from a seemingly empty pot through a hollow table leg and a pump-hose operating under the stage; that a mirror placed at an angle of forty-five degrees under a chair or table will deceive the spectator into believing he can see through the under part of the chair or table; that when the doors of a spiritualist's cabinet are thrown open and nobody is there it doesn't signify that a little girl can not be hitched behind one of the rear doors and that the aforesaid little girl can not thereafter sneak inside and shake a bell and rattle a tambourine; and a whole lot of other such thats.

I have said that there are few new tricks. I have also said that anyone who says that he knows how tricks are done is regarded as being pretty offensive. So now I shall offer you a new trick of my own amateurish invention and make myself pretty offensive by telling you how it is done, thus being doubly offensive.

You first take two empty bottles. You then go to a writing table, and write whatever you will on a sheet of paper. This sheet you fold, place in one bottle, tightly cork the bottle, and place the bottle on a mantel or where you will. You then take a sheet of blank paper, fold it, place it in the other bottle, tightly cork the bottle, and place the bottle in turn any distance you choose from the first bottle. I touch nothing in the meanwhile. All I do is string a connecting piano wire—a loop around each end—from one bottle to the other. After a few minutes I request you to examine the bottles. In the first bottle you find that the sheet of paper on which you have written is blank. In the second bottle you find that the originally blank sheet of paper has your written message on it. (*Loud applause and profound mystification.*)

Explanation. The ink on the writing table, it has been seen to, is vanishing ink. The sheet of paper under the sheet on which you have written is carbonized to take the imprint of what you have written and has been further treated with a coating of invisible ink. The ink in the first bottle rapidly disappears, leaving blank the sheet of paper on which you have written. The heat of the tightly corked second bottle rapidly brings out the impressed invisible ink on the presumably blank sheet of paper.

But what of the piano wire and all that "chop suey" incantation in pig-Latin? You've got it. Like the ostrich in the old riddle, "What is the difference between a steamship, a cow, and an ostrich?", it's just put in to make it harder.

XXVIII

The Theatre in Slacks

The little summer theatres that dot the countryside far and wide like hot-dog stands (and that often provide considerably less nourishment) continue seasonally to operate full blast. It may, accordingly, be of some entertainment and instruction to examine them. As one who has expended considerable time and gasoline over the past six years in attendance upon them, I take the liberty of addressing myself to the business.

We begin at the beginning. The prevalent idea that all summer theatres are crudely converted barns, cow stables, delicatessen stores and garages is far from the fact. Some of them are, but there are others beside which such New York theatres as the Belmont, Daly's and Forty-ninth Street, to say nothing surely of the Davenport, Cherry Lane and Provincetown, are hardly to be called any sweet shakes. For example, the Clinton in Connecticut, the Ridgeway in New York, the Maplewood and certainly the Paper Mill in New Jersey, the Stockbridge and Dennis in Massachusetts, and the Skowhegan in Maine.

Further, the somewhat less prevalent but sufficiently accepted notion that ninety-nine percent of the young ac-

236]

tors visible in the rural playhouses are of the species who
elsewhere would have to protect themselves with nets and
who can subsist from June to September on the tomatoes,
eggs and kohlrabi thrown at them is no nearer to the fact.
While it is true that perhaps fifty percent of the pasture
mimes are nothing to make Guthrie McClintic and Gilbert
Miller jump out of bed at eleven o'clock and frantically
beseech their agents to get busy instanter on contracts,
there are any number who really aren't so terrible. I have
seen not a few who could easily outplay the New York professional companies who have disported themselves in exhibits like *Popsy, Boudoir* and, certainly, the Erwin Pis-
cator *King Lear*. I appreciate that this is not saying much,
but it is at least saying something, considering the obloquy
usually and arbitrarily bestowed on the rusticos.

Further still, while I have seen a great deal of stage
direction on the hen-and-rooster circuit that would need a
whole warehouse of compasses to set it on its proper course,
I have seen some that was quite respectable and as good
as a lot I have engaged on the so-called professional stage.

So much for the rosy side. Now for the other.

The first great weakness of the summer theatre idea is
the summer theatre idea. Why it should be, I don't know,
but the invitation to go to a theatre in summer is rather
akin to an invitation to go to baseball in the winter. It's
uncomfortable; it's out of key with the season; it's just a
little ridiculous. There is something confounding about going to a theatre on a hot July night and looking at actors
sweating themselves to death under the stage lights the
while they aristocratically conduct themselves through
The Second Mrs. Tanqueray or get passionate as all hell in
White Cargo. And there is something even more confounding in ambling out of a summer theatre between the acts

of something like the elegant *The Last Of Mrs. Cheyney* and bumping into a cow.

Getting to one of the summer theatres in the first place is nothing to put you in the properly receptive theatrical frame of mind. If you happen to live in the close neighborhood, very good. But if you do not, not so very good. No one even so little as a mile and a quarter removed from the theatre ever seems to be able to tell you exactly where the theatre is and how to get to it. The result is that when and if you finally arrive at it—after touring the countryside for miles around and successively landing at four remote closed tea-rooms, half a dozen road diners, three dark farm houses (with dogs), several cemeteries, and a woods that looks like a Haitian jungle—you find you have missed the first two acts and might just as well turn right around and go home, that is, if you can find the way back.

Another thing are the soft drinks. Such drinks are generally the only tipples on sale in the temples of warm weather art and, while they may be thoroughly satisfactory in their own eccentric way, they are not always exactly the thing to work you up into the proper, hilarious mood to appreciate something like *Charley's Aunt* or *You Can't Take It With You*. Soft drinks may be seemly for the higher drama, but no one ever laughed himself to death when full of Coca-Cola, strawberry pop or sarsaparilla.

Then there are the ushers. The ushers in the summer theatres are usually recruited from the prettier young girls in the apprentice groups, and if you think a lot of pretty young girls frisking up and down the aisles, saucily flirting their bustles at you, and whispering audibly to one another that they wish they had a date after the show with someone with more than a quarter in his pocket—if you think such-like don't take your mind off what is going on on the stage, you are either eighty years old or mistaken.

The physical structure and environs of many of the theatres only add to the difficulty of a correct reaction to their stage exhibits. At the Bucks County Playhouse in Pennsylvania, for instance, the thin walls are penetrated throughout the evening by the racket of a thunderous rushing stream. When, accordingly, you hear one actor say to another, "It is so quiet here you'd think it was the Sahara desert," and another seriously reply, "You said something there, baby!", you may be forgiven a laugh on which the playwright didn't expect to collect royalties. Similarly, the theatre at Parsippany, New Jersey, being situate close to a large dog kennel, has frequently found its audiences confused as to whether what they were listening to on the stage was *Autumn Crocus* or *Uncle Tom's Cabin.*

If a storm breaks while you are seeing a play in one of the urban theatres, it doesn't much matter; you can't hear it. But in many of the bucolic theatres you can not only hear it but feel it. The roofs of some of these theatres seem to have been especially constructed for super-realistic productions of plays like *Rain,* with the audience cast in the role of Jeanne Eagels. What is more, two hours of loud thunder claps may scarcely be said to be the exactly right accompaniment to a peaceful enjoyment of something like H. V. Esmond's *One Summer's Day* or anything else of the beatific sort, especially when they are preceded by bolts of lightning that shoot through the theatre and momentarily threaten to strike dead everyone in the house.

The selection of plays is another point. At least once or twice during the season the operators of the summer houses evidently think they should give their acting youngsters something to get their teeth into, something as a relief from the conventional light dramatic fare. What then happens is enough to stampede the cows for miles around. Suddenly projecting a troupe of kids, who have already had a tough enough time of it trying to get by with *Peg o' My Heart,* into something like Dostoievski's *Crime and Punishment* isn't calculated to drive the more critical appraisers of histrionic art crazy with delight. Particularly when the youngsters have had only a week in which to rehearse the play, when the director—as is frequently the case—knows no more about Russian character than he has gleaned at dinner one night from watching the waiters at the Kretchma restaurant, and when the leading roles are assigned to a girl and boy whose only dramatic experience antecedent to the present summer was in the third road company of *Life With Father,* in which one played a maid and the other one of the Day brats.

Nor must we overlook the mosquitoes. By no means must we overlook the mosquitoes. They don't overlook us, so it would be impolite to overlook them. If you think it is easy to acquiesce in the romantic mood of some play like, say, *The Animal Kingdom,* while a dozen or so mosquitoes are mistaking your neck and ears for a smörgåsbord, you are more of a Casanova than your wife thinks you are.

The stray bees, warmed into nocturnal virtuosity by the theatre's hot lights, are also no sophomores when it comes to invalidating an audience's mood. I may not be an authority on the drama, but I *am* an authority on the drama in its relation to bees. And I wish to state that even the faint threat of being stung by a bee is enough to take even the greatest drama lover's mind off dramatic art quicker than you can say Bea Lillie. Last summer during a performance of *Margin For Error* in one of the Connecticut rural theatres I kept waving my arms in front of me, by way of chasing off one of the persistent beasts, for such a space of time that all I saw of the play was the scene between the two cops, the bee at that moment having given me a respite by momentarily concerning itself with the duenna in the seat in front of me.

The automobile horns do not help much either. Most of the audience of a summer theatre arrives by car, usually from half an hour to an hour late, and apparently is unanimously of the theory that automobile horns provide a tasty obbligato to the drama. Last year at the Cape Playhouse, in Cape May, New Jersey, I accordingly found an otherwise satisfactory enough performance of *Smilin' Through* orchestrated by enough horns of every description and variety, embracing sirens, clarinet tooters, World's Fair *Sidewalks Of New York* spielers, ordinary honkhonkers and what not else, to greet a visiting foreign dignitary coming up the Bay. In the case of many of the summer theatres, it is just as well to come only to the second act, since you can't hear the first act anyway and since the departures during the third make such a renewed din with their horns that you can't hear that act either.

While, as I have duly allowed, some of the little theatres are as thoroughly comfortable as some of those in New York and other cities, many of them are nevertheless hardly to be compared favorably with the Metropolitan Opera House or a dollar dentist's waiting-room. What I am thinking of particularly are the seats. After some of those seats riding a bucking bronco is like having sat on a feather bolster.

The aforesaid seats are of peculiar and stunning diversity, all of them guaranteed to make your hinterparts feel as if they were afflicted with a vicious case of lumbago that had worked itself down. There are hard wooden benches that project sharp splinters into you. There are

seats on springs which, while you try to adjust your posterior to them, crawl slowly up on you and slide you back
into the slots in their rear. There are seats with ridges in
them that permit you when the evening is over to offer
yourself to the circus as a tattooed man, and at a handsome
honorarium. There are other seats obviously upholstered,
at an outlay of fourteen cents, with corn-cobs, and still
others made of something that looks and certainly feels like
roof-tiling. And one and all are calculated to put their de-
positees in such a frame of mind that *Hellzapoppin* itself
would seem as gloomy as *Rosmersholm*.

And let us not forget the nails. Last summer alone I
ruined ten pairs of pants on those nails. Next summer I
take me along a hammer.

But when the show is over comes the real diphtheria.
For some reason I have never been able to make out, it is
incumbent upon a summer theatre audience at the conclusion of a play to repair en masse to an adjacent dog-
wagon, diner or roadside restaurant and there to wolf down
innumerable wienies or hamburgers, usually to the accompaniment of a juke box blaring out *God Bless America* or
I'll Never Smile Again. Just why the audience should be
under any such compulsion I do not know, but it apparently is. Last summer I myself, notoriously a vegetarian,
figured out that in the course of my study of the summer
drama I had been forced to eat six hundred frankfurters
that I didn't want to eat, to say nothing of five hundred and
twenty-three hamburgers, two hundred of which had been
soused in sour ketchup, one hundred and seven of which
consisted of one part meat to nine parts Bermuda onion, and
the rest of which were made of something that tasted like
a cross between army veal and Shetland wool. The frankfurters weren't so bad—some of them, indeed, were quite

toothsome—but I nevertheless stoutly maintain that forty-two frankfurters is going just a little too far for any one night.

The discussion of the play of the evening that takes place during the frankfurters, hamburgers and renditions of *God Bless America* and *I'll Never Smile Again* is another matter I'd like to bring to your attention. Nobody ever seems to be other than hysterically enthusiastic about the performance. This may be partly due to the fact that the cast is generally hanging around in the dog-wagon or restaurant and is listening in with all ears. Or it may be due to the effect that frankfurters, hamburgers and renditions of *God Bless America* and *I'll Never Smile Again* exercise on the critical faculties.

There's an idea there for the New York producers.

XXIX

Waves of Soap

Six times in as many recent days I haphazardly turned on my radio and heard a male comique reply to a female ditto who asked him if that was cinnamon candy on his lips: "That wasn't no cinnamon candy, lady, that was my wife." And six times I heard the rejoinder greeted with such a loud burst of studio laughter as would have overwhelmed the modesty of the greatest humorists in recorded history. Just what the reaction on the part of the great listening public was, I have no means of knowing, as the Crosley statisticians, who are occasionally no mean comedians themselves, negligently do not include in their researches the relative popular puissance of such mots. Yet I entertain a mild doubt that after hearing the jocosity once, or maybe even twice, the public response to it matched entirely the enthusiasm of the studio-hired guffawers.

It is possible, of course, that I may be in error. I myself, renownedly a creature sadly deficient in a proper sense of humor, have sat no less than seven successive times to the badinage of the night-club zany, Mr. Joe E. Lewis, and each of the seven times have laughed like a fool when he told how he had rubbed gallons of oil on his scalp by way of trying to put hair on his bald spot and how finally he had to give it up because he didn't know what to do with the sardines. But just the same I have me a feeling, the quality of the respective masterpieces of wit aside, that you can't lead a horse or radio audience to the trough too often and still expect it to go on drinking like an Egyptian camel or Irishman.

But it isn't only the constant repetition of facetiæ, good or bad, that induces a slight paralysis of the more sensitive radio ear. In directions apart from humor the impresarios of the ether appear similarly to follow the doctrine of the movie masters, to wit, that if the public is found to like something the astute commercial procedure is to keep on feeding it either that something or a something else pretty much like it ad infinitum. The principle may operate successfully in the case of hot dogs and political philosophies, but just as the movies have lately discovered their mistake in the sharp decline of their audiences so must the radio presently discover, if it has not already, that the one and only prosperous keynote of entertainment of almost any kind is, as always it has been, variety. Repetition, the late Arthur Brisbane once observed, makes reputation—but not always at the box-office.

Herewith is an exact record of what the radio poured into my ear upon one hundred short casual turns of the dial in the week I am writing this, commercial ballyhoo and news broadcasts not included in the hundred.

Twelve repetitions of the musical composition *Intermezzo,* from last year's movie of that name.

Twelve of the *Hut-Sut Song.*

Four of the wisecrack: Lamp that sun-tan, kid!

Seven quizzes of one sort or another.

Six masters of ceremonies remarking flatteringly on the

looks and dresses of introduced women singers.

Five Hawaiian string bands all playing *Sweet Leilani*.

Three snatches of soap operas in which a father told his young daughter he would not interfere with the dictates of her heart but urged her to be sure of that heart before she married the man.

Seven comedians (bandleaders, professional clowns, etc.) who jocularly derogated their personal pulchritude, three of them winding up with: "But, anyway, observe the youthful gleam in my eye!"

Four wheezes to the effect that June's got only thirty days whereas July's got thirty-one, indicating that July must have committed *grand* larceny.

Three waggish allusions to Staten Island as the gem of the ocean. And four to Coney Island as a land of bodies entirely surrounded by water.

Three Hollywood gossipers who allowed, respectively, that Charlie Chaplin and Paulette Goddard were again having emotional trouble, that Charlie Chaplin and Paulette Goddard were seen that day at Catalina and never looked happier together, and that Charlie Chaplin and Paulette Goddard must be in hiding in the desert since no one had heard anything about them or seen them in the last four weeks.

Three different sets of hillbilly singers all singing the same songs.

Three pairs of blackface comics each of whom retailed this one: "Is you Mose?—Mose who?—Mose anything."

Six recorded jazz sessions, all the discs save two being identical.

Four bands with the saxophone player, suddenly given a solo focus, performing whimsically on his instrument.

Four health talks in which the listener was warned to

beware of too many ice-cold drinks in the hot weather, to eat sparingly of red meats during the torrid season, and to wear some head protection in the hot sun by way of safeguarding oneself from sunstroke. Also to bathe frequently and keep the pores open.

Three advisers on book reading who urged that readers not forget the classics what with all these interesting new war books crowding the market.

Three puns on the name of the prizefighter, Billy Conn.

Four joking references to Bull Montana.

I do not exaggerate, as the skeptic who has or hasn't a radio may possibly imagine; that is what I heard; and that is the gospel truth. And it indicates, surely, that when it comes to the lighter phases of entertainment the radio is often in the matter of reiteration somewhat akin to a not particularly engrossing case of hiccoughs.

I am, of course and to repeat, speaking of the radio as an entrepreneur of entertainment in the sense that the word is often and incongruously defined. Its symphony concerts, higher drama hours, news broadcasts and the better like do not fall within the scope of the present critique. A number of such phases of air diversion are of sufficient merit. But the lighter entertainment under immediate dissection is another matter.

The apparent reasons for the debility of this lighter entertainment are, I find from investigation, three in number. The first of these reasons is the radio's fear of offending any portion, however small, of its listeners. The second is the radio's mistake of emulating the movies in the assumption that the intelligence quotient and taste of the great majority of its public are negligible. And the third is the belief, shared by the theatre in its past infancy and by the screen in its present maturity, that if the public is fetched by a thing once there is no reason why it will not be equally fetched by the very same thing a dozen or more times.

As an example of the fear of offending any slightest portion of listeners in any way there is the position of one of the greatest business corporations in the country which has sponsored a radio program for five successive years, which has rejected no less than fourteen different suggestions for an improved program on the ground that there might possibly be something or other in them that would not please someone or other in the radio audience, and which has played safe by repeating for the five successive years simply a band with a tenor and soprano warbler. The band, the tenor and the soprano, furthermore and by way of making the safe doubly safe, are enjoined from playing or singing anything perchance controversial in music or lyrics.

To a considerable degree, this desire on the part of the sponsors—and surely the sustaining programs—to play safe may be understood and even sympathized with when some of the facts are scrutinized. Not long ago, for example, a program extolling Abraham Lincoln drew a large number of offended protests from listeners in the Southern states. And only a short time ago one of the studios was deluged with indignant complaints after it had broadcast a musical program containing the melody of *Maryland, My Maryland,* which outraged the more indefatigable patriots on the score that it was of German origin.

The radio's mistrust of the intelligence and taste of its audience has led it deliberately and intentionally to reduce the quality of its entertainment in all kinds of directions. One of the idiosyncrasies of radio philosophy in this regard is the conviction that the daytime intelligence and taste of its listeners is very considerably lower than the night-time intelligence and taste. The result, as any assaying ear will attest, is that the night programs are almost uniformly of at least a relatively higher grade than the daylight programs. These latter are celebrated throughout the nation for what are known in the trade as soap operas, and if anything was ever farther removed from the entertainment art than one of these soap operas, the Cherry sisters and the drama of the late Wilson Barrett alone excepted, few connoisseurs of the more voltaic cheeses have heard of it.

A soap opera, in the event you have just arrived at Ellis Island and have not yet been educated in the terminology, is a serial play, apparently endless, which recounts, on behalf of the manufacturer of one or another household product, the adventures of a character or group of characters, much in the manner of the comic strip. The more successful soap operas, however, lean to the highly emotional. And most of them follow much the same suspensive pattern. A favorite device, for instance, is to end the day's slice of the serial with the ringing of a telephone and a character's puzzled remark, "Who can that be?" or "What can the message have in store for us?" Another is the receipt of a letter or telegram followed by the wondering query, "What news will it bring?" or "Who can that be from?" And, however often the device be repeated, the impatience of the radio audience for the next day's slice with its explanation seemingly remains boundless. Which may indicate that the hereinbefore metaphor about leading the horse to the trough too often may possibly constitute better æsthetic criticism than practical commercial criticism, which is both embarrassing and a pity.

As an illustration of the essence of the average soap opera or serial, we may take a recent newcomer to the air which goes by the title, *Front Page Farrell*. Farrell is a reporter on a New York newspaper in love with a girl reporter named Sally. Sally, in the instalment aired in the week I am writing this, is wooed by a millionaire whom she does not love but who, in the words of the script, sweeps her off her feet and demands her hand in marriage, which for some inscrutable reason almost drives her poor mother demented. Farrell, somewhat less inscrutably, does not relish the situation either and confronts the millionaire with raised fists, whereupon Sally, the brava, jumps between them. Not having had the heart, courage, patience, strength or despair aurally to pursue my dramatic education beyond this point, I fall back on the intrepid *Variety's* report of what followed.

MILLIONAIRE (*to Sally, hissingly*): "I'll get you yet! When you see other women riding in the sort of fine cars you could have, while you trudge the streets, you'll come back to me!"

FARRELL (*storming*): "How dare you talk to *my* future wife that way? Why, I'll spread your dirty past all over the front page of the *Eagle*. I'll print the dope on that crooked stock deal. I'll expose how that model committed suicide off your yacht. I'll show she didn't fall overboard—she was pushed!"

MILLIONAIRE (*sneeringly*): "You try to smear me and you'll have the same fate she had! I'll ruin you if I have to buy your filthy paper to do it!"

And so on, astagh-fer Allah.

The successful soap opera, *Backstage Wife*, at the moment of writing has foul gangsters keeping the listening housewives on tenterhooks with threats of murder. *Stella Dallas*, another volt, has them speculating anxiously on their own love-lives with their husbands. *David Harum* has them wondering if clever Aunt Polly will free the hero of the suspicion of having murdered his evil butler. *The Ro-*

mance Of Helen Trent agitates them over the coming of Helen's baby and makes them glow over the philosophy that romance begins at thirty-five. *Arnold Grimm's Daughter* has them alarmed because old man Grimm has fallen into the clutches of a feline adventuress. *Life Can Be Beautiful* has them momentarily upset because Patricia, though married, is apparently falling again for an old flame. *Martha Webster* has them agog because its heroine's separated husband is scheming to get his hands on her again. *Valiant Lady* has them by the ears because of its heroine's fear that her husband simultaneously does not love her any longer and may be going insane. *Road Of Life* has them almost frantic with impatience to learn whether Dr. Jim Bent is going to defy everybody and marry his beautiful nurse who is passionately in love with him. *Aunt Jenny's Real Life Stories* has them on their toes with Aunt Jenny's tale of how a female surgeon who is in the dumps because one of her patients has died under her operating knife is regaining faith in herself by performing an appendectomy on her own beloved husband. And *Manhattan At Midnight* is causing them to weep copiously into the kitchen sink because the American husband of a poor little Central European refugee is succumbing to the wiles of a dirty hussy.

[XXX]

The Circus

Sinclair Lewis asked me the other night when it was that I first began to feel stirring within me the critical bacillus. "It must have been around the age of nine or ten," I allowed, "because I was then, as I am now, one of the few boys who never wanted to run away with a circus."

A good, cool, hard look at the old tent may accordingly not be amiss. I have been looking at it—inside, outside, and lying flat on my belly through a slit in the canvas—for more years now than I like to confess to the academicians, and my protracted scrutiny has induced in me some increasing qualms. The first of these is that it is high time somebody thought up some new ideas for it if it is to hold its old place in the public affection. A circus, whatever it be like, is all right for very young kids, just as almost anything else they see for the first or second time is pretty exciting for them. But its endless repetitions cannot fail soon to wean even them from it, to say nothing of all the older kids from fifteen to fifty who either paternally take them to it or go to it solo out of nostalgic impulse.

I have, as I say, been gandering circuses—small, middle and colossal—since Benjamin Harrison was in the White

House. I have visited attendance, man and boy, on almost all of them in that span, from Barnum's to Barnum and Bailey's, from Donaldson and Gregory's to Forepaugh's, and from the Sells-Floto and the Cole Brothers' to the Ringling Brothers', with a whole lot of lesser sawdust opera thrown in for full measure. And while there is no gainsaying I didn't once have a reasonably amusing time at them, at least in the period when my papa still had to crack open my peanuts for me and hold the bottle of pop to my mouth so it wouldn't drip over my lace collar, I have, like many another, found that that amusing time has since become steadily and increasingly lessened.

Why?

Because of all the amusement devices in the cosmos the circus has been most guilty of lack of originality and real inventiveness, and has become largely an annual duplication of itself. It has, true, become more and more expensive and lavish. The present Ringling show, for example, is Hollywoodian in its epic opulence. It has, also true, spared no expense to gather from the four quarters of the globe the best acts available. And it has with the hired aid of celebrated designers, costumers and the like succeeded in giving itself a veneer of ocular attractiveness foreign to it in the days of our childhood—those days when a bareback rider in a white tulle skirt with a violent purple sash and with a pea-green ribbon in her molasses hair represented to us a beauty unequalled by Helen of Troy, Drina De Wolfe and Eleanor Mayo all rolled together, with Della Fox, the Hengler sisters and even the pigtailed love of our life in the house next door added.

But for all the outlay of money and the great improvement in externals the circus, whatever its name and wherever you find it, remains today not perceptibly much different from the circus of forty and more years ago. The old Kiralfy spectacles have disappeared, which is something of a pity, for despite their absurd cheesecloth melodrama, chariot races and grand finales showing Hamo Superbus resplendent in crimson, gold and perspiration accepting the homage of one of the Caesars, there was a kind of kid thrill in them that nothing since about the circus has vouchsafed. But, save for that one exception, the rest adheres more or less rigidly to the pristine formula.

The jugglers today, for instance, may manipulate two more iridescent balls or two more Indian clubs than they did back in Grover Cleveland's day, but jugglers are jugglers and, even if you now throw a light on them that makes the sequins on the Indian clubs shine out in the darkness, when you've seen one you've seen all. The wire-walker who teeters perilously until he finally maneuvers his triumphant balance has been teetering perilously in exactly the same manner for so many decades that you no longer feel a moment's concern for the safety of his life and limb. The genius who trembles dangerously on a perch close to the ceiling and then—with the band suddenly resolved into a breathtaking silence—dives into a net has been doing his stuff too long to induce in us any further trepidation on behalf of his wife and children. And the man who is shot out of a cannon, to the accompaniment of enough chemical smoke to screen the combined navies of America, England, Italy, Japan and Russia, nowadays hardly evokes an Oh! from any youngster not hypocritically given to trying to make his old man believe that he is having a wonderful time.

There are more elephants today than there used to be, but they still lift up their paws as they always have and place them on the rumps of their colleagues. There are more trapeze artists and more tumblers but they do much the same thing trapeze artists and tumblers have been doing since Mark Hanna gave McKinley his first sixty-cent cigar. The equestriennes and their brothers-in-law still dash madly after the prancing horses and leap on and off the horses' backs; the lion tamer still overawes his jungle beasts, except for one duly and carefully trained to growl ferociously until finally he is covertly subdued with a hamburger with onions (no ketchup); and the trained dogs, including the little one who drolly falls off the springboard several times to the sympathetic concern of the audience, still go through their ancient routine, with the aforesaid little dog—"isn't he just a darling?"—at the conclusion of the act mastering the springboard jump and rolling himself up in a rug.

It's all all right the first time and maybe even the second and third times, like college class reunions, *Cavalleria Rusticana* and goat's milk cheese, but the taste gets to be surfeited.

One would think that, however static the other elements of the circus have become, there would at least be some novelty in the clown department. But with negligible exception it isn't so. As a matter of established fact, the favorite clowns of twenty-five, thirty and thirty-five years ago who are still alive are still cavorting in the sawdust ring almost exactly in the fashion they originally did. And the newcomers indicate not much more remarkable humorous ingenuity. A connoisseur of the species of long and assiduous standing, I have over a period of more than five decades observed three and only three mild departures from the primitive hokum. The Ringling circus is the one responsible for the phenomena. In it, one clown has slightly varied the old Jules Tournour clown business by blowing up his ample costume with a concealed bellows and having

it suddenly deflated by a sword in the hands of a zany col-
league, another has a skeleton attached at some distance to
his back which gives the appearance of chasing him panic-
stricken around the ring, and a third ludicrously and without recourse to stilts contrives alternately to shrink and ele-
vate his height.

But the rest of circus clowndom is up to the same old
tricks. The small buggy, in later years metamorphosed into
a Ford, out of which pile seriatim a dozen clowns harks
back to the remote days of the Byrne Brothers' extrava-
ganza, *Eight Bells*. And the clown costumed to give him the
appearance of walking backwards and the brace of clowns
serving as the fore and hindparts of a horse, latterly become
a dachshund, have become as established a part of the
scene as the clown on stilts leading a miniature mutt or the
clown from whose pate sprout small red and green rubber
protuberances.

As if thoroughly aware of the danger gradually attach-
ing to these annual mimeographs, the circus impresarios
exert themselves to devise novelties to stimulate and hold
their trade. And so grateful is their public for even the
slightest relief from the old stuff that the most innocent
dodges are welcomed with an enthusiasm inspired only in
other avenues of life by a hamburger with nuts in it or a
movie in which Garbo for once permits herself to laugh. It
is thus that the introduction, to the accompaniment of
enough lush journalistic publicity to elect Sol Bloom president of the United States, of a minor gorilla horrendously
named Gargantua is sufficient to crowd into the old tent
even sexagenarians who momentarily seem to have forgotten an orang-outan named Goliath who served the same
purpose in Barnum's time. And it is further thus that the
mere announcement of the importation from Havana, that

city of impenetrable and hazardous jungles, of a mate for the beast—judging from her photographs a considerably less ferocious and more normal spouse than Catherine II or Ruth Snyder—will bring in the awed gapers from miles around.

I myself, always ready to give anyone an even break, always ready to believe the best in anything and everybody, and ever searching for the pot of gold at the rainbow's end, two years ago fell for the advance ballyhoo about Gargantua like everyone else, including Arturo Toscanini, Albert Einstein, Charles Evans Hughes, and even Clare Boothe. Personally escorted downstairs by my good friend John Ringling North, boss of the circus and Gargantua's discoverer, I was warned to get not nearer than ten feet to the cage housing the vicious monster, lest he reach through the bars with his gigantic paws and tear me to shreds. He was, I was awesomely apprised, not only the most dangerous beast in captivity but one with an appetite for human flesh even greater than the late Diamond Jim Brady's for filet de boeuf Renaissance.

Deeply impressed and not a little terrified, for all my strained outward show of smooth—nay, even lofty—nonchalance, I duly stood not ten but fifteen feet from the den of the man-eater and, while he glowered and growled at me malevolently from behind the restraining iron bars, sought to sustain my ego by growling at him in turn and making faces. He looked at me steadily for a few minutes and then, as God is my judge, frightened half to death beat it hotfoot to the farthest end of his cage!

Maybe next year, when Gargantua has settled down to married life, they ought to hire me in his place.

When it comes to the freaks, there is to be noted even less novelty and change than in the other established departments. I have been standing under their platforms since the days I wore kilts and believed in Henry George and the Single Tax and, aside from the saucer-mouthed Ubangis, I haven't seen a new kind of freak in all that time. The living skeleton, the tattooed man, the bearded lady, the gutta percha man, the dwarfs, the fire-eater, the sword swallower, the Siamese twins, the tallest man in the world, the two-headed calf, the Circassian lady, the snake charmer, the Albinos, the man who can stick nails into his skin, the glass eater, the fat lady—these and all their direct descendants have been boredly suffering the scrutiny of the equally bored customers since Barnum unearthed the Cardiff giant, that prosperous come-on.

But the big parade before the show begins is the circus' stencil plus. The band in the scarlet fever coats, blue pants and with enough gold braid to wrap up all the Christmas presents in Harlem marches out of the farthest entrance to the sawdust trail and lets go with more brass than George Sylvester Viereck. Following, on foot, come the acrobats, jugglers, rope-walkers and trapeze artists and artistes, their tights modestly concealed in flowing capes. Then the inevitable troupe of Japs in native costume and carrying fancy parasols, with behind them the pure Arabian horses led by a handsome longshoreman accoutered like the leading man in *Lord and Lady Algy*. Now heave into view the elephants, lumbering ponderously along like Middle Western senators, their trunks periodically raised aloft and their trappings aglisten with ten-inch gilt thumb-tacks.

Bringing up the elephants' rear are the equestriennes, regal in long purple cloaks and feathered hats, and following the royal creatures are, for contrast, the clowns, who waggishly wave to the customers and familiarly call out

"Hiyah, Sam" and "Hiyah, Lou" to theoretical friends in the stands. Two of the clowns occasionally pretend to stumble over each other, thereafter elaborately brushing off their frowzy costumes. Another clown licks a big all-day sucker, and another still breaks line, stands momentarily apart from the procession, and gazes with an absurd love-light in his eyes at some imaginary beauty up in Row M.

Now pass in review the ponies, among them a small and very cute one who, like the small dog hereinbefore mentioned, evokes tender comment from the female spectators, and after the ponies, seated majestically aloft on something that looks like a cross between an overly decorated El station and an upside down soda fountain, we behold the show's star daredevil, be he the gent due to be shot out of the cannon, the diver from the ceiling perch, the hero who rides a bicycle through a flaming hoop, or what not.

The camels, who always look as if they had not had a bath since Ptolemy's second birthday, are next and following them parade the freaks, with the inescapable male and female lilliputian (in evening dress and the former smoking a big cigar), stepping briefly out of the ranks to allow the little lady to adjust her long and always troublesome train. More pure Arabian horses and then, bringing up the end, the old steam calliope, tooting the ears off all and sundry.

After the show in the rings is over, there is the visit to the menagerie, which customarily discloses at least half the animals sound asleep and which smells as if someone had cornered the asafetida market and gone simultaneously into the glue factory business. Then you eat two more frankfurters encased in soggy rolls that taste like used Mills Hotel towels, buy a small red banner inscribed with the

name of your favorite city, try to get rid of the taste of the
hot dog rolls by eating an ice-cream cone that tastes in
turn like a frozen hunk of horse liniment flavored with
raspberry, brush several quarts of peanut shells off your
clothes, go home and wait until the circus comes around
next year, when you see and do exactly the same thing.

XXXI

Cabarets

Although complete statistics are not available, what is known as the cabaret floor-show must figure pretty well up in the list of current great American industries. Beginning modestly some three decades ago, it more lately has spread all over the nation, until today it is a rare restaurant, hotel, café or night-club in any city of more than thirty thousand population that at one time or another during the evening does not offer at least some symptom of it.

The floor-show, in case there remains anyone who does not know what it is, is an entertainment (so the entrepreneurs insist) staged in that section of a public eating and drinking establishment between the diners and imbibers on the one hand and the bandstand on the other. It takes on various forms, ranging all the way from a solitary vocalist crooning into an obviously detached microphone to the elaborateness of some such show as the Billy Rose exhibits at the Diamond Horseshoe in New York. And it employs all varieties of entertainers (as the entrepreneurs are fond of describing them) from society débutantes to Harlem darkies and from musical comedy and Hollywood luminaries to French, Mexican, Chinese, Spanish, Hawaiian,

Tennesseean and other such alien divas, dancers and theoretical joy dispensers. Sometimes it is fairly good, but more
often it steenks. Not infrequently, indeed, it is difficult to
tell where the floor-show ends and the welsh rabbit begins.

However, you have no trouble in deciphering where the
floor-show itself begins. It begins with the emergence of a
creature in evening dress known as a master of ceremonies.
You can readily and instantaneously identify this creature,
be it male or female, by its expansive air of happiness.
Nobody in the whole world ever looks so happy for no
reason as a master of ceremonies. Why, no one of course
knows, particularly when all things are considered, and
doubly particularly when they are considered after the so-
called ceremonies are over and have been found out.

The master of ceremonies, wherever you encounter him,
is the direct descendant of a couple of not overly bright
parrots. "Ladies and gentlemen," he beamingly quotes his
forebears, "it is a great pleasure to have you with us tonight
and I know you will all enjoy our little show. I now want
to introduce to you that well-known, lovely and charming
little lady, Tootsie Goldberd, who will entertain you with
some of Cole Porter's latest songs. Now let's all give Tootsie
a great big hand!"

The fact that nobody present, except possibly her agent
sitting at a table near the door, has ever heard of the well-
known Tootsie and the further fact that Tootsie is quickly
observed to be approximately as lovely and charming as a
cold in the nose are politely, or perhaps despairingly, overlooked by the customers, who perfunctorily bestow upon
the artiste the big hand requested.

Tootsie, who usually wears an evening gown that looks
as if it had been made on a bet by an inebriated Ethiopian
couturière aided and abetted by a professional decorator

of drugstore candy boxes duly finishes her act and is followed by another well-known, lovely and charming artiste whom also nobody has ever heard of before and who looks like Tootsie's first cousin. This is the Russian dancer, Vermina. Again, at the solicitation of the happy master of ceremonies, the big hand is forthcoming and Vermina then seizes a dagger out of her left garter and frenziedly chases it around the floor for ten minutes. This, according to the master of ceremonies, whom it has made happier than ever, is symbolism indicating that Vermina's childhood was a tragic one because her paternal uncle had murdered her maternal uncle and because her small brother had thereupon disgustedly left home and joined the Tsar's cavalry. At this point one of the waiters, obviously a Russian, drops a large plate of scrambled eggs and bacon on Vermina's agent, who is sitting at the other table near the door.

The next great excitement on the bill is provided by a well-known, charming and versatile young man who is so obscure he hasn't even got an agent. This artist is Harry Bogenscheider, of a well-known society family in Jasper Falls, Iowa. Harry, who also gets the big hand, seats himself at a wheeled-out small piano and proceeds to dispense a "sophisticated" ditty relating the amours of a boa constrictor and an anchovy. Taking five gratuitous bows, Harry then proceeds to dispense another sophisticated ditty recounting the passion of a nightingale for a lobster, the scene being wittily laid in Newburg. Now six gratuitous bows, and a concluding ditty in which the names of Mrs. Astor, Mrs. Vanderbilt, Herbert Swope and Elsa Maxwell are cleverly and respectively rhymed with pastor, handle her kilt, dope, and back's swell.

Item 4 on the gala program is a decrepit Negro baritone who once appeared in a third *Show Boat* road company and who sings *Ol' Man River* for twenty minutes.

"And now, ladies and gentlemen," glees the happy master of ceremonies, "I have a special big treat for you. Hold your breaths! And that certainly means you, Joe (indicating a customer over in a corner who has a visible jag on), because if you don't, ha ha ha, you'll aphyxiate everybody in the room. But, ha ha ha, as I was saying, ladies and gentlemen, and I want you to realize I'm serious, I am now going to introduce to you someone you all know and love. The lovely and charming star of stage, screen and radio, Miss Maebelle Moots. Come on now everybody, a great big hand for Miss Moots!"

Arrayed in more spangles than the grand transformation scene in *Uncle Tom's Cabin*, Miss Moots, who has never been nearer the stage, screen or radio than a year's subscription to *Variety*, demurely accepts the customers' tribute to her and takes her position at the mike, the lights meanwhile having been impressively lowered and her face and figure glitteringly illuminated with a purple baby spot. "I will try to give you my special arrangement of Cole Porter's *Night and Day*," modestly announces Miss Moots, the while Tootsie Goldberd, who sang it earlier in the evening and who has put on her street dress and is hanging acidly around, gives issue to a critical grunt. The applause for Miss Moots upon her final note, led by the waiters and bus boys to whom her agent has slipped five bucks, overwhelms the modest beauty. "Oh thank you, thank you all so much," she purrs. "And now I'll try to give you my special arrangement of *The Last Time I Saw Paris*."

Miss Moots' wonderful act over, we again have the happy, aye, now overjoyed, master of ceremonies. "That concludes our evening's entertainment," he radiantly rhapsodizes, "and I want to thank you all for enjoying it so much and to say we're here every night at the same time and place and hope you'll all come to see us again. Thank you, and good-night."

There you have a composite picture of the most generally encountered floor-show. Its variations are immaterial. Sometimes Tootsie Goldberd's place will be taken by a pseudo-French diseuse who fondly imagines she compares favorably with Lucienne Boyer and who bats out *Un Peu d'Amour* with enough soulful eyeblinking to shake off her false lashes. Sometimes Vermina's place will be taken by a female American tap dancer with calves developed to the point where they begin faintly to resemble cows. Sometimes in the Negro baritone's spot you will find a passionate Mexican who bawls out his love for a senorita south of the Rio Grande. And sometimes you will discover in Miss Maebelle Moots' stead some other peroxide peach who, being even less competent than Miss Maebelle, will seek to conceal the fact that she hasn't got anything by going in for what is called "audience participation." Audience participation, in the event you do not know, consists in persuading the customers simultaneously to bang loudly on their plates with little wooden hammers and to sing along with the vocalist at the tops of their lungs by way of helping prophylactically to drown out her godawful voice. But whatever minor changes there may be, it always remains much the same show.

Then there are what are known as the smarter floorshows. These evidently get their name from the fact that their entrepreneurs are smarter than the entrepreneurs of the other shows in getting a two dollar cover charge for something essentially the same but only dressed up a little better.

These smarter shows go in in a big way for so-called

ballroom dancers. In place of Vermina and the clog dancer
they offer as their main attraction a male and female dago
or a male and female Spanish-Brooklyn couple in evening
dress who peddle grace with a vengeance. The valse is their
big card. Not the waltz, mind you, but the valse. A valse is
a waltz danced in a dim mauve light and, instead of ending
as a waltz does in the man taking his girl by the arm and
escorting her politely to the bar for a glass of schnapps, it
ends in his grabbing her ferociously around the middle and
swinging her around thirty times as if he wanted to throw
her into the bass-drum.

An incidental feature of these more soigné shows is the
Mexican or Puerto Rican baby who stands in front of the
rumba band and without let-up shakes the maracas for at
least half an hour. After the first ten minutes she augments
the shakes with vibrations of her bosom and hips, thus
hypothetically no end exciting the ethyl desires of potential wine-buyers at the surrounding tables.

The society singer, usually an ex-débutante who was
jilted by the rich boy her parents had their eyes on and who
is now secretly stuck on one of the headwaiters, is another
classy item in the tonier floor exhibits. The chief difference between the society singer and Tootsie Goldberd is
that in comparison Tootsie sings like Flagstad. But that is
not the only shortcoming of the fashionable canaries. In
addition to not knowing how to sing, it seems that a society
singer has eight knees and that all eight of them interfere
with her walking carriage. The approach to and retreat
from the mike by one of the chic dears accordingly take on
the aspect of Leon Errol's old vaudeville act.

The sophisticated male singer who accompanies himself on the piano is as omnipresent in the smarter shows as
he is in the other, the main difference between him and

Harry Bogenscheider being that, whereas Harry rents his dress suit, he owns his. The only other difference is that our more high-toned artist rhymes Astor, Vanderbilt, Swope and Maxwell not with pastor, handle her kilt, dope and back's swell but with faster, gander gilt, nope and tax fell, which is esteemed as vastly wittier.

Nor, before we go on, must we overlook the band leader. The band leader in the cheaper shows is usually a rather ordinary mug who worked his way through a tank-town college by playing the saxophone in the little orchestra at the town's movie house and who considers he has done his necessary all by the customers when he has greased his hair to a shine with vaseline and put on a Tuxedo not more than seven years old. But not so in the case of the sweller joints. The band leader here, resplendent in tails, is a suave bird who apparently has trouble making up his mind whether he has been hired to lead a band or make goo-goo eyes at all the lady customers. Therefore, after wielding his baton for a couple of minutes at his men, who pay not the slightest attention to him, he slowly revolves, faces the trade, and spends the rest of the composition in giving a bad imitation of an irresistible Don Juan, the imitation consisting for the most part in alternating a theoretically intriguing dead pan with a theoretically provocative come-hither look, the said look being negotiated by dreamily half-closing the eyes and pretending to be thinking of Chopin instead of the lousy jazz his band is playing.

Variations in these smart floor shows are hardly corruptive of the above picture. Now and again there will be a gypsy dancer who works herself up into such a succession of perspirational ecstasies that they have to fumigate the premises before the next act can go on. Now and then a Russian violinist or guitar player who is generally advertised as having been a member of the late Tsar's entourage will purvey sad music, the guitarist lifting his voice in song. And occasionally there will be inserted into the proceedings a "comédienne and impressioniste" who will give imitations of Tallulah Bankhead and Katharine Hepburn, or a pair of eccentric comedy dancers like the Hartmans whose climactic humor consists in putting on funny hats. But the general pattern remains inviolate.

A word in conclusion about the décor of floor-shows in the aggregate. In the dumps, colored paper ribbons strung around the walls and a half dozen Chinese lanterns are deemed sufficient. In the slightly more recherché spots the Hawaiian or South Seas motif—customarily interpreted in terms of two artificial palm trees and paper leis for the customers—is a favorite idea. And in the select joints the place is left as is and the waiters simply put on clean shirts every other day.

XXXII

The Carnival Shows

The big cities hardly know them, but they are as regular an annual visitation upon the smaller towns as the Sunday school picnic itself, which, however, in even the most elastic imagination they are rather far from resembling. They are the so-called carnival shows; they flourish most luxuriantly in the period from May to October; and they represent in the aggregate the most egregious entertainment enterprise currently functioning in the Democracy.

The carnival show of the present is an outgrowth and development of the old medicine show of hallowed memory. Way back in the last century the seed was planted when migratory vendors of hypothetical cure-alls alleged to have been brewed from mysterious Indian herbs discovered that their spiels on the wonders of their magical philtres were beginning to lose some of their pristine commercial puissance and when they were driven to amplify their hortatory performances with pitch acts of one species or another. Card tricks were accordingly brought forth to lure the suckers to the kill. A stray Swedish servant girl, questing the romance of the open road and succumbing to the wiles of the therapeutical professor, was smeared with

walnut juice, embellished with beads and chicken feath-
ers, and displayed to the potential trade as a Chippewa
princess, daughter of the big Indian chief responsible for
the occult remedy. Or, after an elaborately furtive, if gratuitous, look to right and left to make certain no constable
was in the environs, the pitchman would electrify the hicks
with a demonstration of a remarkable shoe polish—a box
free to each purchaser of a dollar bottle of the nostrum—
that made a pair of patent leather shoes carefully camou-
flaged with wet flour forthwith look exactly like a pair of
patent leather shoes. "My friends, this mystical shoe polish,
the secret formula of a French monk, will do the same for
those very shoes you are now wearing, whether black, yellow, white, or any other color. Come closer, my friends, as
this is very confidential and we don't want to be overheard
by parties we can't trust. One box of this mystical polish to
each and every one of you absolutely free of charge, and
with it a bottle of Old Sioux Elixir absolutely guaranteed
as to contents and absolutely guaranteed to cure the hives,
mumps, sore feet, diphtheria, neuralgia, rheumatism, gout,
piles, common colds, pneumonia, warts, backache and
smallpox infection at only one dollar the bottle!"

The years passed, and with their passing the medicine
men found even greater need for showmanship. The card
tricks, Swedish Indian princesses, and magical shoe polish
no longer in themselves sufficed to magnetize the hayseeds.
So three-piece bands, academically composed of trombone,
fiddle and drum, acrobats, freaks of one description and
another, hooch dancers, or something of the small circus
sort were rushed into the breach. And then more years
passed and what was once the medicine show became the
carnival show.

While many of these carnivals are conducted in what

is allowed by the trade to be an upright and ethical manner, there are wayward others that have often given the
industry a bad name. Whereas the old medicine shows
swindled the rubes only in the case of the supernatural
panaceas (the shoe polishes, etc., being gratis, not correctly counting), these fly-by-night carnivals bamboozle
them in countless ways. Fixed gambling slot machines,
Japanese roller ball prize games with the top number holes
contractible at the operators' will, ring tossing games with
the prize canes and umbrellas so placed at an angle that
no ring can encircle them, sensational sideshows ("all for
the price of a dime") with the pseudo-sensations calling
for an extra dime or even quarter in an adjoining canvas
partition, weight guessing machines controlled by electrical
wires, prize candy boxes containing silver watches that
may be covertly removed from the exhibition packages by
hooks and elastics concealed in the butchers' sleeves, saucy
French postcards the top and only saucy one of which is
palmed by the vendor upon handing over the set ("put
'em in your pocket quick, please, mister, before a cop
comes!"), and many other like feints and fetches lie in
eager wait. And what money, if any, the jakes have left
when they conclude it is time to go home is meat for the
pickpockets who usually follow such carnivals with the
assiduity of vultures following a desert wanderer in the
visibly last stages of phthisis florida.

However, in recent years the carnivals have made a
show of protecting the yokel's last nickel by putting up
signs solicitously urging him to beware of pickpockets. The
average yokel's idea of being beware of pickpockets is,
pursuant to a technique which he has culled from a plausi-
ble stranger at the previous year's carnival, always to place
your money not in the right hand pants pocket, as here-

tofore and as usual, but in the left hand one. The result is
that no pickpocket has dipped into a yokel's right hand
pants pocket since July 4, 1930.

The carnival show of today in its general aspect is an
amalgam of jitney circus, minor pleasure park and street
fair. The circus' animal acts and acrobats, the pleasure
park's rides and roller coasters, and the street fair's games
of chance, fortune-tellers and candy floss are part and
parcel of it. Among the most profitable of its numerous
and varied concessions are the frozen custard, palmis-
try, pea ball, high-striker, guess-your-age, fishpond, scales,
candy apples, penny arcade, photo gallery, snow cones,
pitch-till-win, midget Tinytown, lead gallery, snake show,
cigarette shooting gallery, bingo, juice stands, cotton
candy, knife rack, bowling alley, souvenir jewelry, super-
Jap hull-less and mammoth yellow popcorn, and dice
wheel. And among the tidiest rube bait figure such literary-
scientific ego-cosmetics as *How To Win At Any Kind of
Speculation, Mental Telepathy, Zodiac Secrets, The New
Dream Book,* and *Love Is Yours For The Asking,* which
costs, as should be expected, a nickel more.

If the carnivals have contributed anything to the great
American amusement culture, it is the diversity of their
rides. The geniuses of the open lot shows have concocted
more and more various devices to rattle the insides out of
a client than the human fancy ever previously dreamed of
after a banquet of welsh rabbits, raw hamburgers and Danish pastry. Aside from the mere Ferris wheel, merry-go-
round, roller coaster, switchback and such antedilu-
vian eye-gougers, brain-spinners and spine-splinterers,
their repertoire of more recherché aches and pains includes
the following: the Roll-o-Plane, Double Whip, Ridee-O,
Tilt-a-Whirl, Loop-o-Plane, Silver Streak, Octopus Ride,

Looper Ride, Dipsy-Doodle, Aerial Joyride, Chair-o-Plane, Parachute Drop, Auto Kid Ride, Motor-Drome, Sunset Slide, Hey-Day, Sky Pilot, Flying Scooter, Whizbang, Caterpillar, Eagle Flight, Whirlspin, Lindy Loop, Airplane Swing, Rocket, Flyoplane and Skysweeper, one and all, save possibly only the Auto Kid Ride, certified to excel the effect of two dozen warm Martini cocktails.

It is in these rides that the carnivals, presently numbering in the higher hundreds, have displayed their prime ingenuity. The rest of the picture remains much the same season after season. For despite the bosses' advertising pleas for novelties in the carnival bible, *The Billboard,* nothing much in the way of newness and originality seems to be available. Yet the fact apparently does not give the bosses overly severe headaches, as the rubes continue to swallow the old, familiar stuff with relish, and to swallow it whole.

Aside from the introduction of girl shows, variously dubbed *Follies, Oriental Beauties, Harem Maids, Night In Paris, Venuses On Parade* and the like, the average carnival of any pretensions that one happens to drop in on nowadays is pretty certain to look exactly like the same carnival of five and ten years ago. The ballyhoo has not changed; the free acts, such as trapeze performers, sway-pole equilibrists, boxing bears, etc., are of a piece with those of yesterday; the awesome banners proclaiming the *Deep Sea Wonders And Curiosities From Neptune's Bed* or the prehistoric monster, the Thesaurus, still draw the crowds into the tent; and the snake, geek, chimp, monkey and other such shows still revel in their grand old perfumes. And the terræ filii still throw away their good dimes, quarters and dollars on roller ball, ring, toss, wheel and raffle games in the fond hope of winning one of the rare and beautiful Ming table lamps—"Worth at least twenty-five dollars, ladies and gents, and fit for an Emperor's palace"—that costs the operators exactly $5.40 a dozen.

This brings us to the actual cost prices of the other rich treasures displayed to the gambling-minded greenhorn. The Vanity-Lite, a favorite prize and boomed to be worth $4.50, costs the operator just eighty-five cents. The thirty-inch silk parasols come to two dollars the dozen. The China-head canes cost six dollars a gross. The patriotic wall plaques may be had for sixty cents the dozen, or $6.50 the gross. The beautiful powder boxes that reap in the dollars are $1.80 a dozen; the fountain pen and pencil sets are $1.90 the dozen sets; and the handsome solid gold pendants, lockets and necklaces cost as little as $1.80 a dozen.

The difference between the prices the carnival hawkers pay for novelties, souvenirs, toys, elixirs and gimmicks and the prices diddled from the customers may be contemplated by the latter, perhaps somewhat wistfully, from the following brief sample list:

1. "Your Name In Raised Coral Colored Letters On A Genuine Tropical Sea-shell Brooch"—cost, two and one half cents complete with printed brooch card and taking just half a minute to assemble with Duco cement. Cost to customer, twenty-five cents.

2. Gold shell bracelet—cost, $1.80 a dozen. Cost to customer, fifty cents.

3. Horn shell necklace on plastic chain—cost, two dollars a dozen. Cost to customer, fifty cents.

4. "Plastic Fruit Knives Each Mounted On A Beautiful Four-colored Card"—cost, sixteen dollars a gross. Nick to buyer, seventy-five cents.

5. Laxated Herb Wonder Medicine—cost, one dollar a pound of water soluble powder that makes two gallons of diuretic laxative, with thirty-two fancy labels thrown in. Cost to constipatee, fifty to seventy-five cents.

6. "Snappy Giant Chewing Gum Boxes," each box containing twenty cellophaned packs of gum—cost, from twenty-five to twenty-eight cents. Cost to emptor, seventy-five cents.

7. Military novelty, "If You Gotta Go, You Gotta Go," patriotic label on box showing army and navy men saluting, box containing miniature metal lavatory and illustration of draftee on the run—cost, $1.50 a dozen. Cost to connoisseur of refined humor, fifty cents.

8. "Sterling Silver Army Rings"—cost, eleven dollars a dozen. Cost to come-on, two dollars each.

9. "La France Floral Plaques"—cost for thirty assorted plaques, $9.75. Cost to ceramics lover, one dollar each.

10. "Fascination Candy," one pound box, cost, twenty-four to the carton, seventeen cents each. Cost to customer, fifty cents.

11. "Imported walking cane with smart crook handle"—cost, seventy-five cents a dozen. Cost to dude, fifty cents.

12. "Diamond rings," large center stone set off with six side stones in silver color mounting with one-thirtieth fourteen karat band, each in a gift box—cost, $3.75 a dozen. Sales price, seventy-five cents to a dollar.

13. Two-blade pocket knife, assorted simulated marble and stag handles—cost, $1.19 a dozen. Selling price, forty cents.

14. Five-piece sport kit, consisting of pair of sun glasses with side shield, pocket comb, bevelled-edge mirror, fingernail file, and simulated leather pig grain case—cost, $1.60 a dozen. Cost to purchaser, thirty-five cents.

15. Night In Hawaii perfume—"The romance of a night in Hawaii is captured and expressed in the tantalizing

aroma of this exquisite perfume; attractively bottled in hour-glass style, fluted design glass container; colorful hand-painted wooden head top over metal screw cap"— cost, seventy-nine cents a dozen. Sales price, fifty cents.

But it still costs only two nickels, a dime, the one-tenth part of a dollar, ladies and gents, and step this way quickly, please, if you want to get in ahead of the crowd, to see John Hanna, the Australian sheep-headed man; Ella Wolfe, who climbs a sword ladder in her bare feet; and Martha Joy, the girl with the horse's head. And if Zambeezi, the pin-headed pigmy, alas went to his Maker last May after a brilliant twenty-year career of gibbering at the carnival trade, let the countryside not be downhearted. His equally pin-headed brother, known to the lots as Illa Ellakoola, happily and mercifully survives him.

XXXIII

Coney Island

Coney Island, that stretch of sand washed by two parts Atlantic ocean and three parts watermelon rinds, cheese sandwich ends and nibs of hot dogs, persists as the archetype of summer playgrounds for the otherwise largely unwashed masses. There are other such proletarian plages, big and small, scattered far and wide throughout Rooseveltania, but none of them is the equal of what has been variously dubbed the Brooklyn Biarritz, the Woolworth Atlantic City and the Frankfurter Waikiki. Its name is familiar to people who have never heard of even Sherlock Holmes or a Ferris Wheel; it represents in the field of hot weather pleasure areas what Niagara Falls represents in that of the democratic honeymoon; yet probably not more than five out of the one hundred and thirty-one millions of Americans have ever seen, much less smelled it. This chapter is accordingly for the benefit and instruction of the other one hundred and twenty-six million.

The experienced five million aforesaid may be divided into three categories. Perhaps six hundred thousand of the number are curiosity seekers who, having heard so much about Coney, have gone down once to have a look and,

after having had it, have considered their life's work in that
particular direction done and have not gone back a second
time. Some two million more are of the sort who visit the
place once, loudly swear that you won't find them there
ever again on a bet, and the next year and each year thereafter annually lose the bet at least once. The rest, or two
million four hundred thousand, are regulars and, when the
temperature hits ninety, all seem to be in attendance at
one and the same time. These two million four hundred
thousand may in turn be divided into two categories. One
hundred and three males among them haven't their shirts
open at the neck and wear neckties.

As for the females in the quota, there is no differentia-
tion. All, except for the children and a sprinkling of fresh
young stenographers and shopgirls, wear either pink or blue
dresses, weigh at least one hundred and eighty-five pounds,
and have sore feet.

Situated on the rim of Brooklyn, New York, and having
a five mile expanse of bathing beach, boardwalk, amusement parks, sideshows and generally enough dust to drive
all the Okies out of Oklahoma in half an hour, Coney is
shown by statistics on any hot July or August day to sell two
million frankfurters, two hundred thousand ice-cream
cones, one hundred and eighty-three thousand hamburgers,
one hundred and seventeen thousand ham and cheese sand-
wiches, sixty-one thousand bags of popcorn and peanuts,
twenty-four thousand toy balloons, twelve thousand small
felt banners with "Coney Island" lettered on them, and at
least half a million beers and soft drinks.

A day's schedule at the resort adheres to a strict formula.
Arriving at, say, noon, the male visitor promptly buys a
hot dog encased in a white roll, smears mustard on it with
a little wooden paddle, and eats it, washing it down with

a bottle of soda pop. After repeating this, he purchases a hamburger, smears ketchup on it, eats it, and downs it with another bottle of the pop. He then rushes into a bath house, gets into his bathing suit, and makes hurriedly for the beach by way of getting there before the crowd does. He regularly discovers, however, that the crowd, which evidently ate its hot dogs and hamburgers at eleven, has beaten him to it, and that by this time the beach has left just about one foot of sand on which to deposit himself.

The divertissements on the beach consist in the following:

1. Eating more hot dogs.

2. Telling children to go and play ball somewhere else as you don't want your eye knocked out.

3. Trying vainly to edge away from the expansive behinds of the mothers surrounding you.

4. Flirting with a stenographer or two.

5. Drinking several more soda pops.

6. And trying to find a bit of space in the ocean in which to wet yourself.

All this consumes the better part of the afternoon.

Along toward five o'clock the visitor gets into his street clothes again, negotiates a couple of more hot dogs and maybe another hamburger, and starts looking around for the stenographer he winked at on the beach. Never being able to find her, the fickle miss, he now winks at the first shopgirl who passes him and, if fortune smiles upon him, beseeches the fair creature to join him for a gala time at Steeplechase Park.

This celebrated Tilyou rendezvous the gay couple enter through a large revolving barrel which promptly dejects them on their rears, to the untold delight of the onlookers. Regaining their equilibrium, they now pass through a door and find themselves on a platform before which hundreds of flat-faced young men sit patiently for hours on end looking at a concealed wind machine blowing the feminine entrants' skirts above their heads. Recovering her social position with a loud squeal, our young miss and her escort presently move off the platform and proceed to a rapidly revolving large disc which sends them both flying off in all directions and makes them so dizzy that when they finally stagger off it they are able to eat only four hot dogs.

Next comes the slide, which projects them through a funnel and again lands them on their already sufficiently tried hinterparts. And so on until they limp out of Steeplechase at six-thirty or thereabout and find themselves again on Surf Avenue. Now, by way of a little refreshment, a few hamburgers and a couple of beers, and a tour of the Japanese rolling ball, cane ringing, and other such prize games along the thoroughfare, with perhaps a sideshow or two thrown in.

Then, Luna Park.

Although much more fancy and elaborate than most such pleasure parks, Luna is not essentially different. First, our young swain and his lady weigh themselves and through the slot get cards telling their fortunes. Strangely enough, both seem to be favored by the fates in exactly the same way. Riches await them, and so does a happy marriage, but they both have to watch their health carefully and beware of large investments in gold mines. By now fast friends, with all these things suddenly found to be shared in common, they proceed to have their silhouettes cut out of black paper, and then, upon the young man's observation that his companion looks so much like Ann Sheridan he can't tell them apart, our couple decide it would be great to take a ride on the roller-coaster.

A roller-coaster, you need hardly be told, is an amusement device that combines all the best features of a nightmare in which you dream you are in imminent danger of falling off a high cliff, an osteopath who takes pleasure in cracking your spinal column, and having your taxicab bumped into by a freight-car. This nevertheless so stimulates the spirits of our young friends that there is nothing to do but try the Shoot the Chutes, which splashes a gallon of water all over them and thus adds to their ineffable happiness.

It is time now for more hot dogs, with some salt water taffy for dessert, the whole accompanied by more soft drinks. Then—howz about a dance, kid?—and on to Terpsichore. After an hour or so of Terps, at the conclusion of which our friends look as if they had been caught in a Pago Pago week's rain, a couple of glasses of lemonade with a ritzy cherry in each, and out for a stroll on the boardwalk. A stroll on the Coney boardwalk on any warm mid-summer night is, however, the equivalent of a leisurely promenade in Macy's basement during a sale of eighty-five dollar fur coats for ten cents. But our young friends find it has its advantages. You can neck freely without anyone noticing you, as everyone is jammed so closely to everyone else that if you don't neck you're likely to be considered a potential pickpocket and be embarrassed no end by being hauled off to the gaol.

Follows a little appetizer of three or four hot dogs and a little apéritif of three or four beers—and ahoy for Cupid's Ride, alias the Love Tunnel! Depositing themselves side by side in a small boat, our couple now glide in ecstatic embrace through dark watery tunnels periodically and startlingly illuminated by papier-mâché tableaux of *Mephistopheles Defying The Angel Gabriel* and *Neptune Rising*

From The Sea. Just why and how such spectacles are calculated to induce in their beholders an uncontrollable amour is not entirely clear to the student of human emotions, yet they apparently do. The ride over, our heaven-blessed pair, wreathed in those esoteric smiles vouchsafed only to the young when in the throes of love, are now ready for the Subway trip home.

The day's schedule for the older and more sedate is much the same, minus only the flirtation and the Cupid's Ride.

For several years, one of the big features at Coney was the cooch and strip-tease sideshows, but latterly certain moral elements determined to make the resort more suitable for what they designate the family trade have, in so far as they have been able, blackballed them. The reason for the parties' moral alarm evades the comprehension. Having in my professional capacity studied the shows at close quarters, I may say that anyone whose morals could be corrupted by them must have a moral quotient of something less than one-tenth of one-half percent.

The Coney strip-tease exhibitions, I discovered, were a marked anti-climax to anything you could see on the five mile beach free of charge. The poor, fusty females who engaged in the art were not only as completely anaphrodisiacal as so many kegs of potassium nitrate but took off fewer of their clothes than the average housewife does when she sits down to a hot-weather roadside picnic. And as for the cooch dancers, all that I laid eyes on indulged in considerably less agitating contortions than any girl on the beach down whose back some card had dropped a piece of ice.

Adjacent to Coney are two other beaches, Manhattan and Brighton by name. They differ from the motherbeach. In the first place, they are more select, which means that they are much smaller and therefore can't hold as many of exactly the same kind of people as Coney can. In the second place, they are embellished with amusement devices on an infinitely smaller scale, which means that visitors have just that much more time for frankfurters, hamburgers and soda pop. And in the third place, they do not boast Cupid's Rides, which is pretty tough on the younger element. But otherwise they are Coneys in miniature, including the aroma.

Like all good things on earth, Coney and its subsidiary beaches have had their problems. Sometimes in the past the city fathers who look after the public health have concluded that an aberrant sewage, to say nothing of all those stale cantaloupe rinds, rubber garters, ham sandwich ends, cast-off underdrawers and other such deposits, contaminated the hither portion of the ocean and that, accordingly, bathing in a first-class garbage can would be somewhat more salubrious. But by running the sewage pipes half-way over to Bremerhaven the ingenious fathers soon rectified matters and today bathing at Coney and its environs is almost as safe, save for an occasional bang in the mouth by an old floating watermelon, as in your residential bathtub. On other occasions, a locust plague of pickpockets has called upon all the wily resources of the police force. And on still others it has been found necessary to haul out the fire departments from miles around to play their searchlights under the boardwalk by way of discouraging the more ardent spooning couples.

But it has never been long before Coney has been its old self again, and lately it seems to be even more its old self than ever.

XXXIV

By and Large

The business of entertaining the people of the United States of America in their leisure hours seems increasingly to be conducted on the principle that most of them who are not already touched in the head might just as well be. The idea, apparently, is that amusement seekers are no longer to be satisfied with simply a good straight play or show, a good plain motion picture, an intelligent radio program, a meritorious bar or restaurant, an interesting sports event or anything else of the sort but, whether they want it or not, arbitrarily have to be given something so eccentric and even pestersome that it is small wonder a lot of hitherto regular folk are beginning to talk like Virginio Gayda, think like Salvador Dali, look like John L. Lewis, and act like Olsen and Johnson, or even Kathleen Norris.

All this is the outcome of the piquant theory that the brethren have suddenly become so blasé in the last year or two—because of the war, the California climate, or something or other—that they will no longer spend even a nickel for amusement unless you treat them as if six lunatic asylum guards had chased them into your place. The notion has spread with such violence that the phenomena springing from it would, if laid end to end, so overcome Mr. Ripley that he would have to go to bed for a year, and would then in despair in all probability commit suicide.

While it is obviously denied me under the tenets of human charity and patriotism to list all these convulsions, I nevertheless give you a rough general impression.

In the No. 1 spot we have beheld the epiphany of what are called odorated motion pictures. A product of the heaven-sent genius of a brace of gentlemen named Laube and Barth, to say nothing of several other masterbrains who have organized themselves under the name of the Aromatix Company, these pictures, far from contenting themselves as heretofore with just telling a story in sight and sound, for extra measure vouchsafe an audience all the relevant incidental smells. If, for example, you see a man on the screen guzzling a whiskey, presto!, a whiff of Bourbon fume pervades the auditorium. If the story calls for the smoking of an evil cigar, you duly sniff the empyreuma of the stogie. If a belle sprays herself with Eau de Brie, it is Eau de Brie that massages your nostrils. And so on. What they are going to do when they come to some such scene as a pig-sty or Berchtesgaden I don't know and shudder to think, but in the meantime, as was recently indicated at the first showing of one of the films at the Vogue Theatre in Detroit, there were enough assorted odors, ranging from everything from Jockey Club perfume to banana oil and something that smelled suspiciously like a pair of socks that a plumber had worn three weeks, to make the outdoor fresh air worth two thousand dollars a cubic inch.

According to *Variety*, about eighty percent of the customers voted on the comment cards handed around that the idea was dandy. Though it did not tell what the rest said, it did report that one gentleman wrote, "What flavor are you going to have left for the bad pictures?" So maybe there is a twenty percent chance left for people who are still perfectly satisfied to look at Maxie Rosenbloom without smelling him.

To continue on the movies, consider the bait they have recently hung out in the great state of Wisconsin. The managements of various houses in that section of the nation, persuading themselves that far fewer people go to a movie theatre to see a movie than to enter into a little amour, have staggered especially constructed so-called love-seats throughout the auditoriums wherein couples who are crazy about each other may be comfortably oblivious of what is going on on the screen and may osculate and embrace each other to their hearts' content. More, by means of the stagger system, the love-seats are so arranged that no pair of cooers will find another pair directly in front or behind them to observe and eavesdrop. Theatres in Milwaukee (the Tosa), East Troy (the Troy), Alma (the Alma) and in other localities have installed the chaises d'amour, and more are presently to follow suit.

That town of Milwaukee, where the idea started, seems to be a prodigy. But in its excess of zeal it appears sometimes to over-reach itself. At the Milwaukee Automobile Show some months ago, for instance, one of the several knockout conceits was to give hourly demonstrations to the audience of the effects of ethyl alcohol, or booze as it is vulgarly known, upon drivers. The volunteers were to be summoned to the platform and given as much liquor as they wished in order to test their reactions. The great idea blew up, however, when the lines of volunteers began to stretch eight times around the block, when the enthusiasm to get at the bottles threatened to necessitate the calling out of the police reserves, and when the Milwaukee County

Safety Commission thereupon cruelly turned thumbs down on the grand notion.

The commercial sponsor of a radio program which advertises the miracles of a flea, fly and bug exterminator called *Flit* was seized not long ago with the fear that its air propaganda was not sufficient unto itself and that the listeners-in had to be galvanized by additional means. Whereupon, after days of profound and extended cogitation and after headscratching of enough intensity to dig halfway down to China, it was decided to release in various American municipalities one fly painted gold and one painted in a less opulent hue and to reward the American citizen who captured the first with a tasty hunk of pelf and the one who caught up with the second with a sweet, if somewhat less handsome, sum. The public responded to the invitation in such surprising proportions that, in the city of Miami, Florida, for example, the reconnaissance succeeded not only in the apprehension of the two prize brutes but in ridding the town of all the other flies in it, estimated to be more than 15,224,816 in number, and with the Chamber of Commerce gratefully congratulating the citizenry on their matchless civic élan.

A restaurant and night club in New York called Uptown Café Society last year deemed it expedient to provide some extra novelty for the putatively jaded clientele of such resorts. Its management reflected on the general situation and took note that a New York restaurant named Leone's which had installed a stream on its premises and let the customers fish for their own trout had packed the place. It also meditated that a night-club, the Stork, had drawn crowds by inaugurating balloon fights in which the customers battled for a hundred or more small balloons some of which contained prizes. It further ruminated that other restaurants and night-clubs had held and drawn trade with such devices as rocking-horse races (El Morocco), lucky number prize cards with each Alexander cocktail (Penthouse), horoscope, palm and physiognomic readings (La Marquise), and the like. So it got busy painting reproductions of the latest designs in ladies' hats, culled from the town's most fashionable milliners, on the mirror behind the bar and advertised that women customers might adjust themselves at the bar in front of them and see how they looked in them. The next day the crowd of women at the bar was fifteen deep.

The strategy of keeping people from dying of ennui has extended even to sports. During a recent football season George Marshall, owner of the Washington professional eleven, concluded that his customers were perhaps not being entertained sufficiently merely by the football games themselves and that something ought to be done to sustain their interest between the halves. So he rushed to a vaudeville booking agency and hired a trick horse named Pansy, along with the horse's three human stooges, to divert the spectators. Pansy apparently earned her salary, for Dan Topping, owner of the Brooklyn Dodgers, subsequently engaged her for a display of her virtuosity between the halves of his team's contest with the New York Giants.

We come to the theatre. Peculiarly self-persuaded that customers no longer relish a normal stage play, however good, the sponsors of something called *Quiet Please* last year instructed the audiences to regard themselves as movie extras figuring in the shooting of a Hollywood picture and to stand up periodically and yell "Bravo!" at the tops of their lungs, to say nothing of applauding loudly when commanded to do so by the actor-director on the stage. The sponsors of an exhibit called *Mr. Big* went those of this *Quiet Please* one better. They arranged that their play should be interrupted every once in a while by discussions with the audience on the part of the actors, stagehands and even ushers.

Ever since *Hellzapoppin* began sitting in the audiences' laps, pelting them with beans, causing spiders to creep down their necks and putting cakes of ice on their knees, the theatrical costermongers have been busy trying to figure out other new ways to drive customers insane in the name of novelty. Thus, Al Jolson in *Hold On To Your Hats*, like Joe E. Brown during his engagement on the road in *Elmer The Great*, comes out, seats himself in a chair, and confides to the audience his intimate personal affairs, including, in Al's case, his marital status, the girl in the company he is going to take out to supper that night, the herring that gave him an awful bellyache the night before, the stocks he bought last Tuesday, the difficulty he is having in finding a laundry that won't ruin his shirts, and his financial dealings with the Shuberts.

Where it is all going and just where it will all stop, there is no telling. Walt Disney has already come forth with a movie (*Fantasia*) that tells audiences what they should be thinking of while listening to music by various composers. What is more, he not only tells them but shows them, which is a little embarrassing to those members of the audience who, instead of obeying Mr. Disney's visual injunction to think of fairies and bluebells, somehow refractorily think of the shapely legs of the girl sitting opposite them, the delicious sirloin with onions they are going to have as soon as the show is over, and the rheumatism in their big toes.

But Disney is only the half of it. Vaudeville theatres like Loew's State put on shows in which well-known movie cuties brought on from Hollywood tell the customers all about themselves and in which well-known newspaper columnists tell the cuties all they won't tell about themselves. The radio seeks to enthral the multitude with questions as to which eighteen paleozoic animals have names beginning with Q, with Handel's concerto grosso in B flat played on xylophones and a harmonica, and with Robert Ripley's exhibition of the five tallest women in the United States whom the listeners can't see. And publishers are getting out books full of such pasted-in items as locks of hair, thumb prints, burnt matches, lipsticks, slices of liverwurst and pieces of string and demanding the purchasers to deduce from them who it was who murdered Basil Burlingame.

Aloha!

A NOTE ON THE TYPE

The text of this book is set in Caledonia, a Linotype face designed by W. A. Dwiggins, the man responsible for so much that is good in contemporary book design and typography. Caledonia belongs to the family of printing types called "modern face" by printers—a term used to mark the change in style of type-letters that occurred about 1800. It has all the hard-working feet-on-the-ground qualities of the Scotch Modern face plus the liveliness and grace that are integral in every Dwiggins "product" whether it be a simple catalogue cover or an almost human puppet.

The book was composed, printed, and bound by H. Wolff, New York.